DAWN & DUSK

RAINBOW
for
ORDINARY TIME

Traditional Hymns,
Psalms, Canticles, Sayings of Jesus,
and Readings on the Christian Life
for Ordinary Time

meditation rendering by
Stephen Joseph Wolf

www.idjc.org

Dawn & Dusk: Rainbow for Ordinary Time
Copyright © 2023   Stephen Joseph Wolf

All rights reserved. No part of this book may be copied or reproduced in any form or by any means, except for the inclusion of brief quotations in a review or the songs understood by the publisher to be in the public domain, without written permission of the publisher.

If you need the masculine pronouns for God in traditional translations, you will not like this rendering. For the holy name *YHVH* or Yahweh, the Hebrew word for "My Lord" (*Adonai*) is used, pronounced *ah-duh-'nigh*, and the Aramaic word *Abba* for Father. See page 512 for the other choices made in this meditation rendering.

HOW TO USE THIS BOOK

I take off my shoes, sit up, offer up my still incomplete awareness of the illusions by which I live, and ask God to speak God's name in the center of my soul.

I make the Sign of the Cross with the Psalm 70 verse and the Doxology: *Glory to the Father and to the Son and to the Holy Spirit, as it was in the beginning, is now, and will be forever.**

I sing a Song.

For each Psalm or Canticle, I recite the Antiphon and then the full poem. If limited by time, I omit the *Psalms* with headings in *italics*, (from the traditional Office of Readings, Daytime, and Night Prayer.)

I choose a Reading, or read a chapter from my Bible using a daily reading plan, and then recite the day's Responsory.

I recite the Gospel Antiphon followed by the Gospel Canticle. (In Morning Prayer instead of the Gsopel Canticle I often use the Gospel Reading of the day from my Bible as indicated with the Antiphon; most people will simply use the Gospel Canticle.) Then come the Doxology **Glory to…*, and then the Antiphon is repeated.

Petitions and Intercessions are provided, and they conclude with the Lord's Prayer and the Sign of the Cross.   - Steve Wolf

ISBN 978-1-937081-72-0   This First Edition
ISBN 978-1-937081-74-4   *Dawn & Dusk Rainbow Prayer*, 775 pp.
(includes also the seasons of Advent, Christmas, Lent & Easter)
ISBN 978-1-937081-73-7   *Rainbow Prayer* (abridged version) 175 pp.

printed and distributed by Ingram Books
published by IDJC Press   www.idjc.org

Dawn & Dusk…for Ordinary Time

	Odd Weeks (ONE)	Even Weeks (TWO)
Sunday Vigil (Sat Evg)	4	253
Sunday Morning	19	267
Sunday Evening	38	288
Monday Morning	51	303
Monday Evening	70	325
Tuesday Morning	85	341
Tuesday Evening	107	365
Wednesday Morning	121	379
Wednesday Evening	141	401
Thursday Morning	155	419
Thursday Evening	175	439
Friday Morning	193	455
Friday Evening	213	475
Saturday Morning	233	489

SOLEMNITIES in ORDINARY TIME	511
ACKNOWLEDGEMENTS, SOURCES & CHOICES	512
INDEX of PSALMS	515
PSALTER COMPARISON	516
INDEX of CANTICLES, READINGS & ANTIPHONS	518
INDEX of SONGS	521

Traditional Doxology recited after each psalm or canticle

Glory to the Father and to the Son and to the Holy Spirit, as it was in the beginning, is now, and will be forever. Amen.

The **Antiphon** is then traditionally repeated after the doxology.

WEEK I
VIGIL of SUNDAY
(Saturday Evening)

+ *God, come to my assistance;*   Psalm 70:2
  Lord, make haste to help me!

  Glory…

A   **Now thank we all our God**
With heart and hands and voi-ces,
Who won-drous things has done,
In whom this world re-joi-ces;
Who from our mo-thers' arms
Has blessed/ us on our way
With count-less gifts of love,
And still is ours to-day.

All praise and thanks to God
Our Ab-ba now be giv-en,
With Son and Spir-it as
They reign in high-est heav-en:
The one e-ter-nal God,
Whom heav-en and earth a-dore!
For thus it was, is now,
And shall be ev-er-more.

111, see Ecclesiastes 50:22-24
Text: Martin Rinckart, 1636,
translation by Catherine Winkworth, 1858, altered
Music: 67 67 66 66, NUN DANKET; Johann Cruger, 1648

DAWN & DUSK 5

B **We gath-er to-geth-er**
  to ask the Lord's bless-ing;
Who chast-ens and hast-ens
  the Way to make known.
The wick-ed op-press-ing
  now cease/ from dis-tress-ing.
Sing prais-es to the Name\;
  God for-gets not God's own.

Be-side us to guide us,
  our God with us join-ing,
Or-dain-ing, main-tain-ing
  do-min-ion div-ine;
So from the be-gin-ning
  the fight/ we were win-ning,
You, Lord, were at our side\,
  all glo-ry be thine!

We all do ex-tol you,
  our Lead-er tri-umph-ant,
And pray that you still our
  De-fend-er will be.
Let your con-gre-ga-tion
  es-cape the trib-u-la-tion;
Your Name be ev-er praised\!
  O Lord, make us free!

132, Text: Dutch:*Wilt heden nu treden*, 1597,
translated by Theodore Baker, 1894, altered
Music: 12 11 12 11 KREMSER; *Nederlandtsche Gedenckclanck*,
by Adrianus Valerius, 1626; arranged and translated
from Dutch to Latin by Edward Kremser, 1877

PSALM 4

Antiphon *You are witnesses of these things,*
the Christ to suffer,
and rise on the third day.   Lk 24:46

When I call, answer me, saving God.
From distress you give me relief.
Be merciful to me and hear my prayer.

Until when, human, will you shame the glory?
Until when will you love delusion and seek the lie?
Know that Adonai set apart the faithful for Adonai
and will hear when I call.

When you tremble in awe, do not sin.
Search in your heart and on your bed, and be silent.
Offer sacrifices of goodness, and trust Adonai.

Many are asking, "Who can show us good?
Adonai, let the light of your faces shine upon us."

You put joy in my heart, more joy
than when their grain and new wine abound.
In the peace of God's face I will lie down and sleep,
for you alone, Adonai, make me dwell in safety.

Glory...   Antiphon

---

50 psalms are unattributed. 73 are
attributed to David (about 1,000 BC), 12 each to
sons of Asaph & Korah, 2 of Solomon and one (Ps 90) to Moses.

VIGIL of SUNDAY (Saturday Evening)

PSALM 61

Antiphon
*Come to me,
all who labor and are burdened,
and I will rest you;
my yoke is gentle
and my burden is light.*   Mt 11:28,30

Hear, God, my cry! Listen to my prayer!
From the edge of the earth I call to you
as my heart grows faint.

To the high rock you lead me
for you are my refuge
and tower of strength against adversity.

I would dwell in your tent for forevers
and take refuge in the shelter of your wings.
For you, God, hearing my vows,
gave inheritance to those revering your name.

You increase the days upon days of the royal one,
and the years for generation and generation,
enthroned in God's presences forever,
appointed and protected in God's love and fidelity.

I will sing praise of your name forever
to fulfill my vows day by day.

Glory...

Antiphon

PSALM 113

Antiphon   *No servant can serve two lords,*
and you cannot serve
God and mammon.   Lk 16:13

Hallelujah!

Praise, you who serve Adonai!
Praise the name Adonai!

Blessed be the name of Adonai
from now and to forevermore.
From the rising of the sun to its setting
praised be the name of Adonai.

Exalted over all the nations is Adonai,
the glory above the heavens.
Who is like our God Adonai,
sitting enthroned on high,
stooping to look down
on the heavens and the earth?

Adonai raises the poor from dust
and lifts up the needy from ash heaps
to sit with royals, the royals of the people,
and settles the childless woman in a home,
a happy mother of children.

Hallelujah!

Glory...   Antiphon

VIGIL of SUNDAY (Saturday Evening)

PSALM 116:10-19

Antiphon *As I, the Lord and Teacher, washed your feet,
   so also are you to wash the feet of each other.*
                                                   Jn 13:14

I believed it and so said, "I am greatly afflicted."
I said when it dismayed me, "Everyone is a liar."

How can I repay to Adonai
all the goodness to me?
I will lift the cup of salvation
and call on the name of Adonai.

My vows to Adonai I will now fulfill
in the presence of all the people.
Precious in the eyes of Adonai
are the saints to the death.

Adonai, I am your servant,
your servant and child of your servant;
you freed me from the chains.
I will offer the sacrifice of thanksgiving
and call on the name of Adonai.

My vows to Adonai I will now fulfill
in the presence of all the people,
in courts of the house of Adonai,
in your midst, Jerusalem.

Hallelujah!

Glory...   Antiphon

PSALM 141

Antiphon *Blessed are the merciful,*
for they will receive mercy.   Mt 5:7

The Beatitudes   Mt 5:3-12
Blessed are the poor in spirit,
for theirs is the reign of heaven.
Blessed are those mourning,
for they will be comforted.
Blessed are the meek,
for they will inherit the earth.
Blessed are those hungering and thirsting
for justice, for they will be satisfied.
Blessed are the merciful,
for they will receive mercy.
Blessed are the clean of heart,
for they will see God.
Blessed are the peacemakers,
for they will be called children of God.
Blessed are those who are persecuted for what is right,
for theirs is the reign of heaven.
Blessed are you when they disrespect and persecute
and tell all the lies against you for my sake;
rejoice and be glad, for great is your reward in the heavens.

VIGIL of SUNDAY (Saturday Evening)

Adonai, I call to you; be quick to come to me.
Hear my voice when I call to you.
May my prayer be as incense set before you,
lifting my hands in evening sacrifice.

Set guard, Adonai, over my mouth.
Keep watch over the gate of my lips.
Let my heart not be drawn to evil matter,
to join in bad deeds with their doers
or to eat of their delicacies.

Let the just person strike me, a kindness,
and rebuke me, as oil on my head;
my head will not refuse this,
my prayer is ever against bad deeds.

Their rulers will drop over cliff edge;
they will learn that my words were well spoken:
"As a farmer breaks up the earth,
bones were scattered at the mouth of Sheol."

But on you, Lord Adonai, are my eyes,
and in you I take refuge;
do not give my self over to death.

Keep me from the hands of the snares
and from the traps of those doing the bad.
When they fall together into their nets,
keep me in safety.

Glory... Antiphon

PSALM 142

Antiphon   *Let the light of you shine before humanity,*
that they may see your good works
and give glory to your Abba in heaven.

Mt 5:16

My voice cries to Adonai;
my voice asks for mercy from Adonai,
before whom I pour out my complaint,
before whom I tell my trouble.
When my spirit grows faint within me
then you know my way.

In the path where I walk they hid a snare for me.
Look right and see: the one with concern for me
has fled away from me for refuge;
there is no one who cares for my life.

I cry to you, Adonai, and say you are my refuge,
my portion in the land of the living.
Listen, El, to my cry, for I am in desperate need.

Rescue me from the strong ones pursuing me;
set my self free from prison to praise your name.
The just ones will gather about me
because you are good to me.

Glory...   Antiphon

Life is a mystery to be lived,
not a problem to be solved.
Soren Kierkegaard

PHILIPPIANS 2:6-11

Antiphon
*Do nothing out of selfishness
or for vainglory,
but humbly deem others
as greater than yourselves.*   Phil 2:3

Christ Jesus, subsisting in the form of God,
did not deem equality with God
something to grab,
but emptied himself,
taking the form of a slave,
becoming in human likeness.

And being found in human fashion,
he humbled himself,
becoming obedient until death,
and death on a cross.

And so God highly exalted him,
and gave to him the name above every name,
that in the name of Jesus
every knee should bend,
of heavenly beings and earthly beings,
and beings under the earth;

And every tongue acknowledge
to the glory of God the Father
that Jesus Christ is Lord.

Glory...   Antiphon

One Chapter-A-Day, to read the whole Bible in 44 months in *Lectio Continua*

One plan: Begin with the shortest Book (2nd John with 13 Verses) and read through to the longest (Isaiah with 66 chapters). Don't skip the footnotes!

PENTATEUCH
- 50 Genesis
- 40 Exodus
- 27 Leviticus
- 36 Numbers
- 34 Deuteronomy

HISTORICAL
- 24 Joshua
- 21 Judges
- 4 Ruth
- 31 1st Samuel
- 24 2nd Samuel
- 22 1st Kings
- 25 2nd Kings
- 29 1st Chronicles
- 36 2nd Chronicles
- 10 Ezra
- 13 Nehemiah
- 14 Tobit
- 16 Judith
- 10 Esther
- 16 1st Maccabees
- 15 2nd Maccabees

WISDOM BOOKS
- 42 Job
- 41 Psalms 1-41
- 31 Psalms 42-72
- 17 Psalms 73-89
- 17 Psalms 90-106
- 44 Psalms 107-150
- 31 Proverbs
- 12 Ecclesiastes
- 8 Song of Songs
- 19 Wisdom
- 51 Sirach

THE PROPHETS
- 66 Isaiah
- 52 Jeremiah
- 5 Lamentations
- 6 Baruch
- 48 Ezekiel
- 14 Daniel
- 14 Hosea
- 4 Joel
- 9 Amos
- 21 vs. Obadiah
- 4 Jonah
- 7 Micah
- 3 Nahum
- 3 Habakkuk
- 3 Zephaniah
- 2 Haggai
- 14 Zechariah
- 3 Malachi

THE GOSPELS
- 28 Matthew
- 16 Mark
- 24 Luke
- 21 John
- 28 Acts

PAULINE LETTERS
- 16 Romans
- 16 1st Corin.
- 13 2nd Corin.
- 6 Galatians
- 6 Ephesians
- 4 Philippians
- 4 Colossians
- 5 1st Thess.
- 3 2nd Thess.
- 6 1st Timothy
- 4 2nd Timothy
- 3 Titus
- 23 vs. Philemon
- 13 Hebrews

CATHOLIC LETTERS
- 5 James
- 5 1st Peter
- 3 2nd Peter
- 5 1st John
- 13 vs. 2nd John
- 15 vs. 3rd John
- 25 vs. Jude
- 22 Revelation

VIGIL of SUNDAY (Saturday Evening)

Note about Readings: A regular Reading is supplied (as below) for each prayer session. Alternatives from the two-year cycles of the Office of Readings and the Lectionary for daily Mass are given each day with Morning Prayer. Another alternative is **lectio continua**, *continuous chapter-a-day reading of the Bible, one book at a time (See page 14).*

READING **ROMANS 11:30-36**

As you then disobeyed God, but now have received mercy by way of these disobediences, so also others have disobeyed in the same mercy so that they also may now receive mercy. For God locked up all in disobedience so that God may show mercy to all. O the depth of riches and wisdom and knowledge of God; how inscrutable the judgments and unsearchable the ways, for who has known the mind of the Lord? Or who has been the Lord's counselor? Or who has given anything to the Lord to be repaid? Because of God, through God, and to God all things are. To God is the doxa-glory for the eons.

RESPONSORY Ps 111:2,4,10

Great are the works of the Lord…
 …pondered by all who delight in them.
Praise enduring for deeds of wonder…
 …pondered by all who delight in them.
Glory to the Father and to the Son and to the Holy Spirit:
 …Great are the works of the Lord,
  pondered by all who delight in them.

Gospel Canticle For Evening
Antiphons

Ordinary Time

YEAR A
Responsorial

Week 3	The Lord is my light and my salvation.	Ps 27
5	The just are a light to the upright.	Ps 112
7	The Lord is kind and merciful.	Ps 103
9	Lord, be my rock of safety.	Ps 31
11	We are his people; the sheep of his flock.	Ps 100
13	For ever I will sing the goodness of the Lord.	Ps 89
15	Seed falling on good ground will yield fruit.	Ps 65
17	Lord, I love your commands.	Ps 119
19	Lord, let us see your kindness.	Ps 85
21	Lord, your love is eternal.	Ps 138
23	If today you hear the voice of the Lord, harden not your hearts.	Ps 95
25	The Lord is near to all who call.	Ps 145
27	The Lord's vineyard is the house of Israel.	Ps 80
29	Give the Lord glory and honor.	Ps 96
31	In you, Lord, I have found my peace.	Ps 131

VIGIL of SUNDAY (Saturday Evening)

Week 33   Blessed are those who fear the Lord.   Ps 128

CANTICLE of MARY (The Magnificat)
LUKE 1:46-55

+ **My soul** is stretched full with praise of the Lord,
and my spirit, beyond joy in God, my Savior,
who chose to lay eyes on this humble servant.

Behold, now and forward,
each and every age will call me blessed,
for the Mighty One did great things to me.

Holy is the name and the mercy
to generations and generations,
the ones fearing the One,

Who scattered the haughty of mind and heart,
pulled the powerful off their high place,
and lifted with dignity the humble in need.

The hungering are filled with good things,
the rich are sent away empty,
and servant Israel is given relief

with a memory of mercy to remember,
the promise spoken to our ancestors,
to Abraham and his descendants forever.

Glory…

Antiphon

INTERCESSIONS

- Lord, make your Church ever new…

- Watch over our pope and bishops…

- Keep us united in our diversity…

- Inspire leaders with your justice…

- Keep married couples in love…

- For respect for the dignity of the human person…

- For a culture of vocations all over the world…

- For all who have died…

- In gratitude for blessings, Abba thank you…

- For the sins of this day, Lord Jesus have mercy…

- With concerns over tomorrow, Holy Spirit help…

CLOSING PRAYER FOR MORNING AND EVENING

Our Fath-er, who art in heav-en;
hal-lowed be thy name.
Thy king dom come, thy will be done
on earth as it is in heav-en.
Give us this day our dai-ly bread
and for-give us our tres-pass-es
as we for-give those who tres-pass a-gainst/ us
and lead us not in-to temp-ta/-tion
but de-liv-er us from e\-vil.
A-men.

WEEK I
SUNDAY MORNING

+ *God, come to my assistance;* Psalm 70:2
  Lord, make haste to help me!

  Glory…

Come, **Ho-ly Spir-it**, who ev-er One
Are with the Fa\-ther and/ the Son;
Come, Ho-ly Spir-it, our souls pos-sess
With your full flood of\ ho-li-ness;
With your full flood of\ ho-li-ness.

In will and deed, by heart and tongue,
With all our pow-ers, your praise/ be sung;
Light up in love our hu-man frame,
Till others catch the\ liv-ing flame;
Till others catch the\ liv-ing flame.

Fa-ther Al-migh-ty, hear now our cry
Through Je-sus Christ\ our Lord/ most high,
Who with the Ho-ly Spir-it and Thee
Do live and reign e\-ter-nal-ly;
Do live and reign e\-ter-nal-ly.

87, Text: attributed to Ambrose of Milan,
Nunc Sancte nobis Spiritus, d.397;
trans. by John Henry Newman, *Tracts for the Times*, 1836, altered
Music: LAMBILLOTTE, LM; with repeat;
Louis Lambillotte, SJ, 1796-1855
Popular melody for: *Come, Holy Ghost, Creator Blest…*

PSALM 1

Antiphon
> *Blessed are the poor in spirit,*
> *for theirs is the reign of heaven.*   Mt 5:3

Blessings are on the human being
who stands not in selfish counsel,
who walks not the way of sinners,
who sits not in the seat of mockers,
but rather delights in the law of Adonai
and meditates on it by day and by night.

This blessed one is like a tree
planted by streams of water
which yields fruit in the season
and its leaf withers not
and prosperity finds what this one does.

Not so those who do the bad,
but rather like the chaff blown in the wind
those who do the bad
will be unable to stand in the judgment
nor sinners in the assembly of the just.

Adonai watches over the way of the just
and bad ways will perish.

Glory...   Antiphon

A tree gives glory to God by being a tree.
See *New Seeds of Contemplation* by Thomas Merton

PSALM 2

Antiphon　*Wind blows where it will;*
you hear its sound not knowing
from where it comes and goes away;
so with everyone
who is born of the Spirit.　　　Jn 3:8

Why do nations rage and peoples plot vanity?
Rulers of the earth make their stand
and rulers gather together
against Adonai and the anointed of Adonai:
"Let us break their chains,
let us throw off their fetters."

The One enthroned in the heavens laughs,
the Lord scoffs and rebukes them.
In anger and in wrath the Lord terrifies them.
"I indeed installed my ruler
on my holy mountain of Zion.

I will proclaim a decree of Adonai who said,
'You are my son, this day I am your father.
Ask of me and nations are your inheritance,
and your possession to the ends of earth.
You will rule them with a scepter of iron
and dash them to pieces of what potters make.'

Psalm 2, continued

> Rulers, now be wise!
> Royals of earth, be warned!
> Serve Adonai with fear; rejoice with trembling!
> Kiss my son, lest he be angry
> and you be destroyed
> for in a moment he can flare up in wrath.
>
> Blessings on all who take refuge in God."

Glory...

Antiphon   *Wind blows where it will;*
you hear its sound not knowing
from where it comes and goes away;
so with everyone
who is born of the Spirit.   Jn 3:8

The contemplative life provides
an area, a space of liberty, of silence,
in which possibilities are allowed to surface
and new choices become manifest.

See *The Intimate Merton*, by Thomas Merton

PSALM 63:1-8

Antiphon *Watch ready, for you know
neither the day nor the hour.*   Mt 25:13

God, you are my God; you I earnestly seek.
My soul, she thirsts for you,
my body, he longs for you,
as in a land with no water, dry and weary.

So in the sanctuary I saw you,
beheld you in your power and glory.
Your love is better than life itself;
my lips will glorify you.

So I will praise you in all the ways I am alive;
calling your name I will lift up my hands.
As with fatness and richness,
my soul will be satisfied;
with singing lips my mouth will sing praise.

When I remember you on my bed,
through night watches I think of you,
you who are my help;
then in the shadow of your wings I sing.
My very self stays close to you;
your right hand upholds me.

Glory...

Antiphon

PSALM 93

Antiphon   *Do you ask if I am a ruler from yourself
or have others told you about me?*   Jn 18:34

Adonai reigns, robed in majesty;
robed is Adonai and armed with strength.

The world is firmly established;
she cannot be moved.
Your throne was set up from long ago;
from eternity you are.

The seas lifted up, Adonai,
the seas lifted up their voice;
the seas lifted up their pounding.

More than thunders of great waters
or mighty breakers of the sea,
mighty in the height is Adonai.

Your statutes stand very firm;
your house, Adonai, is adorned in holiness
for length of days.

Glory...

Antiphon

---

*O God,
your sea is so great
and my boat is so small.*
Breton fishing prayer

DANIEL 3:57-90

Antiphon *Taking the five loaves and the two fishes,*
looking up to heaven, he blessed, and broke,
and gave them to the disciples
to set before the crowd. Lk 9:16

Bless the Lord, all you works of the Lord,
exalt and sing praise to forever.
Angels of the Lord, bless the Lord,
You heavens, bless the Lord,
All you waters above the heavens, bless the Lord,
All you powers, bless the Lord,
Sun and moon, bless the Lord,
Stars of heaven, bless the Lord.

All you rain and dew, bless the Lord,
All you winds, bless the Lord,
You fire and heat, bless the Lord,
You ice and cold, bless the Lord,
You dews and falling snows, bless the Lord,
You snows and frosts, bless the Lord,
You nights and days, bless the Lord,
You light and darkness, bless the Lord,
You lightning and clouds, bless the Lord.

DANIEL 3:57-90, continued

Let the earth bless the Lord,
exalt and sing praise to forever.
You mountains and hills, bless the Lord,
All things growing in the ground, bless the Lord,
You seas and rivers, bless the Lord,
You springs and rain, bless the Lord,
You sea monsters and swimmers, bless the Lord,
All you birds of the air, bless the Lord,
All you wild beasts and cattle, bless the Lord,
You sons and daughters, bless the Lord.

O Israel, bless the Lord,
exalt and sing praise to forever.
You priests of the Lord, bless the Lord,
You servants of the Lord, bless the Lord,
You spirits and souls of the just, bless the Lord,
You holy and humble in heart, bless the Lord,
Hananiah, Azariah, and Mishael, bless the Lord,
exalt and sing praise to forever...

Give thanks to the Lord, who is good,
whose mercy endures to forever.
Bless the God of "gods"
all you who worship the Lord;
sing praise and give thanks to the One God
whose mercy endures to forever.

(No doxology)

SUNDAY MORNING

Antiphon   *Taking the five loaves and the two fishes,*
   looking up to heaven, he blessed, and broke, and gave
   them to the disciples to set before the crowd.   Lk 9:16

PSALM 148

Antiphon   *This I command,*
   that you love one another.   Jn 15:17

Hallelujah!

Give praise from the heavens!
Give praise in the heights.
Give praise all you angels.
Give praise all you hosts.

Give praise sun and moon.
Give praise all stars shining.
Give praise, you heavens of the heavens
and waters above the heavens.

Let them praise the name Adonai,
who commanded and they were created,
who set them in place forever,
to forever the decree Adonai gave,
not to pass away.

Praise Adonai, you earth,
you sea creatures and all in the deep,
lightning and hail, snow and cloud,
wind of the storm, all who do Adonai's bidding,

Psalm 148, continued

you mountains and hills,
fruit trees and cedars,
wild animals and all cattle,
small creatures and birds of flight,

you rulers of the earth and the nations,
royals and all people ruling on earth,
young men and young women,
old folks and children:

Let them praise the name Adonai
whose name alone is exalted,
whose splendor is above earth and the heavens,

who raised a horn for the people,
praise of all the saints,
of the sons and daughters of Israel,
of people close to the Lord.

Hallelujah!

Glory...

Antiphon *This I command,
that you love one another.* Jn 15:17

Grace wakes us up when we're ready.
Sr. Helen Prejean, October 28, 2011

PSALM 149:1-6,9c

Antiphon *John the Baptist told his disciples, this joy of mine is full; it is fitting for the Christ to increase and for me to decrease.*   Jn 3:30

Hallelujah!

Sing to Adonai a new song,
praise in the assembly of saints.
Let Israel rejoice in their Maker,
let the people of Zion be glad in their ruler.

Let them praise the name
with dance, tambourine and harp.
Let them make music for Adonai
who delights in Adonai's people.

Adonai crowns humble ones with salvation.
Let the saints rejoice in honor,
Let them sing for joy on their beds.
Praises of God be in their mouths
and a two-edged sword in their hands.

Retribution on the nations
and punishment on the peoples
binding royalty in restraint
and nobility in rings of iron:
the judgment decreed for them,
such is the glory of the saints.

Hallelujah!

Glory...   Antiphon

DAWN & DUSK WEEK I

OFFICE of READINGS

	Odd Years	**Even Years**
Trinity	1 Corinthians 2:1-16	1 Corinthians 2:1-16
CorpusChristi	Exodus 24:1-11	Exodus 24:1-11
week 3	Romans 8:1-17	Genesis 18
5	1 Corinthians 1:1-17	Genesis 39
7	1 Corinthians 10:14-11:1	2 Corinthians 1:1-14
9	James 2:1-13	Galatians 1:1-12
11	Joshua 24	Isaiah 44:21-45:3
13	1 Samuel 5 & 6	Nehemiah 3 & 4
15	2 Samuel 1	Job 1
17	1 Kings 9	Job 28
19	2 Kings 4:8-44	Jonah 1 & 2
21	Ephesians 4:17-24	Titus 1
23	Amos 7	2 Peter 1:1-11
25	Isaiah 6	Tobit 1
27	Isaiah 22:1-14	Sirach 1
29	2 Kings 22 & 23	Sirach 26
31	2 Kings 24 & 25	Wisdom 8
33	Ezekiel 16	1 Macabees 4

MASS READINGS

	Year A	**Year B**	**Year C**
Trinity Sunday	Exodus 34:4b-6,8-9 2 Corin 13:11-13	Deut 4:32-34,39-40 Romans 8:14-17	Prov 8:22-31 Romans 5:1-5
Corpus Christi	Deut 8:2-3,14b-16a 1 Corin 10:16-17	Exodus 24:3-8 Hebrews 9:11-15	Gen 14:18-20 1 Corin 11:23-26
Wk 3	Isaiah 8:23 - 9:3 1 Corin 1:10-13,17	Jonah 3:1-5,10 1 Corin 7:29-31	Neh 8:2-4a,5-6,8-10 1 Corin 12:12-30
5	Isaiah 58:7-10 1 Corin 2:1-5	Job 7:1-4,6-7 1 Cor 9:16-19,22-23	Isaiah 6:1-2a,3-8 1 Corin 15:1-11

SUNDAY MORNING

	Year A	Year B	Year C
7	Lev 19:1-2,17-18 1 Corin 3:16-23	Is 43:18-19,21-22,24b-25 2 Corin 1:18-22	1 Sm 26:2,7-9,12-13,22-23 1 Corin 15:45-49
9	Deut 11:18,26-28,32 Romans 3:21-25,28	Deut 5:12-15 2 Corinth 4:6-11	1 Kings 8:41-43 Gal 1:1-2,6-10
11	Exodus 19:2-6a Romans 5:6-11	Ezekiel 17:22-24 2 Corinth 5:6-10	2 Sam 12:7-10,13 Galat 2:16,19-21
13	2 Kgs 4:8-11,14-16a Romans 6:3-4,8-11	Wis 1:13-15;2:23-24 2 Cor 8:7,9,13-15	1 Kgs 19:16b,19-21 Gal 5:1,13-18
15	Isaiah 55:10-11 Romans 8:18-23	Amos 7:12-15 Ephesians 1:3-14	Deut 30:10-14 Coloss 1:15-20
17	1 Kings 3:5,7-12 Romans 8:28-30	2 Kings 4:42-44 Ephesians 4:1-6	Gen 18:20-32 Coloss 2:12-14
19	1 Kings 19:9a,11-13a Romans 9:1-5	1 Kings 19:4-8 Eph 4:30-5:2	Wisdom 18:6-9 Hebr 11:1-2,8-19
21	Isaiah 22:19-23 Romans 11:33-36	Josh 24:1-2a,15-17,18b Eph 5:21-32, or 2a,25-32	Isaiah 66:18-21 Heb 12:5-7,11-13
23	Ezekiel 33:7-9 Romans 13:8-10	Isaiah 35:4-7a James 2:1-5	Wisdom 9:13-18b Philemon 9-10,12-17
25	Isaiah 55:6-9 Phil 1:20c-24,27a	Wis 2:12,17-20 James 3:16 - 4:3	Amos 8:4-7 1 Timothy 2:1-8
27	Isaiah 5:1-7 Philippians 4:6-9	Genesis 2:18-24 Hebrews 2:9-11	Hab 1:2-3;2:2-4 2 Tm 1:6-8,13-14
29	Isaiah 45:1,4-6 1 Thess 1:1-5b	Isaiah 53:10-11 Hebrews 4:14-16	Exodus 17:8-13 2 Tim 3:14-4:2
31	Mal 1:14b-2:2b,8-10 1 Thess 2:7b-9,13	Deut 6:2-6 Hebrews 7:23-28	Wis 11:22-12:2 2 Thess 1:11-2:2
33	Prov 31:10-13,19-20,30-31 1 Thess 5:1-6	Daniel 12:1-3 Heb 10:11-14,18	Mal 3:19-20a 2 Thess 3:7-12

READING **REVELATION 7:9-12**

I saw, behold, a crowd too great to number, out of every nation and tribe and people and tongue, standing before the throne and before the Lamb clothed in white robes and with palms in their hands.

They cried out with a loud voice saying,
Salvation to our God sitting on the throne, and to the Lamb.

And all the angels stood around the throne with the elders and the four living creatures, and fell on their faces before the throne and worshipped God, saying
Amen, blessing and glory and wisdom and thanks and honor and power and strength to our God to the eons of the eons. Amen.

RESPONSORY Lk 18:13, 22:69

Lord Jesus Christ, Son of the living God...
...*have mercy on us.*

You are seated at the right hand of the Father...
...*have mercy on us.*

Glory to the Father and to the Son and to the Holy Spirit:
...*Lord Jesus Christ, Son of the living God,
have mercy on us.*

---

*Looking for a great short read? Find
'Way of a Pilgrim,' about the Jesus Prayer:
Lord, Jesus Christ, have mercy on me, a sinner.*

Gospel Canticle For Morning
Antiphons

YEAR B
Responsorial

Ordinary Time

Trinity Sunday	Blessed the people the Lord has chosen.	Ps 33

    A- John 3:16-18   **B-** Mt 28:16-20   **C-** Jn 16:12-15

Corpus Christi	I will take the cup of salvation, and call on the name of the Lord.	Ps 116

    A- John 6:51-58   **B-** Mk 14:12-16,22-26   **C-** Lk 9:11b-17

Week

3   Teach me your ways, O Lord.   Ps 25

    A- Matt 4:12-23   **B-** Mark 1:14-20   **C-** Lk 1:1-4; 4:14-21

5   Praise the Lord
    who heals the brokenhearted.   Ps 147

    A- Matt 5:13-16   **B-** Mark 1:29-39   **C-** Luke 5:1-11

7   Lord heal my soul
    for I have sinned against you.   Ps 41

    A- Matt 5:38-48   **B-** Mark 2:1-12   **C-** Luke 6:27-38

9   Sing with joy to God our help.   Ps 81

    A- Matt 7:21-27   **B-** Mark 2:23-3:6   **C-** Luke 7:1-10

11   Lord, it is good to give thanks to you.   Ps 92

    A- Matt 9:36-10:8   **B-** Mark 4:26-34   **C-** Lk 7:36 - 8:3

13   I will praise you Lord
    for you have rescued me.   Ps 30

    A- Matt 10:37-42   **B-** Mark 5:21-43   **C-** Luke 9:51-62

DAWN & DUSK WEEK I
Antiphons & Gospel Reading for Sundays in Odd Weeks, cont.

Week

15 Lord, let us see your kindness,
and grant us your salvation. Ps 85
A- Matt 13:1-23 **B-** Mark 6:7-13 **C-** Lk 10:25-37

17 The hand of the Lord feeds us. Ps 145
A- Matt 13:44-52 **B-** John 6:1-15 **C-** Luke 11:1-13

19 Taste and see the goodness of the Lord. Ps 34
A- Matt 14:22-33 **B-** John 6:41-51 **C-** Lk 12:32-48

21 Taste and see the goodness of the Lord. Ps 34
A- Matt 16:13-20 **B-** John 6:60-69 **C-** Lk 13:22-30

23 Praise the Lord, my soul! Ps 146
A- Matt 18:15-20 **B-** Mark 7:31-37 **C-** Lk 14:25-33

25 The Lord upholds my life. Ps 54
A- Matt 20:1-16a **B-** Mark 9:30-37 **C-** Luke 16:1-13

27 May the Lord bless us
all the days of our lives. Ps 128
A- Matt 21:33-43 **B-** Mark 10:2-16 **C-** Luke 17:5-10

29 Lord, let your mercy be on us. Ps 33
A- Matt 22:15-21 **B-** Mark 10:35-45 **C-** Luke 18:1-8

31 I love you, Lord, my strength. Ps 18
A- Matt 23:1-12 **B-** Mark 12:28b-34 **C-** Luke 19:1-9

33 You are my inheritance, O Lord! Ps 16
A- Matt 25:14-30 **B-** Mark 13:24-43 **C-** Luke 21:5-19

CANTICLE of ZECHARIAH (The Benedictus)
LUKE 1:68-79

+ Blessed be the Lord the God of Israel
who chose a people to visit with redemption,
and raised salvation in the house of David,
saving strength from God's own servant,

speaking from the age of the prophets
through the mouth of the holy prophet:
Salvation out of enmity,
even out of those who hate us,

to show our ancestors how mercy works, -
and to remember the holy promise of the Lord,
the covenant made for our ancestor Abraham,
calming our fear and making us free
to serve with holy justice before God all our days.

And you also child -
will be called a prophet of the Most High
for you will go before the Lord to prepare his way
and give to people a knowledge of salvation
known in accepting forgiveness of their sins.

From the tender mercy of our God,
the sun rising from the height will visit with light
for those who sit in the dark or shadow of death
and to guide our feet into the way of peace.

Glory...

Antiphon

PETITIONS FOR THE CONSECRATION TO GOD
OF THE DAY AND ITS REST

- For the Church and her ministry and apostolates…
- For secular authorities and all serving as stewards…
- For people who are poor or sick or in sorrow…
- For peace and the basic needs of each human being…
- For acceptance of the gift of the infinite love of God…
- For the blessings of faithful Sabbath rest…
- In gratitude for blessings and grace…
- For those who have asked for my prayer…
- For those for whom I have promised to pray…
- For those who weigh on my heart…

CLOSING PRAYER FOR MORNING AND EVENING

Our Fath-er, who art in heav-en;
hal-lowed be thy name.
Thy king dom come, thy will be done
on earth as it is in heav-en.
Give us this day our dai-ly bread
and for-give us our tres-pass-es
as we for-give those who tres-pass a-gainst/ us
and lead us not in-to temp-ta/-tion
but de-liv-er us from e\-vil.
A-men.

SUNDAY MORNING

HYMN, TE DEUM

You are God: we praise you;
You are the Lord; we acclaim you;
You are the eternal Father: all creation worships you.

To you all angels, all the powers of heaven,
Cherubim and Seraphim, sing in endless praise:
Holy, holy, holy, Lord, God of power and might,
heaven and earth are full of your glory.

The glorious company of apostles praise you.
The noble assembly of prophets praise you.
The white-robed army of martyrs praise you.

All over the world the holy church acclaims you:
Father, of majesty unbounded,
your true and only Son, worthy of all worship,
and the Holy Spirit, advocate and guide.

You, Christ, are the royal of glory,
the eternal Son of the Father.

When you became human to set us free
you did not spurn the Virgin's womb.

You overcame the sting of death,
and opened the reign of heaven to all believers.

You are seated at God's right hand in glory.
We believe that you will come and be our judge.

Come then, Lord, and help your people,
bought with the price of your own blood,
and bring us with your saints
to glory everlasting. Amen.

WEEK I
SUNDAY EVENING

+ *God, come to my assistance;*   Psalm 70:2
  Lord, make haste to help me!

  Glory...

A

Praise God, from whom all bless-ings flow;
Praise God, all crea-tures here be-low;
Praise God a-bove, ye heav'n-ly host,
Praise Fa-ther, Son, and Ho-ly Ghost.

For maj-es-ty and migh-ty deeds,
With blast of horn and tam-bou-rine,
With harp and dance and flute and string,
Let ev'-ry hu-man breath now sing.

Give praise to reach the migh-ty dome,
Give praise with cym-bals, crash-ing sound,
Give praise with lyre and bless-ed skill,
Praise God to wake the ho-ly hill.

Praise God, from whom all bless-ings flow;
Raise hands, all crea-tures here be-low;
Praise God, our Fa-ther and the Son
And Ho-ly Spir-it, Three in One.

120, Text: from Psalm 150; verse 1 by Thomas Ken, 1695, altered;
verses 2,3 by Stephen J. Wolf, 2009
Music: OLD HUNDREDTH, LM, Louis Bourgeois,
first published in *Genevan Psalter*, 1551

B

Ho-ly God\, we praise/ your Name;
Lord of all\, we bow\ be-fore you!
All on earth\ your scep/-ter claim,
All in heav-en a-bove\ a-dore you;

   In-fin/-ite\ your vast do/-main,
   Ev-er-last\-ing is\ your reign.

Hark! The loud\ cel-es/-tial hymn
An-gel choirs\ a-bove\ are rais-ing,
Cher-u-bim\ and ser/-a-phim,
In un-ceas\-ing chor\-us prais-ing;

   Fill the/ heav-ens with sweet ac/-cord:
   Ho-ly, ho\-ly, ho\-ly Lord.

Ho-ly Fa\-ther, Ho/-ly Son,
Ho-ly Spir\-it, Three\ we name you;
While in ess\-ence on/-ly One,
Un-div-i\-ded God\ we claim you;

   And a/-dor\-ing bend the/ knee,
   While we en-ter the mys\-ter-y.

96, Text: Ignaz Franz, *Grosser Gott*, about 1774,
translated by Clarence Walworth, 1858, altered
Music: 78 78 77 GROSSER GOTT,
Katholisches Gesangbuch, Vienna, 1774

PSALM 91

Antiphon	*It has been written,* *"not on bread alone* *shall the human live."*	Lk 4:4

One who dwells in the shelter of Elyon,
in the shadow of Shaddai, will find rest.
I will say of Adonai, my refuge, my fortress:
in my God do I trust.

Surely the Lord will save you
from fowler snare, from deadly pestilence.
With the feather of the Lord you will be covered,
and under those wings you will find refuge,
shield and rampart, the fidelity of the Lord.

You will have no fear of terror at night
nor of arrows flying by day,
of pestilence stalking in the darkness,
nor of plague that destroys at midday.

A thousand may fall at your side,
and ten thousand at your right hand;
near to you they will not come.

Observe with your eyes, simply watch;
punishment of doers of the bad you will see.
Make Adonai, who is my refuge,
make Elyon your dwelling.

SUNDAY EVENING

Harm will not befall you,
nor will disaster come near your tent.
God's own Angels, the Lord will command
to guard you in all of your ways.

In their hands they will lift you up;
your foot will not strike against the stone.
Upon lion and cobra you will tread,
you will trample the great lion and serpent.

"Because you love me, I will rescue you,
I will protect all who know my Name.
You will call upon me and I will answer.
I am with you in trouble;
I will deliver you and honor you.

In length of days I will satisfy you,
and show you my salvation."

Glory...

Antiphon

Psalm 91 is often used for night prayer
with the Canticle of Simeon (Luke 2:29-32 on page 144)
and the antiphon:

Protect us Lord as we stay awake, watch over us as we sleep
that awake we may keep watch with Christ
and asleep rest in his peace.

or *Lord, save/ us! Save/ us while\ we are a-wake\,*
pro-tect us while we are a-sleep, that we may keep our watch/
with Christ/, and when we sleep\, rest/ in his\ peace.

PSALM 64

Antiphon *Abba, forgive them,*
for they know not what they do.   Lk 23:34

Hear my voice, O God, in complaint;
threatened by enmity, you protect my life.
You hide me from conspiracies,
from the noisy crowd of people doing bad things,

who sharpen their tongue like the sword,
aim their arrow of harmful words,
and shoot from ambush the innocent person;
they shoot suddenly and without fear.

They encourage those who plan harm,
and they talk of hidden snares,
saying, "who will see them?"
They plot injustices they call "the perfect plan!"
Surely the human mind and heart are cunning.

But God will shoot sudden arrows
striking down those plans.
Their ruin will be by their own tongues;
all who see them will shake heads at them.

All humanity will fear,
then come to proclaim the work of God,
and ponder the deeds of God.
Let the just rejoice and take refuge in Adonai;
let all the upright of heart give praise.

SUNDAY EVENING

Glory…

                                          Antiphon

PSALM 110:1-6a,7

Antiphon   *Give them food yourselves.*   Lk 9:13a

Adonai said to my Lord:
"Sit at my right hand
until I make enmity
as a footstool for your feet."

A scepter of your might
Adonai will extend from Zion,
and rule in the midst of enmity!

Your troops are willing on the day of your battle.
In holy majesty from the womb of the dawn,
to you is the dew of your youth.
Adonai pledged in a mind unchanging,
"You are a priest to forever
in the order of Melchizedek."

The Lord is at your right hand
and will crush rulers on the day of wrath,
will judge the nations…
and will drink from a brook on the way
with head lifted up in it all.

Glory…

                                          Antiphon

PSALM 111

Antiphon *Stretching out his hand right away,
Jesus took hold of Simon, and said,
Little-faith, why did you doubt?*   Mt 14:31

Hallelujah!

I will extol Adonai with all my heart
in the assembled council of the upright.
Great are the works of Adonai,
pondered by all who delight in them.

Glorious and majestic are the deeds,
and this wise design endures to forever.
Remembered are the deeds of wonder
by gracious and compassionate Adonai,

providing food for ones fearing the One,
remembering the covenant to forever,
and having shown power at work,
giving the people the lands of the nations.

Faithful and just is the handiwork of Adonai,
whose precepts are worthy of trust.
Steadfast are they forever to forever,
done with fidelity and honesty.

Redemption is sent for Adonai's people;
ordained to forever is the covenant.
Holy and awesome is the Name.

The beginning of wisdom is fear of Adonai,
good understanding for all who live by it.
Praise endures to eternity.

Glory...

Antiphon

PSALM 114

Antiphon   *I tell you, forgive; not seven times,
but to seventy times seven.*   Mt 18:22

When Israel came out from Egypt,
the house of Jacob
free from people of another tongue,
Judah became as God's sanctuary,
and Israel God's dominion.

The sea looked and fled, the Jordan turned back.
The mountains skipped like rams
and hills like a flock of lambs.

What to you, sea, that you fled?
Jordan, that you turned back?
Mountains, that you skipped like rams?
You hills, like a flock of lambs?

Tremble, earth, at the presences of the Lord!
Tremble at the presences of the God of Jacob,
who turned rock into pools of waters,
hard rock into springs of waters.

Glory...

Antiphon

REVELATION 19:1b,2a,5b,6b,7

Antiphon

*We are an Easter people
and* **alleluia** *is our song.*   St. Augustine

Alleluia!
Salvation and glory and power are to our God,
whose judgments are true and just.

Alleluia!
Praise our God, all you servants of the Lord,
you small and you great, who hold God in awe.

Alleluia!
The Lord is reigning, our God, the Almighty.
Let us rejoice and let us exult,
and we will give the glory to the Lord.

Alleluia!
The day has come
for the marriage of the Lamb,
and the bride has prepared herself.

Glory...

Antiphon

The normal way we become best friends is by spending so much time with each other that we become happy to accomplish nothing but to waste time together. The best definition of prayer is wasting time with God, who is the good kind of jealous for this kind of time, and so Jesus says, 'I call you friend.'   See John 15

SUNDAY EVENING

READING   **2 CORINTHIANS 1:3-7**

Blessed be the God and Father of our Lord Jesus Christ, Father of compassion and God of all comfort, comforting us in all our affliction that we may be able to comfort those in every affliction, through the comfort by which we ourselves are comforted by God. As the sufferings of Christ abound in us, so through Christ also abounds our comfort.

Now when we are afflicted, it is on behalf of your comfort and salvation; when we are comforted, it is on behalf of your comfort enduring in the same sufferings which we also suffer. Our hope for you is firm, knowing that as you partake in the sufferings, so also you partake of the comfort.

RESPONSORY   Ps 138:5,4

May all creation sing of your ways...
   ...for great is your glory.
And praise the words of your mouth...
   ...for great is your glory.
Glory to the Father and to the Son and to the Holy Spirit:
   ...May all creation sing of your ways,
   for great is your glory.

Comfort (parakleseos) can mean
comfort - consolation - encouragement,
and is related to a name Jesus gives for the
Holy Spirit as helper or advocate pleading for us.

Gospel Canticle For Evening
Antiphons

Ordinary Time Week		YEAR C Responsorial
3	Your words, Lord, are Spirit and life.	Ps 19
5	In the sight of the angels I will sing your praises, Lord.	Ps 138
7	The Lord is kind and merciful.	Ps 103
9	Go out to all the world and tell the good news.	Ps 117
11	Lord, forgive the wrong I have done.	Ps 32
13	You are my inheritance, O Lord.	Ps 16
15	Turn to the Lord in your need.	Ps 69
17	Lord, I called for help and you answered me.	Ps 138
19	Blessed the people the Lord has chosen.	Ps 33
21	Go out to all the world and tell the good news.	Ps 117
23	In every age O Lord you have been our refuge.	Ps 90
25	Praise the Lord who lifts up the poor.	Ps 113
27	If today you hear his voice, harden not your hearts.	Ps 95
29	Our help is from the Lord.	Ps 121
31	I will praise your name forever, my king and my God.	Ps 145

33   The Lord comes to rule the earth with justice. Ps 98

CANTICLE of MARY (The Magnificat)
LUKE 1:46-55

+ **My soul** is stretched full with praise of the Lord,
and my spirit, beyond joy in God, my Savior,
who chose to lay eyes on this humble servant.

Behold, now and forward,
each and every age will call me blessed,
for the Mighty One did great things to me.

Holy is the name and the mercy
to generations and generations,
the ones fearing the One,

Who scattered the haughty of mind and heart,
pulled the powerful off their high place,
and lifted with dignity the humble in need.

The hungering are filled with good things,
the rich are sent away empty,
and servant Israel is given relief

with a memory of mercy to remember,
the promise spoken to our ancestors,
to Abraham and his descendants forever.

Glory…

                                                    Antiphon

INTERCESSIONS

- For those who have gone before us marked with the sign of faith…

- In gratitude for blessings…;   Abba thank you.

- For the sins of this day…;   Lord Jesus have mercy.

- With concerns over tomorrow…;   Holy Spirit help.

THE ROAD AHEAD   Thomas Merton

My Lord God,
I have no idea where I am going.
I do not see the road ahead of me.
Nor do I really know myself,
and the fact that I think I am following your will
does not mean that I am actually doing so.
But I believe that the desire to please you
does in fact please you.
And I hope I have that desire in all that I am doing.
I hope that I will never do
anything apart from that desire.
And I know that if I do this
you will lead me by the right road,
though I may know nothing about it.
Therefore I will trust you always though
I may seem to be lost and in the shadow of death.
I will not fear, for you are ever with me,
and you will never leave me to face my perils alone.

OUR FATHER…

WEEK I
MONDAY MORNING

+ *God, come to my assistance;*   Psalm 70:2
  Lord, make haste to help me!

  Glory...

From all that dwell be/-low the\ skies,
Let the Cre-a-tor's praise a-rise;
Let the Re-deem/-er's/ Name\ be\ sung,
Through ev-'ry land, by ev-'ry tongue.

E-ter-nal are your/ mer-cies\, Lord;
E-ter-nal truth at-tends your Word.
Your praise shall sound/ from/ shore\ to\ shore,
Till suns shall rise and set no more.

In ev-'ry land be/-gin the\ song;
To ev-'ry land the strains be-long;
In cheer-ful sounds/ all/ voi\-ces\ raise,
And fill the world with loud-est praise.

92, see Psalm 117
Text: Isaac Watts, *The Psalms of David*, 1719;
Robert Spence, *Pocket Hymn Book*, 1780, altered
Music: DUKE STREET, LM; John Hatton, 1793

PSALM 9

Antiphon *Foxes have holes and birds of the sky nests,
but the Son of Humanity has no place
where his head may lay.* Lk 9:58

I will praise Adonai with all my heart;
I will tell of all the wonderful things.
I will be glad and rejoice in you,
I will sing praise to your name, Most High.

When enmity turns back
it stumbles before you
for you upheld my right and my cause;
you sat on the throne judging justly.

You rebuked nations, you destroyed bad ways;
their name you blotted out to forever and ever.
Enmity is overtaken by endless ruin;
cities are uprooted and their memories perish.

Adonai reigns to forever,
set up on the throne for judgment
to judge the world in fairness
and to govern peoples with justice.

Adonai is the refuge for the oppressed,
the stronghold in times of trouble.
Those who know your name will trust in you,
for you never forsake seekers of Adonai.

MONDAY MORNING

Sing praise to Adonai, enthroned in Zion.
Proclaim the deeds among the nations
for the One who can avenge violence remembers
and does not ignore the cry of the afflicted.

Have mercy on me, Adonai,
and see the persecution of enmity.
Lift me up from the gates of death
that I may declare all of your praises
in the gates of your daughter Zion.
I will rejoice in your salvation.

Nations fell into the pit they dug;
in the net that they hid are their own feet caught.
Adonai is known by justice;
bad ways get snared in their handiwork.

The nations forgetting God return to Sheol,
but the needy will not be forgotten
nor will the hope of the afflicted ever perish.

Arise Adonai; let not the human triumph.
Let the nations be judged in your presences.
Strike the nations, Adonai,
and let them know their humanity.

Glory...   Antiphon

Live always, monk, as if you were to die tomorrow
but treat the body as if to live on with it for many years to come.
See *Praktikos* (#29) by Evagrius Ponticus

PSALM 5

Antiphon *If someone wishes to sue you*
to get your tunic,
let that one take also the cloak.   Mt 5:40

Give ear to my words, Adonai;
consider my sighing.
Listen to the sound of my cry for help,
for to you I pray, my Ruler and my God.

Hear, Adonai, my morning voice;
with my morning request before you, I wait.

You are not pleased with doings of the bad,
nor can the doers dwell with you.
The arrogant cannot stand before your eyes.
You hate when wrong is done, you destroy lies,
you abhor bloodshed and deceit.

By the greatness of your mercy, Adonai,
I will come into your house,
In reverence I will bow in your holy temple.

Lead me in your justice, Adonai;
because of enmity
make straight before me your way.

MONDAY MORNING

Their mouth is not to be trusted,
their heart is destruction,
their throat an open grave,
and their tongue speaks deceit.

If you, God, declare them guilty
let their fall be by their intrigue;
let them be banished if they have sinned,
if they have rebelled against you.

But let all who take refuge in you be glad;
let them sing for joy forever.
You spread protection over them
that they may rejoice in you and love your name.

You bless the just, Adonai,
surrounding them with favor as a shield.

Glory...

                                                                         Antiphon

---

It's letting go
of the sense that the past
should have been any different or better.
See *The Tricky Part* by Martin Moran

PSALM 84

Antiphon *Why do you look for me?*
Do you not know that I have to be
in my Abba's house?   Lk 2:49

How lovely are your dwellings,
Adonai Sabaoth!
My soul she yearns and even faints
for the courts of Adonai;
my heart and my flesh cry out for God alive.

Even the sparrow found a home
and the swallow a nest for her
where she may settle her young ones
near your altar, Adonai Sabaoth,
my Ruler and my God.

Blessed are the dwellers in your house,
ever they praise you.
Blessed are the ones whose strength is in you,
who make a pilgrimage in their hearts.

Passing through the Baca Valley,
springs are found,
pools covered over with autumn rains.
They go from strength to strength
and appear before God in Zion.

MONDAY MORNING

Adonai, God Sabaoth, hear my prayer!
Listen, God of Jacob. God, our shield, look!
Look on the face of your anointed one!

Better is one day in your courts
than a thousand elsewhere.
Better to be doorkeeper in my God's house
than to dwell in tents of those who do the bad,

for God Adonai is sun and shield.
Adonai bestows grace and honor,
withholding no goodness
from blameless walkers.

Adonai Sabaoth,
blessed is the one trusting in you.

Glory...

Antiphon

Psalm 84
is often used
for the blessing
of a new sacred space.

ISAIAH 2:2-5

Antiphon

*Blessed are the peacemakers,
for they will be called
sons and daughters of God.*

Mt 5:9

In the last of the days
the mountain of Adonai's temple
will be established as chief of the mountains,
raised above the hills.

All the nations will stream to it.
Many peoples will come and say,
"Come, let us go up to the mountain of Adonai,
to the house of the God of Jacob,
who will teach us the ways
so we may walk in the path."

Indeed, from Zion the law will go out
and from Jerusalem the word of Adonai,
who will judge between the nations
and settle disputes for many peoples.

They will beat their swords into plowshares
and their spears into pruning hooks.
Nations will not take up the sword against nations,
and they will train for war no more.

House of Jacob, come!
Let us walk in Adonai's light.

Glory...

Antiphon

1 CHRONICLES 29:10b-13

Antiphon   *Every thing we have to give
is from you, our God.*   1Chr 29:14b

Praise be to you, Adonai, God of Israel,
our Abba from everlasting to everlasting.

To you, Adonai, are the greatness and power
and glory and majesty and splendor
for all in the heavens and on the earth.

To you, Adonai, are the reign
and exaltation as head over all,
and wealth and honor from before you.

And you rule over all in your hand,
strength and power in your hand,
to lift up and give strength to all.

Now, our God, we give thanks to you
and praise your name and your glory.

Glory…

Antiphon

---

*I want
not the things
you have, but you.*
Paul to the Corinthians   2 Cor 12:14

PSALM 29

Antiphon *A voice out of heaven:*
this is my Beloved Son
in whom I am well pleased.   Mt 3:17

Ascribe to Adonai, you in the heavens,
acknowledge Adonai as glory and strength.
Give to Adonai the glory of the Name.
Worship Adonai in holy splendor.

The voice of Adonai over the waters,
the God of glory thunders.
Adonai over mighty waters,
the voice of Adonai in power and majesty,
the voice of Adonai breaking cedars,

Adonai breaks the cedars of Lebanon
and makes Lebanon leap like a calf
and Sirion like a young bull.

The voice of Adonai strikes flashes of lightning,
the voice of Adonai shakes the desert,
Adonai shakes the desert of Kadesh.

The voice of Adonai makes the deer give birth
and strips the forests bare,
and all in the temple cry, "glory."
Adonai sits over the flood
and Adonai is enthroned as Ruler to forever.

May Adonai give strength to the people;
may Adonai bless the people with peace.

Glory... Antiphon

God is not nice. God is not an uncle. God is an earthquake.
Hasidic saying

PSALM 96

Antiphon   *Render to Ceasar the things of Ceasar,*
           and to God the things of God.   Mt 22:21

Sing to Adonai a new song!
Sing to Adonai, all the earth!
Sing to Adonai and praise the name!
Proclaim salvation from day to day!

Declare among the nations the glory of the Lord!
Among all the peoples the marvelous deeds,
for great is Adonai, greatly being praised,
the one to be feared above all so-called "gods."

For all "gods" of the nations
are do-nothing idols,
but Adonai made the heavens,
splendor and majesty and strength and glory
in the holy sanctuary.

Ascribe to Adonai, families of nations!
Acknowledge Adonai as glory and strength!
Give to Adonai the glory of the Name!

Bring offerings and come into the courts!
Worship Adonai in holy splendor!
Tremble in the presence all you earth!

Say among the nations, "Adonai is our ruler!"
Firmly set, the world cannot be moved
and peoples will be judged with equity.

Let the heavens rejoice and the earth be glad.
Let the sea resound and all its fullness.
Let the fields and all that is in them be jubilant
and all the trees of the forests sing for joy

before Adonai who comes,
who comes to judge the earth,
who will judge the world and its peoples
with justice and honesty.

Glory…

Antiphon

---

*Praying the
psalms continually
ponders and proclaims
the action of God in the history
of salvation.*   Pope Paul VI, 1970

OFFICE OF READINGS and FIRST READING AT MASS

	Odd Years	**Even Years**
1 readings	*Romans 1:1-17*	*Genesis 1:1-2:3*
mass	**Hebrews** 1:1-6	**1 Samuel** 1:1-8
3 rdgs	*Romans 8:18-39*	*Genesis 19*
mass	Hebrews 9:15,24-28	2 Samuel 5:1-7,10
5 rdgs	*1 Corinthians 1:18-31*	*Genesis 41*
mass	**Genesis** 1:1-19	1 Kings 8:1-7,9-13
7 rdgs	*1 Corinthians 11:2-16*	*2 Corinthians 1:15-2:11*
mass	**Ben Sira** 1:1-10	James 3:13-18
9 rdgs	*James 2:14-26*	*Galatians 1:13-2:10*
mass	**Tobit** 1:1a-2;2:1-9	**2 Peter** 1:2-7
11 rdgs	*Judges 2 & 3*	*Ezra 1 & 2 & 3*
mass	2 Corinthians 6:1-10	1 Kings 21:1-16
13 rdgs	*1 Samuel 7 & 8*	*Nehemiah 5 & 6*
mass	Genesis 18:16-33	**Amos** 2:6-10,13-16
15 rdgs	*2 Samuel 2 & 3*	*Job 2*
mass	**Exodus** 1:8-14,22	**Isaiah** 1:10-17
17 rdgs	*1 Kings 10*	*Job 29 & 30*
mass	Exodus 32:15-24,30-34	Jeremiah 13:1-11
19 rdgs	*2 Kings 5*	*Jonah 3 & 4*
mass	Deuteronomy 10:12-22	**Ezekiel** 1:2-5,24-28c

MONDAY MORNING

	Odd Years	**Even Years**
21 rdgs	*Ephesians 4:25-5:7*	*Titus 2*
mass	**1 Thess** 1:2b-5,8b-10	**2 Thess** 1:1-5,11b-12
23 rdgs	*Amos 8*	*2 Peter 1:12-21*
mass	Colossians 1:24-2:3	1 Corinthians 5:1-8
25 rdgs	*Isaiah 3*	*Tobit 2*
mass	**Ezra** 1:1-6	**Proverbs** 3:27-34
27 rdgs	*Isaiah 30:1-18*	*Sirach 2*
mass	**Jonah** 1:1-2:1,11	**Galatians** 1:6-12
29 rdgs	*Nahum 1 & 2 & 3*	*Sirach 27 & 28*
mass	Romans 4:20-25	Ephesians 2:1-10
31 rdgs	*Jeremiah 38*	*Wisdom 9*
mass	Romans 11:29-36	Philippians 12:1-4
33 rdgs	*Ezekiel 17*	*2 Macabees 12*
mass	**1 Maccabees** 1:10-15,41-43,54,57,62,64	**Revelation** 1:1-4;2:1-5a

READING **2 THESSALONIANS 3:7-13**

You yourselves know how good it is to imitate us. We were not idle among you, nor did we eat bread as a gift from anyone, but by labor and struggle by night and by day working, to not be a burden on any of you, not that we have no authority, but so that we ourselves might give to you an example to imitate.

2 Thessalonians 3, continued

Even when we were with you, we gave you as a charge that if anyone does not wish to work, neither let that one eat. For we hear of some walking among you idly, not working but walking around the work, and to such we charge and exhort in the Lord Jesus Christ that from your quiet working you may eat bread. And you, brothers and sisters, do not lose heart in doing good.

RESPONSORY   Ps 72:18,19

Blessed be the Lord, the God of Israel...
  ...*blessed from now and to forever.*
The One alone doing marvelous deeds...
  ...*blessed from now and to forever.*
Glory to the Father and to the Son and to the Holy Spirit:
  ...*Blessed be the Lord, the God of Israel;*
  blessed from now and to forever.

Gospel Canticle For Morning

Antiphon   *Blessed be the Lord our God.*

Gospel Reading for Monday of

Week			
1	Mark 1:14-20	13 Matt 8:18-22	25 Luke 8:16-18
3	Mark 3:22-30	15 Mt 10:34 - 11:1	27 Lk 10:25-37
5	Mark 6:53-56	17 Matt 13:31-35	29 Lk 12:13-21
7	Mark 9:14-29	19 Matt 17:22-27	31 Lk 14:12-14
9	Mark 12:1-12	21 Matt 23:13-22	33 Lk 18:35-43
11	Matt 5:38-42	23 Luke 6:6-11	

CANTICLE of ZECHARIAH (The Benedictus)
LUKE 1:68-79

+ **Blessed be** the Lord the God of Israel
who chose a people to visit with redemption,
and raised salvation in the house of David,
saving strength from God's own servant,

speaking from the age of the prophets
through the mouth of the holy prophet:
Salvation out of enmity,
even out of those who hate us,

to show our ancestors how mercy works, -
and to remember the holy promise of the Lord,
the covenant made for our ancestor Abraham,
calming our fear and making us free
to serve with holy justice before God all our days.

And you also child -
will be called a prophet of the Most High
for you will go before the Lord to prepare his way
and give to people a knowledge of salvation
known in accepting forgiveness of their sins.

From the tender mercy of our God,
the sun rising from the height will visit with light
for those who sit in the dark or shadow of death
and to guide our feet into the way of peace.

Glory...

                                                      Antiphon

MONDAY MORNING

PETITIONS FOR THE CONSECRATION TO GOD
OF THE DAY AND ITS WORK

- For the Church and her ministry and apostolates…

- For secular authorities and all serving as stewards…

- For people who are poor or sick or in sorrow…

- For peace and the basic needs of each human being…

- For justice for migrant workers and refugees…

- For starving children awakening our conscience…

- For people living in subhuman conditions…

- For human beings enslaved or unjustly imprisoned…

- For laborers where treated as mere tools for profit…

- For good work for all to do in dignity…

- In gratitude for blessings and grace…

FOR WORKERS IN
OFFICES, SHOPS & MARKETS

adapted from the
Book of Blessings

O God, lead all who plan and conduct business to
wise and honest decisions and give them the grace
to carry them out fairly for the common good.
Like the Carpenter, may all who skillfully transform
the things you have created know their dignity
and be fulfilled in making human lives better.
And may buyers and sellers
embody justice and charity and find joy
in the progress of the whole earthly city.

OUR FATHER…

LECTIO DIVINA
lek'-see-oh div-ee'-nuh

1. *Lectio* – Read the passage of the word of God with attention, silently, aloud, or in a whisper. If drawn to a word or phrase or image, stop.

2. *Meditatio* – Breathe. Repeat the word or phrase or image over and over as you breathe. Let it sink into your mind, heart, soul and strength. Savor the word. Ask just one question: *Why this? What do you wish to say, Lord?*

3. *Oratio* – Be not afraid to enter into a spontaneous and loving dialogue with God. Talk to God as you would talk to your closest most intimate friend. Be totally honest about what you are thinking and feeling. Are any memories provoked? What do you want to say to God who loves you just the way you are? You may be drawn to praise, thanksgiving, contrition, petition, desires, decisions, resolutions, commitments, dedications... God is interested in everything you have to say and will not judge you. You get to decide whether you will integrate this Word of God into your heart, life and work, or whether you will reject it or dismiss it as of no worth or value to you.

4. *Contemplatio* – For the remainder of the time you have set aside, go back to the word, phrase or image. Breathe. Relax. Simply repeat the word, phrase or image over and over. When distracting thoughts or feelings enter your mind (they will), go back to your word. There is nothing to accomplish; just give this time to the God who loves you. Sitting in God's presence in this silence, you are making an act of faith that God is working in you in God's own time and way. When your time is up, offer a prayer of gratitude. Many people who do *Lectio Divina* find regular journaling helpful.

WEEK I
MONDAY EVENING

+ *God, come to my assistance;* Psalm 70:2
Lord, make haste to help me!

Glory…

For the/ beau-ty of the earth,
For the glo-ry of the skies,
For the/ love which from our birth
O-ver and a-round us lies.
Lord of all, to you we raise
This our song of grate-ful praise.

For the/ beau-ty of each hour,
Of the day and of the night,
Hill and/ val-ley, tree and flow'r,
Sun and moon and stars of light.
Lord of all, to you we raise
This our song of grate-ful praise.

For the/ joy of ear and eye,
For the heart and mind's de-light,
For the/ mys-tic har-mo-ny
Link-ing sense to sound and sight.
Lord of all, to you we raise
This our song of grate-ful praise.

For the/ joy of hu-man love,
Bro-ther, sis-ter, par-ent, child,
Friends on/ earth and friends a-bove,
Sa-cred res-pite from the wild.
Lord of all, to you we raise
This our song of grate-ful praise.

For your/ peo-ple ev-er-more
Lift-ing ho-ly hands a-bove,
Off-'ring/ up on ev-'ry shore
Faith and sac-rif-i-cial love.
Lord of all, to you we raise
This our song of grate-ful praise.

Per-fect/ gift of pres-ence thine
Won-drous gift so free-ly giv'n,
Gra-ces/ hu-man and div-ine,
Peace on earth and joy in heav'n.
Lord of all, to you we raise
This our song of grate-ful praise.

94, Text: Lyra Eucharistica, 1864;
Folliot S. Pierpoint, 1864, altered
Music: 77 77 77, DIX, Conrad Kocher, 1838;
adapted by William H. Monk, 1823-99

When God looks at us God sees Jesus,
and only Jesus, the innocent, guiltless Jesus.
See *Who Told You That You Were Naked?* by John Jacob Raub

PSALM 7

Antiphon *Why do you see*
the piece of dust in your neighbor's eye
but ignore the wood beam
in your own eye? Lk 6:41

My God, **Adonai**, in you I take refuge;
save me and deliver me from all who pursue me.
Like lions they want to tear me up,
rip my self to pieces with no one to save me.

My God, Adonai, if I deserve this,
if there is guilt on my hands,
if I did wrong to one at peace with me,
or if I robbed without cause from an adversary,

then let that one pursue my self
and overtake my life
and trample my honor to the ground;
let that one put me down in the dust.

Arise, Adonai, rise up in your anger
against the rages of enmity.

Awake, my God, and decree your justice
and let the assembly of peoples gather to you;
rule over us from the height.
Let Adonai be the judge of the peoples.

Judge me, Adonai, as you judge me in justice,
as you judge my integrity, Most High.
May violence end now and the just be secure;
search our minds and hearts, God of justice.

My shield, God Most High,
saves the honest of heart,
and judges each day with justice,
holding the threat of wrath.

If none repent, they will sharpen their sword
and bend their bow with string and make ready
with weapons of death and flaming arrows.
See, trouble is conceived and evil is pregnant,
then comes to birth disillusionment.

They dig holes and scoop them out
but fall into the pits they made.
Their trouble recoils on their heads;
on their heads their violence makes landing.

I give thanks for the justice of Adonai
and sing praise to the name of Most High Adonai.

Glory...

Antiphon

---

*The old joke is that though the psalmists seem to suffer from
paranoia, nevertheless somebody might truly be out to get them.*

PSALM 71

Antiphon *Amen I tell you
that no prophet is acceptable
in their native place.*   Lk 4:24

In you, Adonai, I take refuge;
to forever, let me not be shamed.
In your justice you rescue and deliver me.
Turn your ear to me and save me!

Be to me as a rock, and a refuge to go to always.
Command that I be saved,
for you are my rock and my fortress.
My God, deliver me
from the hands and from the grasp
of doers of the cruel bad,

for you are my hope, Lord Adonai,
my confidence since my youth.
I have relied on you from birth,
from my mother's womb you brought me forth;
my praise is ever to you.

To many I became like a portent
but you are my strong refuge.
My mouth is filled all the day
with praise of your splendor.
Cast me not away at my time of old age;
forsake me not when my strength is gone.

MONDAY EVENING

Enmity speaks against me;
waiting on my life, conspirers together say,
"God has forsaken that one! Pursue to seize,
for no one is coming to the rescue!"

God, be not far from me.
God, come quickly to help me!
May accusations against me perish in shame.
May scorn and disgrace
cover the desire to do harm.

But I will hope always and add praise of you.
My mouth will tell of your just deeds,
all the day of your salvation,
though I know not its measure;

I will come in mighty acts of Lord Adonai;
I will tell of your singular justice.
You taught me, God, since my youth;
to this day I declare your marvelous deeds.

Even in my old age and gray hair
you do not forsake me, God,
till I delcare your power to this generation,
your might to all yet to come,
and your justice to the heavens,
you, God, who have done great things.
Who, God, is equal to you?

Psalm 71, continued

Though you let me see troubles, many and bitter,
you will again let me live.
And from the depths of the earth
you will again raise me up.
You will restore my honor
and you will again comfort me.

With the harp instrument I will praise you
and your faithfulness, my God;
I will sing praise to you with lyre,
Holy One of Israel.

My lips will shout for joy
when I sing praise to you,
even my self whom you redeemed.

Also my tongue will tell
all the day of your justice,
for desires of some to harm me
are in shame and confusion.

Glory…

Antiphon *Amen I tell you
that no prophet is acceptable
in their native place.* Lk 4:24

---

*Psalm 71
is known as a
song of the elders.*

PSALM 11

Antiphon *Blessed are you poor,*
for yours is the reign of God.   Lk 6:20b

In Adonai I take refuge.
How can you say to my self,
"Flee, bird, to your mountain
for look, doers of bad now bend their bow,

they set their arrow on the string
to shoot from the shadow at the upright of heart.
When the foundations are destroyed,
what can the upright do?"

Adonai is in the holy temple,
on Adonai's throne in the heavens
with eyes observing, examining
the sons and daughters of humanity.

Adonai examines the good and the bad,
hating in the soul the love of violence,
and will rain onto bad ways
coal and sulphur on fire
and scorching wind, the lot of their cup,

for Adonai is just, loving justice;
we will see the faces of the Just One.

Glory…

Antiphon

PSALM 15

Antiphon
*Blessed are the clean of heart,
for they will see God.*   Mt 5:8

Adonai, who may dwell in your tent sanctuary?
Who may live on your holy mountain?
One walking without blame, one doing the right,
speaking the truth in the heart,

whose tongue does not slander,
who does no wrong to a neighbor,
who casts no slur on a mutual human,
in whose eyes vile acts are despised

while those who fear Adonai are honored,
whose sworn oath is not changed even to pain,
who lends money without usury,
and accepts no bribe against the innocent.

One faithful in these
will be unshaken to forever.

Glory...

Antiphon

---

*Humans, you have been told
what is good and what Adonai requires of you:
do justice, love goodness, and walk humbly with your God.*

Micah 6:8

PSALM 123

Antiphon *Talitha koun;*
little girl, I say to you, arise.   Mk 5:41

I lift up my eyes to you,
sitting in the heavens.
As eyes of a servant are
to the hand of a master,

as the eyes of a maid
are to the hand of a mistress,
see, our eyes are to Adonai
till our God shows to us mercy.

Have mercy on us, Adonai, have mercy on us,
for we have endured much contempt.
Much ridicule from proud ones
and contempt of arrogant ones
have we ourselves endured.

Glory…

Antiphon

Consider what it means to
be a baptized follower of Jesus:
Lifegiver Priest, Soldier Prophet,
Footwasher Royal, and Beloved Lover.
See *God's Ones* by Stephen Joseph Wolf

PSALM 124

Antiphon   *One finding one's own life will lose it,
and one losing one's own life for my sake
will find it.*   Mt 10:39

If Adonai was not for us, let Israel now say,
if Adonai was not for us
when human beings attacked against us,
then they would have swallowed us alive
when their anger blazed against us.

Then the floods would have engulfed us,
the torrents would have swept over our selfs,
and the raging waters would have swept over us.

Praise be to Adonai,
who did not let us be torn by their teeth.
Our selfs, like a bird,
escaped from the snare of fowlers.

The snare being broken we escaped.
Our help is in the name of Adonai,
the Maker of heavens and earth.

Glory...   Antiphon

---

*Take off your sandals... Offer whatever still-incomplete
awareness of illusions that you can... Then let Jesus pray...*
See *Too Deep For Words* by Thelma Hall

EPHESIANS 1:3-10

Antiphon *Jesus called to himself the Twelve and began to send them out two by two.* Mk 6:7a

Blessed be the God and Abba
of our Lord Jesus Christ,
who has blessed us in Christ
with every spiritual blessing in the heavens.

God chose us in Christ
before the foundation of the world,
to be holy and free of blemish before him.

In love, God gave us a destiny:
as parents adopt, through Jesus Christ himself,
in accord with the good pleasure of God's will
to the praise of the glory of grace
by which we are favored as God's beloved.

In Christ we have the redemption
through his blood, the forgiveness of sins,
in accord with the riches of his grace
which he made abound to us.

In all wisdom and intelligence
the mystery of God's will is made known to us
in accord with God's good pleasure and purpose:

A stewardship of the fullness of time,
heading up all things in Christ,
the things in the heavens and the things on earth.

Glory...   Antiphon

READING — **COLOSSIANS 1:9b-14**

May you be filled with the full knowledge of God's will in all wisdom and spiritual understanding, to walk worthily and all-pleasing to the Lord in every good work bearing fruit, and growing in the full knowledge of God, be empowered with all power as the glory of God is mighty, and endure all long-suffering with joy.

Give thanks to the Father who has made you fit for your part of the lot of the saints in light, who delivered us out of the authority of darkness and transitioned us into the reign of his beloved Son, in whom we have redemption, the forgiveness of our sins.

RESPONSORY — Ps 41:5

You, Lord, are the one who can heal me…
  …*for it is you I have grieved.*
Lord, show to me your mercy…
  …*for it is you I have grieved.*
Glory to the Father and to the Son and to the Holy Spirit:
  …*You, Lord, are the one who can heal me,*
    for it is you I have grieved.

Come Holy Spirit,
take hold of my life, and
sign me with your holy love;
give me your gifts, confirm me in faith.
Spirit come.

Serafina Di Giacomo

CANTICLE of MARY (The Magnificat)
LUKE 1:46-55

Antiphon *My soul is stretched full*
with praise of the Lord.

+ **My soul** is stretched full with praise of the Lord,
and my spirit, beyond joy in God, my Savior,
who chose to lay eyes on this humble servant.

Behold, now and forward,
each and every age will call me blessed,
for the Mighty One did great things to me.

Holy is the name and the mercy
to generations and generations,
the ones fearing the One,

Who scattered the haughty of mind and heart,
pulled the powerful off their high place,
and lifted with dignity the humble in need.

The hungering are filled with good things,
the rich are sent away empty,
and servant Israel is given relief

with a memory of mercy to remember,
the promise spoken to our ancestors,
to Abraham and his descendants forever.

Glory…

Antiphon

INTERCESSIONS

- Lord, keep married couples in love…

- Grow our youth in wisdom and grace…

- For respect for the dignity of the human person…

- For all who have died…

- In gratitude for blessings, Abba thank you…

- For the sins of this day, Lord Jesus have mercy…

- With concerns over tomorrow, Holy Spirit help…

PRAYER OF SAINT FRANCIS

Lord, make me an instrument of your peace.
Where there is hatred, let me sow love.
Where there is injury, pardon.
Where there is discord, unity.
Where there is doubt, faith.
Where there is error, truth.
Where there is despair, hope.
Where there is sadness, joy.
Where there is darkness, light.
O Divine Master, grant that I may not so much seek
to be consoled as to console,
to be understood as to understand,
to be loved as to love.
For it is in giving that we receive.
It is in pardoning that we are pardoned.
And it is in dying that we are born to eternal life.

OUR FATHER…

WEEK I
TUESDAY MORNING

+ *God, come to my assistance;* Psalm 70:2
  Lord, make haste to help me!

  Glory...

Lord of all be-ing, throned a-far,
Your glo-ry flames from sun and star;
Cen-ter and soul of ev-'ry sphere\\,
And yet to lov-ing hearts how near.

Sun of our life, your liv-ing ray
Sheds on our path the glow of day;
Star of our hope, your gen-tle light\\
Shall ev-er cheer the long-est night.

Lord of all life, be-low, a-bove,
Whose light is truth, whose warmth is love;
Be-fore the bril-liance of your throne\\
We ask no lus-ter of our own.

Give us your grace to make us true,
And kind-ling hearts that burn for you,
Till all your liv-ing al-tars claim\\
One ho-ly light, one heav-'nly flame.

108, Text: Oliver Wendell Holmes, 1809-1894
Music: JESU DULCIS MEMORIA, LM; Model 1
Popular melody for: *O Radiant Light, O Sun Divine*

PSALM 10

Antiphon *New wine is put
into fresh wineskins.*   Mk 2:22

Why, Adonai, do you stand distant
and hide in times of the trouble?
In arrogance doers of the bad hunt the weak
and are caught in schemes they devise.

Doers of the bad boast of what their hearts crave,
blessing the greedy and reviling Adonai.
In pride they point their nose away
and seek God in none of their thoughts.

Their haughty ways prosper always,
your laws are kept at a distance,
and they sneer at all who oppose them.

They say to themselves
"I will not be shaken, but happy,
untroubled for generations to come."
Their mouths are full of curses, lies and threats,
trouble and bad things kept under their tongue.

They lie in wait to ambush villages and murder,
their secret eyes on the innocent victim.
They lie in wait to ambush like a lion,
undercover lying in wait to catch the helpless,
they catch and drag the helpless off in their nets.

TUESDAY MORNING

The victims are crushed and collapse,
falling under their strength.
They say to themselves "El has forgotten,
with faces covered, and sees nothing anymore."

Arise, Adonai! God, lift up your hand!
Do not forget the helpless ones.
For why do those doing bad revile God and say,
to themselves, "God will not call an accounting"?

But you do see trouble and grief,
and consider taking the matter in hand;
to you the victims commit themselves,
to you, the helper of orphans.

Stop the arm of the doer of the bad;
call to account lest bad things be kept secret.
Adonai rules forever and ever;
the nations will vanish from the land.

You hear, Adonai, the desire of the afflicted;
you encourage their heart and open your ear
to defend the orphaned and the oppressed.
May humanity repeat no terror on the earth.

Glory…

Antiphon

A subordinate caste accepts a survival mechanism in which
people must become attuned to the people with power over them
and learn to adjust themselves to their expectations to please them
See *Caste: the Origins of Our Discontents* by Isabel Wilkerson.

PSALM 68

Antiphon *When you are invited, take the lowest place;*
one exalting the self will be humbled,
and one humbling the self will be exalted.

Lk 14:10,11

May God arise
and may enmity flee and be scattered.
As smoke is blown, let it blow;
as wax melts before fire
may bad ways perish from before God.

But may just ones be glad
and rejoice before God;
may they be happy with joy.
Sing to God! Sing praise to the name!
Extol the Rider of the Clouds,
and rejoice in the name Adonai,

Abba of the fatherless
and defender of widows,
God dwelling in holiness.
God sets the lonely into a family
and leads prisoners forth with songs,
but ones rebelling live on sun-scorched land.

TUESDAY MORNING

When you went out before your people, God,
when you marched through the wasteland,
the earth shook and heavens poured rain
before the One God of Sinai,
before God, the God of Israel.

You gave a shower of abundances, God,
on your inheritance;
even the weary you refreshed.
Your people settled in her, God;
you provided for the poor from your bounty.

The Lord announced the word,
a great company of proclaimers.
Rulers and armies flee, they flee,
and in resident camps the plunder is divided.

While you sleep among campfires
wings of dove are sheathed with silver
and her feathers with the shine of gold.
When Shaddai scatters the rulers,
the scattering is like snow on Zalmon.

A majestic mountain, the mountain of Bashan,
a rugged mountain is the mountain of Bashan.
Why gaze in envy, you rugged mountains,
at the mountain God chooses for the reign,
indeed where Adonai will dwell to forever?

Psalm 68, continued

Chariots of God are tens of thousands,
thousands of the multitude
into the Sinai sanctuary.
You ascended to the height and led captive;
you received gifts from human beings,
and even from those rebelling,
to your dwelling, God Adonai.

The Lord is being praised day by day,
bearing our burden is El our Savior.
Our El, the El of salvation,
the Lord Adonai is the escape from death.
Surely God will silence the plans of enmity,
in the crown of their hair where sins go on.

The Lord says, "From Bashan I will bring,
I will bring from depths of the sea,
that you may wash your foot in their defeat
and the tongues of your dogs have their share."

They view your processions, God,
processions into the sanctuary
of my God and my Ruler.
Singers are in front, followed by musicians
among girls playing tambourines.

In great congregations, praise God;
praise Adonai in the assembly of Israel!
There little Benjamin leads the royals of Judah,
their throng the royals of Zebulun and Naphtali.

TUESDAY MORNING

You, God, summoned your power.
Show strength, God, as you did for us!
Because of your temple at Jerusalem,
to you the rulers will bring gifts.

Rebuke the beast of the reeds,
the herd of bulls among calves of nations;
being humbled with bars of silver,
nations that delight in wars are scattered.
Envoys from Egypt will come;
Ethiopia will submit their hands to God.

Peoples of the earth, sing to God!
Sing praise to the Lord, the Rider in the skies,
the ancient heavens, see!
The voice thunders, the voice of might.

Proclaim the power of God over Israel,
the majesty and power in the skies.
Awesome are you, God, in your sanctuary;
the God of Israel gives power and strengths
to the people praising God.

Glory...

Antiphon *When you are invited, take the lowest place;*
one exalting the self will be humbled,
and one humbling the self will be exalted.
                                                Lk 14:10,11

Last ones will be first,
and first ones will be last.   Lk 13:30

PSALM 24

Antiphon *She will bear a son,*
and you will name him Jesus;
he will save his people from their sins. Mt 1:21

TUESDAY MORNING

The earth and everything,
the world and all who are alive are Adonai's,
God who founded the earth on the seas
and established the earth on the waters.

Who may ascend to the mountain of Adonai?
And who may stand in the holy place?
The clean of hand and pure of heart
who do not lift the soul to an idol
and do not swear by falsehood
will receive the blessing from Adonai
and vindication from the God who saves.

Such is the generation of ones who seek,
who seek your faces, God of Jacob.

Lift up your heads, you gates;
lift up, you ancient doors,
that the Crown of glory may enter.

Who is this Crown of glory?
Adonai, strong and mighty,
Adonai, mighty of battle.

Lift up your heads, you gates;
lift up, you ancient doors,
that the Crown of glory may enter.

Who is this Crown of glory?
Adonai Sabaoth is the Crown of glory.

Glory...

Antiphon

PSALM 85

Antiphon
*Take courage;
it is me. Come.*   Mt 14:27,29

You showed favor, Adonai, to your land;
you restored the fortune of Jacob.
You forgave the iniquity of your people;
you pardoned all of their sin.
You set aside all of your wrath;
you turned from your fierce anger.

Restore us, God of our salvation!
And put away your displeasure toward us.
Will you be angry with us to forever?
Will you prolong your anger
to generation and generation?

Will you not revive us again
that your people may rejoice in you?
Show us, Adonai, your unfailing love
and grant us your salvation.

I will listen to what El Adonai will say,
promising peace to the people, even to the saints,
but not letting them return to folly.
Surely near to those in awe is their salvation,
the glory to dwell in our land.

Love and Fidelity meet;
Justice and Peace kiss.
Fidelity springs forth from the earth
and Justice looks down from the heavens.

Indeed Adonai will give the good
and our land will yield her harvest,
Justice going forward to prepare the way
for the steps of the Lord.

Glory…

Antiphon

TOBIT 13:1b-8

Antiphon *Behold,
I make all things new.*   Rev 21:5b

Blessed be God who lives forever
and the reign of our God for all ages,
who scourges but then has mercy,
casts down to the deepest grave
and brings up from the great abyss.
No one can escape this hand.

Israelites, acknowledge before the nations
God who has scattered you among them
and even there shown you great mercy.

Let God be exalted by every living being
because our Lord is our God,
our Father and God forever.

Though scourged for your iniquities,
mercy will be on you all;
you will be gathered from all the nations
among whom you have been scattered.

With all your heart and soul
turn with honesty to the Lord
who will turn the face to you
and no longer hide.

See now what has been done for you,
and with full voice praise Adonai.
Bless the Lord of justice
and exalt the Ruler of the ages.

In the land of my exile I acknowledge the Lord
and make known to a sinful nation
this power and majesty:
"Turn, you sinners, and do right before the Lord,
who may look upon you with favor and mercy."

My God, I will exalt you
and rejoice in the Ruler of Heaven.
Let all speak of this majesty
in Jerusalem with exaltation.

Glory...

Antiphon

What the prophet
does is not so much predict
the future as to so accurately describe
the present that it becomes clear what is going
to happen unless we change our collective ways.

ISAIAH 26:1b-4,7-9,12

Antiphon *My soul yearns for you in the night;*
within me my spirit longs for you.

Our city is strong;
salvation makes walls and rampart.
Open gates, so the just nation may enter,
the one keeping faiths.

Your steadfast mind will keep peace,
peace because of trusting.
Trust in Adonai to forever,
for in Yah Adonai is the Rock of eternities…

The path of justice is level;
the Upright One smooths the way of the just.
Yes, in the way of your laws, Adonai, we wait,
for your name and your renown
are the desire of our heart.

My soul yearns for you in the night;
within me my spirit longs for you.
Just as your judgments are on the earth,
so people of the world learn justice…

Adonai, you establish for us peace;
indeed all we have accomplished
you did for us.

Glory… Antiphon

PSALM 33

Antiphon *Where your treasure is,
there also will your heart be.*   Lk 12:34

Sing joyfully to Adonai, you just,
for praise is fitting for the upright.

Praise Adonai with a harp,
make music on the lyre of ten.
Sing a new song with skill
and play with a shout of joy.

For true is the word of Adonai
and all the faithful deeds done.
The earth is full of the goodness of Adonai,
who loves justice and integrity.

The heavens were made by the word of Adonai
and all their hosts by the breath of the mouth,
as one gathers in a heap the waters of the sea,
as one puts into the deep of the storehouses.

Let all the earth, let them fear,
let all alive in the world revere Adonai
who spoke and it came to be,
who commanded and it stood firm.

Adonai foils the plans of the nations
and thwarts the designs of peoples.
The plan of Adonai stands firm to forever,
heartfelt thoughts to generation and generation.

Psalm 33, continued

Blessed is the nation for whom Adonai is God,
the people chosen for this inheritance.
From the heavens Adonai looks down and sees
all sons and daughters of Adam and Eve,

and from the place of dwelling watches
all those alive on the earth.
The one who formed our heart
knows all our deeds.

No ruler is saved by the size of an army;
no warrior escapes by greatness of strength.
The horse is a vain hope for deliverance;
despite greatness of strength it cannot save.

See the eye of Adonai on those who place
their fear and hope in the unfailing love
that delivers them from death
and keeps them alive in famine.

Our being waits for Adonai,
who is our help and our shield,
in whom our heart rejoices,
the holy name in whom we trust.

Adonai, may you rest on us your unfailing love
even as we hope in you.

Glory…

Antiphon	*Where your treasure is,*	
	there also will your heart be.	Lk 12:34

PSALM 67

Antiphon
*Woman (of Canaan),
great is your faith
let it be done as you desire.* Mt 15:28

May God be gracious to us and bless us,
may God's faces shine upon us.
How else can your ways be known on the earth
and your salvation among all the nations?

May the peoples praise you, God,
may the peoples praise you, all of them.

May the nations be glad and sing for joy
for you rule the peoples
and guide nations of the earth into justice.

May the peoples praise you, God,
may the peoples praise you, all of them.

The land will yield her harvest, God will bless us,
and all the ends of the earth will revere our God.

Glory...

Antiphon

---

*Pondering that DNA studies
reveal that the common ancestors of
the human race were from somewhere in Africa,
where do I imagine the garden of Eden might have been?*

OFFICE OF READINGS and FIRST READING AT MASS

	Odd Years	**Even Years**
1 readings	*Romans 1:18-32*	*Genesis 2:4-25*
mass	Hebrews 2:5-12	1 Samuel 1:9-20
3 rdgs	*Romans 9:1-18*	*Genesis 21*
mass	Hebrews 10:1-10	2 Samuel 6:12b-15,17-19
5 rdgs	*1 Corinthians 2*	*Genesis 42*
mass	Genesis 1:1-19	1 Kings 8:22-23,27-30
7 rdgs	*1 Corinthians 11:17-34*	*2 Corinthians 2:12-3:6*
mass	Ben Sira 2:1-11	James 4:1-10
9 rdgs	*James 3:1-12*	*Galatians 2:11-3:14*
mass	Tobit 2:9-14	2 Peter 3:12-15a,17-18
11 rdgs	*Judges 4 & 5*	*Ezra 4 & 5*
mass	2 Corinthians 8:1-9	1 Kings 21:17-29
13 rdgs	*1 Samuel 9*	*Nehemiah 7 & 8*
mass	Genesis 19:15-29	Amos 3:1-8;4:11-12
15 rdgs	*2 Samuel 4 & 5*	*Job 3*
mass	Exodus 2:1-15a	Isaiah 7:1-9
17 rdgs	*1 Kings 11*	*Job 31*
mass	Ex 33:7-11;34:5b-9,28	Jeremiah 14:17-22
19 rdgs	*2 Kings 6*	*Zechariah 9*
mass	Deuteronomy 31:1-8	Ezekiel 2:8-3:4

TUESDAY MORNING

	Odd Years	**Even Years**
21 rdgs	*Ephesians 5:8-20*	*Titus 3*
mass	1 Thessalonians 2:1-18	2 Thess 2:1-3a,13-17
23 rdgs	*Amos 9*	*2 Peter 2:1-8*
mass	Colossians 2:6-15	1 Corinthians 6:1-11
25 rdgs	*Isaiah 5:8-30*	*Tobit 3*
mass	Ezra 6:7-8,12b,14-20	Proverbs 21:1-6,10-13
27 rdgs	*2 Kings 18*	*Sirach 3*
mass	Jonah 3:1-10	Galatians 1:13-24
29 rdgs	*2 Chronicles 35 & 36*	*Sirach 29 & 30 & 31*
mass	Rom 5:12,15b,17-19,20b-21	Ephesians 2:12-22
31 rdgs	*Jeremiah 32*	*Wisdom 10 & 11*
mass	Romans 12:5-16a	Philippians 2:5-11
33 rdgs	*Ezekiel 18*	*1 Macabees 6*
mass	**2 Maccabees** 6:18-31	Revelation 3:1-6,14-22

READING **ROMANS 13:11-14**

Know that this is the time (the *kairos*), the hour for you to be raised out of sleep, for now our salvation is nearer than when we became believers. The night has advanced and the day draws near. Let us cast off therefore the deeds of the darkness, and let us put on the armor of the light.

As in the new day, let us walk not in revellings to drunken bouts, not in sex to excesses, not in strife to jealousy, but put on the Lord Jesus Christ, and as for the flesh, give its lust no room to think.

RESPONSORY Ps 71:1,5

In you, Lord, I take refuge...
 ...you, Lord, are my hope.
My trust, O Lord, from my youth,...
 ...you, Lord, are my hope.
Glory to the Father and to the Son and to the Holy Spirit:
 ...In you, Lord, I take refuge; you, Lord, are my hope.

Gospel Canticle For Morning

Antiphon *God raised salvation in the house of David.*

Gospel Reading for Tuesday of
Week			
1	Mark 1:21-28	**13** Matt 8:23-27	**25** Luke 8:19-21
3	Mark 3:31-35	**15** Matt 11:20-24	**27** Lk 10:38-42
5	Mark 7:1-13	**17** Matt 13:36-43	**29** Lk 12:35-38
7	Mark 9:30-37	**19** Mt 18:1-5,10,12-14	**31** Lk 14:15-24
9	Mark 12:13-17	**21** Matt 23:23-26	**33** Luke 19:1-10
11	Matt 5:43-48	**23** Luke 6:12-19	

CANTICLE of ZECHARIAH (The Benedictus)
LUKE 1:68-79

+ **Blessed be** the Lord the God of Israel
who chose a people to visit with redemption,
and raised salvation in the house of David,
saving strength from God's own servant,

speaking from the age of the prophets
through the mouth of the holy prophet:
Salvation out of enmity,
even out of those who hate us,

to show our ancestors how mercy works, -
and to remember the holy promise of the Lord,
the covenant made for our ancestor Abraham,
calming our fear and making us free
to serve with holy justice before God all our days.

And you also child -
will be called a prophet of the Most High
for you will go before the Lord to prepare his way
and give to people a knowledge of salvation
known in accepting forgiveness of their sins.

From the tender mercy of our God,
the sun rising from the height will visit with light
for those who sit in the dark or shadow of death
and to guide our feet into the way of peace.

Glory...

Antiphon

PETITIONS FOR THE CONSECRATION TO GOD OF THE DAY AND ITS WORK

- For the Church and her ministry and apostolates…

- For secular authorities and all serving as stewards…

- For people who are poor or sick or in sorrow…

- For peace and the basic needs of each human being…

- For those who weigh on my heart…

SUSCIPE of MOTHER CATHERINE McAULEY

My God, I am yours for time and eternity.
Teach me to cast myself entirely
into the arms of your loving providence,
with the most lively, unlimited confidence
in your compassionate, tender pity.
Grant me, O most merciful Redeemer,
that whatever you ordain or permit
may be acceptable to me.
Take from my heart all painful anxiety;
suffer nothing to sadden me but sin,
nothing to delight me but the hope of coming
to the possession of you, my God and my all,
in your everlasting reign.

OUR FATHER…

WEEK I
TUESDAY EVENING

+ *God, come to my assistance;* Psalm 70:2
  Lord, make haste to help me!

Glory…

What a Friend we have in Je-sus,
All our sins and griefs to bear!
What a priv-i-lege to car-ry
Ev-'ry-thing to God in prayer!
Oh, what peace we of-ten for-feit,
Oh, what need-less pain we bear,
All be-cause we do not car-ry
Ev-'ry-thing to God in prayer!

Glo-ry be to God the Fa-ther,
Son, and Spir-it ev-'ry-where.
Glo-ry be as the Be-got-ten
Son of Ab-ba hears our prayer
At the right hand of the Fa-ther,
Lamb of God, our mer-cy home.
Fa-ther, Son and Ho-ly Spir-it,
Glo-ry be to you a-lone.

133, Text: based on Matthew 21:22; Joseph Scriven, 1865;
verse 2 Stephen J. Wolf, 2011
Music: FRIEND; Charles C. Converse, 1868

PSALM 14

Antiphon   *If we say we have no sin, we deceive ourselves;*
if we confess our sins,
God is faithful and forgiving.   1 John 1:8,9

The fool says in the heart, "There is no God."
They are corrupt, vile are their deeds;
no one is doing good.

Adonai looks down from the heavens
on sons and daughters of Adam and Eve
to see if even one is wise enough to seek God.

All turned aside together to corruption;
no one is doing good, not even one.

Will doers of the bad never learn?
Devouring my people as they eat bread,
they do not call on Adonai.

There they are, in dread of dread,
for God is in the company of the just.
They frustrate the hopes of the poor,
but in Adonai the poor find refuge.

Who from Zion could bring salvation to Israel?
When Adonai restores the fortune to the people,
let Jacob rejoice, let Israel be glad.

Glory...

Antiphon

PSALM 74

Antiphon

*The Son of Humanity
took our infirmities
and bore our diseases.*

Mt 8:17
Isaiah 53:4

Why, God, do you reject us to forever?
Your anger smolders
against sheep of your pasture.
Remember your people you gathered of old,
your tribe of heirs you redeemed,
Mount Zion where you dwelt.

Lift high your steps through everlasting ruin,
the enmity destruction to the sanctuary.
Enmity roared in your meeting place
and set up their standard signs.

They behaved like ones raising axes
through a thicket of trees,
and now her carved panels
they smashed with axe and hatchet.
They sent your sanctuary to the ground with fire
and defiled the dwelling place of your Name.

Psalm 74, continued

They said in their heart, "We will crush them."
Completely they burned in the land
all the places to worship God.
We see no miraculous signs;
there is no longer a prophet among us.
Until when? No one knows.

Until when, God,
will enmity mock and revile your name?
To forever?
Why do you hold back your hand,
even your right hand
from the fold of your bosom?

But God, my Ruler from of old,
bringing salvation onto the midst of the earth,
you split open the sea by your power,
you break the heads of dragons in the waters.

You crushed the heads of Leviathan,
giving him as food
to people and desert creatures.
You opened up streams and springs
and dried up everflowing rivers.

To you is the day and to you is the night,
and you established the moon and the sun.
You set all the boundaries of the earth;
summer and winter were made by you.

TUESDAY EVENING

Remember how enmity mocks Adonai,
and foolish people revile your name.
Do not hand over to the wild beast
the life of your dove;
remember to forever
the life of your afflicted ones.

Scary places of the land
are haunted with violence.
So have regard for your covenant.
Let not the oppressed retreat, nor the disgraced;
may the poor and the needy praise your name.

Rise up, God! Defend your cause!
Remember the all-day mockery of fools.
Ignore not the clamor of enmity
nor those in continual uproar.

Glory…

Antiphon *The Son of Humanity
took our infirmities
and bore our diseases.* Mt 8:17
Isaiah 53:4

---

*Lamentations are part of many of the psalms,
but perhaps the most used little psalm of
lamentation has but one word, 'shit!'*

PSALM 20

Antiphon
The Spirit of the Lord is upon me;
the Lord anointed me
to evangelize the poor
and sent me
to proclaim release to captives,
sight to the blind,
and freedom to the crushed,
to proclaim a year
of the Lord's acceptance.

Lk 4:18
and see Isaiah
61:1-2 & 58:6

—
What
is justice? The
root of justice is in the
awareness that God created an
abundance intended as a blessing for all.
If anyone is denied their just due of this abundance
our God has given for us all, that is injustice. The ancient
Hebrew test for whether we live in a just society is to ask how
the widows, orphans, and alien strangers in our midst are doing.

Deal with your neighbor with justice; oppress no alien, orphan,
or widow; shed no innocent blood; and follow no other "god."
Jeremiah 7:5b,6

TUESDAY EVENING

May Adonai answer you on the day of distress.
May the name of the God of Jacob protect you,
send you help from the sanctuary,

support you from Zion,
remember all of your sacrifices,
accept your burnt offerings,
give to you as your heart desires,
and make all of your plans succeed.

We will shout for joy at your victory
and lift a banner in the name of our God;
may Adonai grant all your requests.

Now I know
that Adonai saves the chosen anointed
and answers from the holy heavens
with a strong hand of saving powers.

Some trust in the chariot
and others in the horses,
but we in the name of our God Adonai.
They kneel and they fall,
but we rise up and stand firm.

Adonai, save the ruler;
answer us on the day we call.

Glory...   Antiphon

In the name of the Abba and
of the Son and of the Holy Breath of God

PSALM 21:2-8,14

Antiphon *Jesus and his disciples ate at the house of Levi
and with them tax collectors and sinners;
many from there followed him.* Mk 2:15

In your strength, Adonai, the crown rejoices,
and in your victory; how great is the joy!
You granted the desire of their heart
and did not withhold the request of their lips.

Indeed, you welcomed them with rich blessings
and placed on their head a crown of pure gold.
They asked from you life
and you gave length of days forever and ever.

Great is the glory through your victory;
on them you bestowed splendor and majesty.
Surely you granted them blessings for eternity
making them glad with joy in your presences,

for the ruler trusting in Adonai will be unshaken
through the unfailing love of the Most High…
Be exalted, Adonai, in your strength!
We will sing and we will praise your might.

Glory…

Antiphon

Being homosexual is not a crime.
Pope Francis, January 24, 2023

PSALM 125

Antiphon *If you know to give good gifts to your children,*
how much more will the heavenly Abba
give the Holy Spirit to all who ask.   Lk 11:13

They who trust in Adonai are like Mount Zion;
not to be shaken, they endure to forever.

As mountains surround around Jerusalem,
so Adonai surrounds around the people
from now and to forevermore.

Indeed the sceptor of bad doings
will not remain over the lot of the just
lest the hands of the just be used for the bad.

Do good, Adonai, to the good,
even to those honest in their hearts!
But those who turn to bad ways
Adonai will banish with doers of the bad.

Peace be upon Israel!

Glory…

Antiphon

A salty parish priest retiring to his
home town made sandwiches to give away
in a park. Cash that another priest sent to help was
returned with a note, 'Make your own damn sandwiches.'

PSALM 131

Antiphon
*Scribes and Pharisees
preach and do not do it;
they put on human shoulders
heavy burdens bound,
but are unwilling
to lift a finger to move them.* Mt 23:3b,4

Adonai, my heart is not proud
and my eyes are not haughty
and I am not busied with the great matters,
with things so wonderful as to be beyond me.

But indeed I have become still
and quiet in my soul
like a child with a mother, being weaned.
Like one being weaned is my soul within me.

Israel, put your hope in Adonai
from now and to forevermore.

Glory…

Antiphon

---

*As a child rests in
their mother's arms, this is
how my soul rests in you, O God.*

God uses parents to reveal to children something (not everything, but something) about who God is.

TUESDAY EVENING

REVELATION 4:8b,11; 5:9,10,12,13b

Antiphon
*Holy, Holy, Holy,
Lord God Almighty
who was and is and is to come.* Rev 4:8b

Worthy are you, our Lord and our God,
to receive the glory and honor and power,
for you have created all things,
and by your will all things were created and are.

Worthy are you to receive the scroll and unseal it
for you were sacrificed, and by your blood
ransomed for God those from every
tribe and tongue and people and nation.

You made of them for our God
a realm of royals and priests,
and thus will they reign over the earth.

Worthy is the Lamb, sacrificed to receive
the power and riches and wisdom and strength
and honor and glory and blessing.

Glory... Antiphon

---

*Thomas Merton's friend Robert Lax: 'What you
should say is that you want to be a saint... Don't you
believe that God will make you what God created you to be,
if you will consent to let God do it? All you have to do is desire it.'*
See *The Seven Storey Mountain* by Thomas Merton

READING **1 JOHN 3:1-2**

See what manner of love the Father has given to us, that we may be called children of God, and we are. The world does not know us because it did not know him. Beloved, now we are children of God, and what we shall be has not yet been shown. We know that when it is shown, we shall be like him because we shall see him as he is. Everyone who carries this hope is made pure as God is pure.

RESPONSORY Ps 100:5

The love of the Lord endures to forever…
 …*for God is good.*
Faithful love to all generations,…
 …*for God is good.*
Glory to the Father and to the Son and to the Holy Spirit:
 …*The love of the Lord endures to forever, for God is good.*

CANTICLE of MARY (The Magnificat)
LUKE 1:46-55

Antiphon
*My spirit is beyond joy
in God, my Savior*

+ **My soul** is stretched full with praise of the Lord,
and my spirit, beyond joy in God, my Savior,
who chose to lay eyes on this humble servant.

Behold, now and forward,
each and every age will call me blessed,
for the Mighty One did great things to me.

Holy is the name and the mercy
to generations and generations,
the ones fearing the One,

Who scattered the haughty of mind and heart,
pulled the powerful off their high place,
and lifted with dignity the humble in need.

The hungering are filled with good things,
the rich are sent away empty,
and servant Israel is given relief

with a memory of mercy to remember,
the promise spoken to our ancestors,
to Abraham and his descendants forever.

Glory...

Antiphon

INTERCESSIONS

- For a culture of vocations all over the world…
- For all who have died…

- In gratitude for blessings…; Abba thank you.
- For the sins of this day…; Lord Jesus have mercy.
- With concerns over tomorrow…; Holy Spirit help.

PRAYER FOR GENEROSITY   Saint Ignatius of Loyola

Lord, teach me to be generous,
to serve you as you deserve,
to give and not to count the cost,
to fight and not to heed the wounds,
to toil and not to seek for rest,
to labor and not to ask reward,
save knowing that I do your will.

OUR FATHER…

---

*It is quite possible for a human
to have none but the purest thoughts
and yet be so distracted mulling over them
that one remains the while far removed from God.*

See *Chapters on Prayer* (#55) by Evagrius Ponticus

WEEK I
WEDNESDAY MORNING

+ *God, come to my assistance;* Psalm 70:2
  Lord, make haste to help me!

  Glory…

A

A-ma-zing\ Grace! How sweet the sound
That saved a\ wretch like me.
I once\ was\ lost, but now/ am\ found,
Was blind, but\ now I see.

'Twas grace that\ taught my heart to fear,
And grace my\ fears re-lieved.
How prec\-ious\ did that grace/ ap\-pear
The hour I\ first be-lieved.

Through ma-ny\ dan-gers, toils, and snares,
I have al\-rea-dy come.
'Tis grace\ hath\ brought me safe/ thus\ far,
And grace will\ lead me home.

When we've been\ there ten thou-sand years,
Bright shi-ning\ as the sun,
We've no\ less\ days to sing/ God's\ praise
Than when we'd\ first be-gun.

77, Text: John Newton, 1779
Music: NEW BRITAIN, CM, composer unknown;
Virginia Harmony, 1831

B

As Ab-ba loves you, Je-sus you love us
Tell-ing us to re-main in your love
In your com-mand to love one an-oth-er
As you have loved us, call-ing us friends.

You are the vine and we are your branch-es;
Let Ab-ba prune us so we bear fruit.
Your word re-mem-b'ring, lov-ing each oth-er
As you have loved us, call-ing us friends.

No great-er love has one than to lay down
One's ver-y life for e-ven a friend.
We you have cho-sen, lov-ing each other
As you have loved us, call-ing us friends.

We have been with you from the be-gin-ning;
To tes-ti-fy in Spir-it and truth
In word and ac-tion, lov-ing each oth-er
As you have loved us, call-ing us friends.

81, Text: from John 15, Stephen J. Wolf, 2007, 2016, public domain
tribute to the priesthood of Charley Giacosa
Music: BUNESSAN 5554 D, Scots Gaelic melody
Popular melody for *Morning Has Broken*

PSALM 18:2-30

Antiphon *You shall love the Lord, your God*
with all your heart and soul and mind,
and your neighbor as yourself.   Mt 22:37,39
see also
Dt 6:5 & Lev 19:18

I love you, Adonai, my strength,
my rock Adonai, my fortress and deliverer;
in my God and Rock I take refuge,
my shield and horn, my salvation and stronghold.

I call out praise to Adonai
and am saved from enmity.

They tangled me in cords of death
and overwhelmed me in torrents of destruction.
Cords of Sheol coiled around me
and snares of death confronted me.

In my distress I called "Adonai,"
I cried for help from my God,
who heard from the temple my voice;
my cry went into these ears.

The earth trembled and quaked
and foundations of mountains shook
and trembled because of anger.
Smoke rose from the nostrils
and fire from the mouth consumed blazing coals.

Psalm 18, continued

The heavens parted
and dark clouds came down under the feet.
Mounted on the cherub,
flying and soaring on wings of wind,
a canopy of darkness covered all around,
dark waters in the clouds of the skies.

From the brightness of the presence
the clouds advanced hailstone and lightning bolts.
Adonai thundered from the heavens,
the voice of the Most High resounding
as hailstone and lightning bolts.

Arrows shot, scattering them all;
with great lightning bolts they are routed.
Valleys of waters were exposed
and foundations of earth laid bare
at your rebuke, Adonai,
at the blast of the breath of your nostril.

You reached from on high and took hold of me
and drew me out from the deep waters;
you rescued me from enmity
and from those too strong, too powerful for me.

They confronted me in the day of my disaster
but Adonai was my support,
brought me out to the spacious place,
and rescued me because of delight in me.

Adonai dealt with me as my ways are upright,
rewarded me as my hands are clean,
for I kept to the ways of Adonai.
Indeed all of God's laws are before me
and I did not turn from those decrees.

Blameless before God, on guard against sin,
in the sight of Adonai I am rewarded
as my ways are just and my hands are clean.

To the faithful you show yourself faithful,
to the honest you show yourself honest,
and to the pure you show yourself pure,

but to the crooked you show yourself shrewd,
for you save humble people
but bring low the eyes of the haughty.

Indeed you make my lamp burn;
my God Adonai makes light in my darkness.
Indeed with you I can advance against troops,
with my God I can scale a wall.

Glory...

Antiphon *You shall love the Lord, your God
with all your heart and soul and mind,
and your neighbor as yourself.* Mt 22:37,39
& Dt 6:5, Lev 19:18

---

*Our lives become a parchment; our sufferings and our actions
are the ink. The workings of the Holy Spirit are the pen, and with
it God writes a living gospel.* Jean-Pierre de Caussade, Jesuit

PSALM 89:2-38

Antiphon

*One loving father or mother
or son or daughter
more than me
is not worthy of me.* Mt 10:37

Forever will I sing the great love of Adonai;
with my mouth I will make known
your fidelity to generation and generation.
Indeed I will declare forever love standing firm,
your faithfulness established in the heavens.

"I made a covenant with my chosen ones,
sworn to my servant David.
I will establish your line to forever,
and to generation and generation
I will make firm your throne."

The heavens praise your wonder, Adonai,
and your fidelity in the holy assembly.
For who in the sky can compare to Adonai;
who is like Adonai among heavenly beings?

God is greatly feared in the council of holy ones
and is awesome over all who surround around.
Adonai Sabaoth, who is like you?
Mighty Adonai, your fidelity is around you.

You rule over the surging of the sea;
when waves mount up you still them.
You crushed Rahab like the slain
and scattered enmity
with the arm of your strength.

To you are the heavens and to you is the earth;
the world and all her fullness you founded.
North and South you created;
Tabor and Hermon sing for joy at your name.

To you is the arm strong with power;
your hand is exalted, your right hand.
Justice and Judgment
are the foundation of your throne;
Hesed-Love and Fidelity go before your faces.

Blessed are people who learn to acclaim Adonai;
they walk in the light of your presences.
In your name they rejoice all the day
and in your judgment they exult,

for you are the glory of their strength
and by your favor you exalt our horn.
Indeed Adonai is our shield
and the Holy One of Israel is our Ruler.

Once in a vision you spoke to your faithful ones:
"I bestowed strength on a warrior;
I raised from the people a young man.

Psalm 89, continued

I chose David my servant,
I anointed him with my sacred oil,
and my hand will sustain him;
surely my arm will strengthen him.

Enmity will not subject him to tribute
and people doing the bad will not oppress him.
Before him I will crush foes
and strike down adversity,

and my fidelity and my love are with him,
and through my hands will his horn be exalted.
And I will set his hand over the sea
and his right hand over the rivers.

He will call out to me: 'You are my Father,
my God and Rock of my salvation.'
I will also appoint him firstborn
and most exalted among rulers of the earth.

I will maintain my love for him to forever
and my unfailing covenant with him.
I will establish his line to forever
and his throne as days of the heavens.

If his sons and daughters forsake my law
and do not follow my statutes,
if they violate my decrees
and keep not my commands,

then I will punish their sins with the rod
and their iniquity with floggings.
But I will not take my love from them,
nor will I ever betray my fidelity.

I will not violate my covenant
nor will I alter the utterance of my lips.
Once I swore by my holiness;
I will not lie to David:

His line will continue to forever
and his throne like the sun before me.
Like the moon it is established forever,
a faithful witness in the sky."

Glory...

Antiphon *One loving father or mother*
or son or daughter
more than me
is not worthy of me. Mt 10:37

Hounded by somebody about something,
a brother said, 'You are on it, but here is my list:
God, family, job, parish, etc... I want to keep you on it,
but you will not be first on my list. Can I keep you on my list?'

PSALM 36

Antiphon — *Blessed are your eyes for they see
and your ears for they hear
what many prophets and just ones
longed to see and hear.* Mt 13:16,17a

An oracle of sin in the midst of my heart:
There is no fear of God in the eyes of a sinner,
whose own eyes are full of self-flattery,
who hates to detect sin.

Words of this mouth are bad and deceitful:
Ceasing to be wise or do good,
they plot the bad while still in bed
and commit to a course of the no-good
and reject nothing that is wrong.

Adonai, to the heavens is your love
and your fidelity to the skies.
Your justice is like the mountains,
your judgment, deep and great;
human and beast you preserve, Adonai.

How priceless is your unfailing love.
High ones and humans find refuge
in the shadow of your wings.

They feast on the abundance of your house;
in the river of your delights you give them drink.
With you is the fountain of life,
and in your light we see light.

Continue your love to those who know you
and your just defense of the honest of heart.
Let the foot of pride not come to me
nor the hand of bad ways drive me away.

See, doers of the bad lie fallen;
they are thrown down, unable to rise.

Glory…

Antiphon

*True
Humility
is the grace of
awareness of how I am
created uniquely in God's
image, seeing myself as neither
better than I am nor less than I am.
Humility is reality; pride is an illusion.
Debasement of the self is also an illusion.*

JUDITH 16:1,13-15

Antiphon *O Lord, you are great and glorious,*
wonderful in strength, invincible.

Begin a song to my God with timbrels;
sing to my Lord with cymbals.
Sing to my Lord a new song;
exalt and acclaim the name.

I will sing to my God a new song;
O Lord, you are great and glorious,
wonderful in strength and unbeatable.

Let your every creature serve you,
for you spoke, and they were made.
You sent forth your spirit,
and they were created;
no one can resist your word.

Mountain foundations are shaken by waters
and rocks melt like wax at your glance.
But to those who fear you, you show mercy.

Glory…

Antiphon

To sing is
to pray twice.
Saint Augustine

WEDNESDAY MORNING

ISAIAH 33:13-16

Antiphon *Blessed is the one who works justice*
and speaks honesty.

Hear what I have done, you who are far away!
And acknowledge my power, you who are near.

Sinners are terrified in Zion
and trembling grips the godless.
Who of us can dwell in fire that consumes?
Who of us can dwell in everlasting burning?

One working justice and speaking honesty,
rejecting the gains of extortion,
waving off acceptance of the bribe,
stopping ears from hearing of bloodshed,
shutting eyes to not gaze on the bad:

That one will dwell on the heights
in a mountain fortress refuge,
supplied with bread and waters never-failing.

Glory...

Antiphon

If you can figure out its name, it may be helpful to then
choose a daily church bell or alarm ringtone to remind you
to simply remember once a day what your personal vocation is.

See *Discovering Your Personal Vocation* by Herbert Alphonso, Jesuit
(If this helps to ponder it, I think mine is *holy honesty*. – SJW)

PSALM 47

Antiphon *Behold, I am with you all the days
until the completion of the eon.*   Mt 28:20

All you nations, clap your hands!
Shout to God with cries of joy!
How awesome, Most High Adonai.

The great Ruler over all the earth
subdued nations under us
and peoples under our feet,
and chose for us an inheritance,
the pride of Jacob the beloved.

God ascended with shouts of joy,
Adonai amid sound of trumpet.
Sing praises to God, sing praises.
Sing praises to our Ruler, sing praises.

For God, Ruler of all the earth, sing praises.
God reigns over the nations,
God sits on the holy throne.

Nobles of nations assemble
with the people of the God of Abraham.
The shields of the earth belong to God
who is greatly exalted.

Glory...

Antiphon

PSALM 98

Antiphon   *I will give you a mouth and wisdom that will not be contradicted or withstood.*   Lk 21:15

Sing to Adonai a new song
who has done marvelous things,
working salvation at the right hand and holy arm.

Adonai made known salvation,
justice revealed for the eyes of the nations.
Love is remembered
and fidelity to the house of Israel

and all the ends of the earth see
the salvation of our God.
Shout for joy to Adonai, all you earth!
Break into song and sing praise.

Make music to Adonai with harp,
with harp and the sound of singing,
with trumpets and blast of ram horn:
Shout for joy before Adonai, the Ruler.

Let the sea resound, the fullness of the world,
and those living in her.
Let the rivers clap hands,
let the mountains sing together for joy

before Adonai who comes to judge the earth,
who will judge the world with justice
and peoples with equity.

Glory...   Antiphon

OFFICE OF READINGS and FIRST READING AT MASS

	Odd Years	**Even Years**
1 readings	*Romans 2:1-16*	*Genesis 3*
mass	Hebrews 2:14-18	1 Samuel 3:1-10,19-20
3 rdgs	*Romans 9:19-33*	*Genesis 22*
mass	Hebrews 10:11-18	2 Samuel 7:4-17
5 rdgs	*1 Corinthians 3*	*Genesis 43*
mass	Genesis 2:4b-9,15-17	1 Kings 10:1-10
7 rdgs	*1 Corinthians 12:1-11*	*2 Corinthians 3:7-4:4*
mass	Ben Sira 4:11-19	James 4:13-17
9 rdgs	*James 3:13-18*	*Galatians 3:15-4:7*
mass	Tobit 3:1-11,16	**2 Timothy** 1:1-3,6-12
11 rdgs	*Judges 6*	*Haggai 1*
mass	2 Corinthians 9:6-11	1 Kings 2:1,6-14
13 rdgs	*1 Samuel 11*	*Nehemiah 9:1-21*
mass	Genesis 21:5,8-20	Amos 5:14-15,21-24
15 rdgs	*2 Samuel 6*	*Job 4*
mass	Exodus 3:1-6,9-12	Isaiah 10:5-7,13-16
17 rdgs	*1 Kings 12:1-19*	*Job 32 & 33*
mass	Exodus 34:29-34	Jeremiah 15:10,16-21
19 rdgs	*2 Kings 7 & 8*	*Zechariah 10*
mass	Deuteronomy 34:1-12	Ezekiel 9:1-7;10:18-22

WEDNESDAY MORNING

	Odd Years	**Even Years**
21 rdgs	*Ephesians 5:21-33*	*1 Timothy 1*
mass	1 Thessalonians 2:9-13	2 Thessa 3:6-10,16-18
23 rdgs	*Hosea 1 & 3*	*2 Peter 2:9-22*
mass	Colossians 3:1-11	1 Corinthians 7:25-31
25 rdgs	*Isaiah 7*	*Tobit 4 & 5*
mass	Ezra 9:5-9	Proverbs 30:5-9
27 rdgs	*2 Kings 19*	*Sirach 4*
mass	Jonah 4:1-11	Galatians 2:1-2,7-14
29 rdgs	*Habakuk 1 & 2*	*Sirach 35*
mass	Romans 6:12-18	Ephesians 3:2-12
31 rdgs	*Jeremiah 30*	*Wisdom 12 & 13*
mass	Romans 13:8-10	Philippians 2:12-18
33 rdgs	*Ezekiel 20*	*1 Macabees 9*
mass	2 Maccabees 7:1,20-31	Revelation 4:1-11

READING **TOBIT 4:15a,16a,18a,19**

What you yourself dislike do not do to anyone else. Give some of your food to the hungry and some of your clothing to the naked. Seek advice from every wise person. At all times bless and ask the Lord God that your ways may be made straight and that your plans may prosper.

RESPONSORY Ps 25:4

Push and pull my heart…
 …*as is your will, my Lord.*
Keep my feet on your path…
 …*as is your will, my Lord.*
Glory to the Father and to the Son and to the Holy Spirit:
 …*Push and pull my heart, as is your will, my Lord.*

Gospel Canticle For Morning

Antiphon *Show us, Lord, how mercy works, and remember your holy covenant.*

Gospel Reading for Wednesday of
Week **1** Mark 1:29-39   **13** Matt 8:28-34   **25** Luke 9:1-6
    3 Mark 4:1-20   **15** Matt 11:25-27 **27** Luke 11:1-4
    5 Mark 7:14-23   **17** Matt 13:44-46 **29** Lk 12:39-48
    7 Mark 9:38-40   **19** Matt 18:15-20 **31** Lk 14:25-33
    9 Mark 12:18-27 **21** Matt 23:27-32 **33** Lk 19:11-28
   11 Matt 6:1-6,16-18 **23** Luke 6:20-26

CANTICLE of ZECHARIAH (The Benedictus)
LUKE 1:68-79

+ **Blessed be** the Lord the God of Israel
who chose a people to visit with redemption,
and raised salvation in the house of David,
saving strength from God's own servant,

speaking from the age of the prophets
through the mouth of the holy prophet:
Salvation out of enmity,
even out of those who hate us,

to show our ancestors how mercy works, -
and to remember the holy promise of the Lord,
the covenant made for our ancestor Abraham,
calming our fear and making us free
to serve with holy justice before God all our days.

And you also child -
will be called a prophet of the Most High
for you will go before the Lord to prepare his way
and give to people a knowledge of salvation
known in accepting forgiveness of their sins.

From the tender mercy of our God,
the sun rising from the height will visit with light
for those who sit in the dark or shadow of death
and to guide our feet into the way of peace.

Glory...

Antiphon

PETITIONS FOR THE CONSECRATION TO GOD OF THE DAY AND ITS WORK

- For the Church and her ministry and apostolates…

- For secular authorities and all serving as stewards…

- For people who are poor or sick or in sorrow…

- For peace and the basic needs of each human being…

COME HOLY SPIRIT Cursillo

Come, Holy Spirit, fill the hearts of your faithful,
And kindle in us the fire of your love.

Send forth your Spirit and we shall be created,
And you shall renew the face of the earth.

Let us pray:

O God, who by the light of the Holy Spirit
did instruct the hearts of the faithful, grant,
that by the same Holy Spirit
we may be truly wise
and ever rejoice in her consolations,
through Christ our Lord.

OUR FATHER…

84, Text: Ephesians 1:3-14, Stephen J. Wolf, 2008,
with gratitude to the Institute for Priestly Formation
Music: 8787D, HYMN TO JOY, Ludwig van Beethoven, d. 1827;
adapted by Edward Hodges, 1824
Popular melody for: *Joyful, Joyful, We Adore Thee*

WEEK I
WEDNESDAY EVENING

+ *God, come to my assistance;*   Psalm 70:2
  Lord, make haste to help me!
  Glory...

A   **Bles-sed be the God and Fa-ther**
Of our Lord/ Je-sus Christ,
Who has blessed us in the Christ\,
bless-ings in their Spir-it breath.
As God chose us in the Mes-si-ah
be-fore/ found-ing sky or earth,
To be ho-ly, clean of blem-ish,
in God's eye: a-dop-tion worth.

In the Son we have re-demp-tion,
God's for-give-ness of our sin,
By the rich-es of his grace\
lav-ished on us gath-ered in.
Giv-ing wis-dom, know-ledge/, vis-ion,
mys-t'ry/ of the Fa-ther's will,
Sum-ming up all things in Je-sus,
fa-vored in the full-ness sent.

In our hear-ing of the gos-pel
word of our sal-va\-tion,
One by one we too were cho-sen,
joined as part-ners with the Son.
By the prom-is'd Ho-ly/ Spir-it,
signed and/ sealed as heirs of God,
God's pos-ses-sion, God's re-demp-tion,
God's be-lov-ed, Ab-ba's own.

B

There's a wide/-ness in God's mer\-cy
Like the wide-ness of\ the sea;
There's a kind/-ness in God's jus\-tice
Which is more than lib\-er-ty.
There is plen\-ti-ful re-demp\-tion
In the blood/ that has\ been shed;
There\ is joy\ for all\ the mem//\-bers
In the sor\-rows of the Head.

For the love/ of God is broad\-er
Than the meas-ures of\ our mind,
And the heart/ of the E-ter\-nal
Be-yond won-der-ful\ and kind.
If our love\ were but more simp\-le
We might take/ him at\ his word,
And\ our lives\ would be\ thanks-giv//\-ing
For the good\-ness of the Lord.

Troub-led souls/, why will you scat\-ter
Like a crowd of fright\-ened sheep?
Fool-ish hearts/, why will you wan\-der
From a love so true\ and deep?
There is wel\-come for the sin\-ner
And more gra/-ces for\ the good;
There\ is mer\-cy with\ the Sa//\-vior,
There is heal\-ing in his food.

114, Text: Frederick W. Fabor, 1814, 1863, altered
Music: 87 87 D, HYFRYDOL; Rowland Prichard, 1811-1887
Popular melody for: *Love Divine, All Love Excelling*

PSALM 70

Antiphon *You have heard it said,*
an eye for an eye and a tooth for a tooth;
but I say to you, do not resist a doer of bad;
when someone strikes you on the right cheek,
give the other as well.   Mt 5:38,39

God, come to save me;
Adonai, make haste to help me!
May plans to seek my life
be shamed and confused;

may the desire for my ruin
be turned back in disgrace
and ones saying "aha!, aha!"
turn back in shame.

May all who seek you
rejoice in you and be glad
and may lovers of salvation say always,
"Let God be exalted."

Yet I am poor and needy, God,
come quickly to me and do not delay,
Adonai, my help and deliverer.

Glory...   Antiphon

An eye for an eye makes the whole world blind.
attributed to Gandhi

PSALM 17

Antiphon *The Lord is God of the living.* Lk 20:38

Alternate Now, Master, you set free your servant
according to your word in peace;
my eyes have seen the salvation,
which you have prepared
before the face of all the peoples,
a light for revelation to the nations
and glory for your people, Israel.

Lk 2:29-32
Canticle of Simeon
*(often used in night
prayer, see pg 41)*

Hear, **Adonai**, a just plea; listen to my cry.
Give ear to my prayer, from lips without deceit.
May my vindication come from you;
may my eyes see right things.

You probe and examine my heart in the night,
you test me and find nothing wrong.
By resolve my mouth will not sin.

By the word of your lips
my human deeds are kept from violent ways.
Holding my steps to your paths
my feet did not slip.

WEDNESDAY EVENING

I call on you, El, for you will answer me.
Give ear to me and hear my prayer.
Show the wonder of your great saving love;
at your right hand are refugees from adversity.

Keep me as the apple daughter of your eye.
You hide me in the shade of your wings
from those who assail me in enmity,
surrounding around my life.
They close their callous hearts,
they speak their arrogant mouth.

Now they surround our tracks;
their eyes are alert, ready to throw to the ground.
They are like a lion, hungry to tear prey,
like a great lion crouching to ambush.

Rise up, Adonai!
Confront and bring down their ways.
Rescue my self by your sword, Adonai,
by your hand from humans,
humans of the world whose reward is this life.

As for those who are cherished by you,
their belly is full, sons and daughters are plenty,
and they store up their wealth for their children.

May justice let me see your faces
and be satisfied waking up to your likeness.

Glory…

Antiphon

PSALM 27

Antiphon
*Come after me,
and I will make you
fishers of human beings.*   Mt 4:19

Adonai is my light and my salvation.
Whom shall I fear?
Adonai is the stronghold of my life.
Of whom shall I be afraid?

When people doing the bad
advance against me to devour my flesh,
when enmity and adversity go against me,
they will stumble and fall.

Though an army encamp against me,
my heart will not fear.
Though war break out against me,
in this I will be confident.

One thing I ask of Adonai:
to seek and to dwell in Adonai's house,
to gaze on Adonai's beauty
all the days of my life as a seeker in the temple.

I will be kept safely dwelling,
hidden in the shelter of the tabernacle,
on the day of trouble set high upon rock.

WEDNESDAY EVENING

Then will my head be lifted above enmity,
and I will sacrifice at the tabernacle
the sacrifice of shouts of joy.

I will sing and make music to Adonai.
Hear, Adonai, my voice calling;
be merciful; answer me.
To you my heart says, "My face seeks you."

Your faces, Adonai, I will seek.
Hide not your faces from me;
turn not away from your servant in anger.

You are my help;
neither reject nor forsake me,
God of my salvation.
Even if my father and my mother forsake me,
you, Adonai, will take me in.

Teach me your way, Adonai,
and lead me through oppression to level paths.
Do not give me over to the desires
of enmity rising with false witnesses
and breathers of violence.

Still I am confident: I will see
the goodness of Adonai in the land of the living.
Wait for Adonai!
Take courage and strengthen your heart.
And wait for Adonai!

Glory...   Antiphon

PSALM 28:1-3,6-9

Antiphon *Pray for all, even for those in authority,
that our living may include
quiet and dignity.*   1 Tim 2:2

To you I call, my Rock Adonai,
turn not to me a deaf ear.
For if you remain silent, away from me,
then I will be like one going into the pit.

Hear the sound of my cries for mercy
calling to you for help as I lift my hands
toward the Holy Place of your Holiness.

Drag me not away with those who do the bad,
who speak cordiality with their neighbors
but with malice in their heart.

Praised be Adonai,
who heard the sound of my cries for mercy.
Adonai, my strength and my shield,
in whom my heart trusts,
I am helped and my heart leaps for joy
and in my song I will give thanks.

Adonai is the strength
and the saving refuge of the anointed.
Save your people! Bless your inheritance!
Be their shepherd and carry them to forever!

Glory...   Antiphon

PSALM 126

Antiphon *What do you wish me to do for you?*
  ...Go, your faith has healed you. Mk 10:51,52

When Adonai restored Zion out of captivity
we felt like people in a dream.
Then our mouth was filled with laughter,
and our tongue with a song of joy.

Then they said among the nations
"Their Adonai did great things for them."
Adonai did great things for us;
we were full of joy.

Restore our good fortune, Adonai,
like streams in the Negev desert.
Sowers are now in tears;
they will reap with a song of joy.

Going out, the sower goes out weeping,
carrying seeds for the sowing.
Returning, the sower will return
carrying sheaves with a song of joy.

Glory...

Antiphon

God our Savior desires that all
humans be saved and come to know the truth.
1 Timothy 2:3b,4

PSALM 127

Antiphon *Look at the birds of heaven and see:*
they do not sow or reap or gather into barns
and your heavenly Abba feeds them.   Mt 6:26

If Adonai does not build the house,
the builders labor in vanity.
If Adonai does not watch over the city,
the watcher stands guard in vain.

It is vanity to rise early or stay up late,
or to eat the bread of hard toil;
the Lord provides as the beloved get their sleep.

See, heritage of Adonai!
Sons are a reward, and daughters of the womb.
Like arrows in the hand of a warrior,
so are children of one's youth.

Blessed are they whose quivers are full of them;
they will not be shamed
when they speak with enmity at the gate.

Glory…

Antiphon

The Catechism…says that Catholics are called to treat
(LGBTQIA+ people) with respect, compassion, and sensitivity.
See *Building a Bridge* by James Martin, SJ, CCC #2358

COLOSSIANS 1:12-20

Antiphon *Who follows me will have the light of life.* Jn 8:12c

Give joyful thanks to the Abba who made you fit
for your part of the lot of the saints in light,

who delivered us out of the authority of darkness,
transitioning us into the realm of the beloved Son
in whom we have redemption,
the forgiveness of our sins.

The Son is the image of the invisible God,
the firstborn of all creation.
In him all things were created,
in the heavens and on the earth,
the visible and the invisible,
whether thrones, lordships, rulers or authorities.

All creation has come to be through and for him.
He is before all things,
and in him all things hold together.

He is the head of the body, the church,
and the beginning, the firstborn from the dead,
so that in all things he may hold the first place.

In him all the fullness was well pleased to dwell,
and through him reconciliation to himself
of all things on earth and things in the heavens,
making peace through the blood of his cross.

Glory... Antiphon

READING   **JAMES 1:19-27**

Know, my beloved brothers and sisters; let every human be swift to hear, slow to speak, and slow to be angry, for human anger does not work toward God's righteous ways. So put away all filthiness and unnecessary waste and receive in meekness the word planted in you that is able to save your souls.

Become doers of the word (the *logos*) and not hearers only misleading yourselves. The hearer of the word who is not a doer is like a human seeing in a mirror one's face of birth, and seeing oneself, goes away right away and forgets what sort he or she is.

But the one who looks into the perfect law of freedom and remains, becoming not a forgetful hearer but a doer of the work, blessed in the doing will this one be. Any who think themselves religious and do not bridle their tongue but deceive their heart, vain is their religion.

This is religion clean and undefiled before the God and Father: to visit orphans and widows in their affliction, and to keep oneself unspotted by the world.

RESPONSORY   Ps 26:11,9

Redeem me, my Lord and my God,...
   ...and in your grace have mercy.
Sweep me not with those doing badness...
   ...and in your grace have mercy.
Glory to the Father and to the Son and to the Holy Spirit:
   ...Redeem me, my Lord and my God,
   and in your grace have mercy.

CANTICLE of MARY (The Magnificat)
LUKE 1:46-55

Antiphon *The Mighty One has done*
great things for me.

+ **My soul** is stretched full with praise of the Lord,
and my spirit, beyond joy in God, my Savior,
who chose to lay eyes on this humble servant.

Behold, now and forward,
each and every age will call me blessed,
for the Mighty One did great things to me.

Holy is the name and the mercy
to generations and generations,
the ones fearing the One,

Who scattered the haughty of mind and heart,
pulled the powerful off their high place,
and lifted with dignity the humble in need.

The hungering are filled with good things,
the rich are sent away empty,
and servant Israel is given relief

with a memory of mercy to remember,
the promise spoken to our ancestors,
to Abraham and his descendants forever.

Glory...

Antiphon

INTERCESSIONS

- For all who have had a hard day at work...
- For all who have died...

- In gratitude for blessings...; Abba thank you.
- For the sins of this day...; Lord Jesus have mercy.
- With concerns over tomorrow...; Holy Spirit help.

PRAYER in an ADDICTIVE CULTURE

> God of mercy,
> your Son ministered to all who came to him.
> Give strength to your sons and daughters
> who have lost their health and freedom
> to the slavery of addiction.
> Give them your grace in the work of recovery
> and bring them to the freedom of sobriety.
> To those who care for them,
> grant wisdom to know when to help
> and the patient love that perseveres.
> Amen.

OUR FATHER...

> 117, Text: Psalm 23, Henry W. Baker, 1868, altered
> Music: ST. COLUMBA, CM; Gaelic Folk Melody
> Popular melody for: *O Breathe On Me, O Breath Of God*

WEEK I
THURSDAY MORNING

+ *God, come to my assistance;*   Psalm 70:2
Lord, make haste to help me!

Glory...

The/ King of Love my/ Shep-herd is,
Whose/ good-ness fails me// nev-er;
I noth-ing lack if I am his
And he is mine for-ev-er.

Where/ streams of liv-ing/ wat-er flow,
Our/ ran-somed souls he// leads us,
And where the ver-dant pas-tures grow,
with food cel-es-tial feeds us.

Per/-verse and fool-ish/, do I stray,
But/ yet in love he// seeks me
To on his shoul-der gent-ly lay
And home, re-joic-ing, bring me.

You/ spread a ta-ble/ in our sight
Your/ unc-tion grace be//-stow-ing;
And, oh! the tran-sport of de-light
With our cup ov-er-flow-ing.

And/ so through all the/ length of days
Your/ good-ness fails us// nev-er.
Good Shep-herd, may we sing your praise
With-in your house for-ev-er!

PSALM 18:31-51

Antiphon   *Hear, Israel,*
                     the Lord our God is One.   Mk 12:29

The ways of God are perfect,
the word of Adonai is flawless,
a shield for all who need refuge.
For who is God besides Adonai?
And who is the Rock except our God?

God arms me with strength,
makes my way good,
makes my feet like the deer
and makes me to stand at full height,
training my hands for the battle;
my arms can bend a bow of bronze.

You give to me your shield of victory,
your right hand sustains me,
stooping to make me great.
You broaden my path beneath me
so my ankles do not turn.

I pursued and overtook enmity
and did not turn back until its defeat…
They fell beneath my feet.

You armed me with strength for the battle
and made the adversity bow at my feet.
You turned back enmity and brought its defeat.

They cried for help, but no one saved them.
Adonai did not answer them.
I beat them as dust in the wind;
like mud in the streets I poured them out.

You delivered me from attacks of people,
you made me as a head of nations;
people I knew not became subject to me.
Hearing me in their ear they obey.

Foreigners cringe before me, losing heart,
trembling out of strongholds.

Adonai is alive and praised;
may my Rock be exalted, my saving God.
God gives victory to me
and subdues nations under me,

saving me from enmity,
and rescuing me from violence.
I praise you, Adonai, among the nations,
and to your name I will sing praise.

You make great victories of your king
with unfailing kindness to David, your anointed,
and his descendants to forever.

Glory... Antiphon

If I expect another human to love me perfectly, then
I am expecting them to be God, and I will be disappointed.
See *Bread for the Journey* by Henri Nouwen

PSALM 89:39-53

Antiphon
*Who does not take their cross
and follow after me
is not worthy of me.*   Mt 10:38

Lord, you have rejected and spurned,
you were angry with your anointed one.
You renounced the covenant of your servant,
the crown you defiled in the dust.

You broke through all of the walls
and reduced the strongholds to ruin.
Those passing on the way plundered
and the neighbors were full of scorn.

You exalted the right hand of adversity
and made enmity rejoice.
You turned back the edge of our sword
and did not support us in the battle.

You put an end to the splendor
and cast the throne to the ground.
You cut short the days of youth
and covered us over with shame.

Until when, Adonai?
Will you hide yourself to forever?
Will your wrath burn like fire?
Remember how fleeting am I!

For what futility you created the human race,
sons and daughters of Adam and Eve!
What human can live and not see death,
or save the self from the power of Sheol?

Where, Lord, are your former great loves,
your fidelity sworn to David?
Remember, Lord,
the mockery of your servants!

I bear this in my heart
from many nations, Adonai:
the mockery of enmity,
the mockery of the steps of your anointed one.

Blessed be Adonai to forever.
Amen and amen.

Glory...

Antiphon

My Cross:

Part of the faith journey
is to figure out what my cross is.
Hint: everyone carries a core wound.
Then I can run away from it, try to give
it to someone else, pretend to know nothing
about it, try to bury it, or take it up and follow Jesus.

PSALM 57

Antiphon

This is my comandment,
that you love one another
as I have loved you.   Jn 15:12

Have mercy on me, God, have mercy on me,
for in you my soul takes refuge
and in the shade of your wings I take refuge
until disasters pass.

I cry out to God Most High,
to El who fulfills me,
who sends from the heavens and saves me
and rebukes the one pursuing me.

God sends love and fidelity to my self;
in the midst of ravenous lions I lie,
in the midst of human beings
with teeth and spear and arrows and tongues,
their sharp swords.

Be exalted, God, above the heavens,
your glory over all the earth.

For my feet they spread a net
and my self was bowed down.
Before me they dug a pit
and fell inside it themselves.

THURSDAY MORNING

My heart is steadfast, Elohim,
my heart is steadfast;
I will sing and make music.

Awake, my soul!
Wake up the harp and the lyre;
I will wake up the dawn.

I will praise you among the nations, Lord;
I will sing of you among the peoples,
for great to the heavens is your love
and to the skies is your fidelity.

Be exalted above the heavens, God,
your glory over all the earth.

Glory…

Antiphon

---

*You feel
you are hedged
in; you dream of escape;
but beware of mirages. Do not
run or fly away in order to get free:
rather dig in the narrow place which has
been given you; you will find God there and
everything. God does not float on your horizon,
but sleeps in your substance. Vanity runs, love digs.
If you fly away from yourself, your prison will run with
you and will close in because of the wind of your flight; if
you go deep down into yourself it will disappear in paradise.*
See *Homo Viator (Human Wayfarer)* by Gabriel Marcel

PSALM 87

Antiphon *The Abba and I are one.* Jn 10:30

On the holy mountain
is the foundation of Adonai,
who loves the gates of Zion
more than all of Jacob's dwellings.
Glorious things are being said of you, city of God.

"I will record Rahab and Babylon
among those who know me;
see Philistia and Tyre with Ethiopia:
this one was born there!"

But of Zion it will be said,
"One and another were born in her,
and the Most High will establish her."

Adonai will write when registering peoples,
"This one was born there."
And making music they will sing,
"All of my fountains are in you."

Glory...

Antiphon

*In the Bible
a mountain is often
a meeting place with God.*

JEREMIAH 31:10-14

Antiphon *They will be my people and I will be their God*
for they will return to me with all their heart.

Jer 24:7b

Hear, nations, the word of Adonai;
proclaim it to distant coastlands and say:
"The One who scattered Israel
will gather them and watch them
as one who is shepherd to a flock."

For Adonai will ransom and redeem Jacob
from the hand of those with more strength.

They will come and they will shout
up on the height of Zion
and they will rejoice in the bounty of Adonai,
the grain and new wine and oil,
and younglings of the flock and herd;
and they themselves like a well-watered garden
will sorrow no more, not again.

Then the maiden will be glad in dance,
and young men together with the old.
I will turn their mourning into gladness;
I will comfort them, replacing sorrow with joy.
I will satisfy with abundance the self of the priests
and my people will be filled with my bounty,
declares Adonai.

Glory... Antiphon

ISAIAH 40:10-17

Antiphon *A voice of one cried out in the desert:*
prepare the way of the Lord.   Mk 1:3

See! Sovereign Adonai comes with power,
and with a ruling arm.
See! And with reward
accompanied with recompense.

Like a shepherd tending the flock
and gathering lambs in the arms,
carrying them in the heart
and leading gently those with young.

Who can measure the waters in a hand's hollow?
or mark off the heavens with handbreadths?
or hold the dust of the earth in a basket?
or weigh mountains on a scale
or hills in a balance?

Who has understood the mind of Adonai?
What human has given counsel or instruction,
or whom was consulted for enlightenment
and teaching about what is right
and teaching knowledge?
Who can show the path of understanding?

Surely nations are like drops in a bucket
and are regarded as dust on a scale.
Surely islands are weighed like fine dust.

Even Lebanon is not sufficient to make fire,
nor their animals sufficient for burnt-offering.
Before God, all the nations are as nothing,
regarded as worthless and less than nothing.

Glory…

Antiphon

God questions:
*Where were you when
I founded the earth? Have
you in your days ordered morning
and shown the dawn its place? How
is the lightning sent and the east wind
scattered over the earth? Who has wisdom
to count the clouds? Do you know the time
of birth of a mountain goat? Do you give strength
to the horse? Does the eagle soar at your command?*
And Job answers: *Surely I have spoken without understanding of things more wonderful than me I cannot know. I retract my words and repent in dust and ash.* See Job 38-42

PSALM 48

Antiphon

*Take nothing on the way
except a staff, sandals,
and a single tunic.*

Mk 6:8

Great is Adonai, greatly being praised
in the city of our God, on the holy mountain,
beautiful height, the joy of all the earth,

Mount Zion, the upmost heights,
sacred mountain, the city of the Great Ruler.
God in the citadels is shown as a fortress when,
see, the rulers join forces and invade together.

They saw, were astounded, and fled in terror;
trembling seized them, pain
like a woman in labor.
By the east wind you destroyed
ships of Tarshish;

just as we heard, so we saw in the city
of Adonai Sabaoth, in the city of our God.
God makes her secure to forever.

In your temple we meditate
on your unfailing love.
Like your name, God, so your praise
goes to the ends of the earth;

your right hand is filled with justice.
Mount Zion rejoices
because of your judgments;
the villages of Judah are glad.

Walk about Zion! Go all around!
Count her towers!
Consider at heart her ramparts!
View her citadels!
So that you may tell to the next generation:
This God, our God, forever and ever
will guide us to the always.

Glory...

                Antiphon

---

*Emperor
Constantine's
Edict of Milan in
313 AD diminished
the general risk of being
a martyr, which had been
seen by many as the highest
form of Christian life. And so
some sought to pattern their lives
after Jesus' 40 days of temptation in
the desert, but in desert caves in Egypt
and Syria praying primarily the psalms. Over
time others began to live in nearby caves seeking
spiritual direction from the one they would treat as
a kind of father or abba, such as Saint Anthony of Egypt.*

PSALM 99

Antiphon *Were not ten lepers cleansed?*
And this one foreigner alone
gives glory to God?   Lk 17:17

Adonai reigns; let the nations tremble.
The One sits enthroned on the cherubim;
let the earth shake.

Great in Zion is Adonai,
and exalted over all of the nations.
Let them praise your great and awesome name,
"Holy are you, and mighty."

The Ruler of justice loves you
and establishes equity and justice,
having done what is right in Jacob.

Exalt Adonai, our God!
And worship at the feet on the footstool,
"Holy are you, and mighty."

Moses and Aaron were among the priests,
and Samuel among those calling the name,
calling on El Adonai, who answered them,
who spoke to them from the pillar of cloud.
They kept the statutes and decrees given to them.

Adonai, our God, you answered them.
You were the one Forgiving El to them,
though punishing their misdeeds.

Exalt Adonai our God!
And worship at the holy mountain,
for holy is our God Adonai!

Glory...

Antiphon

OFFICE OF READINGS and FIRST READING AT MASS

	Odd Years	**Even Years**
1 readings	*Romans 2:17-29*	*Genesis 4*
mass	Hebrews 3:7-14	1 Samuel 4:1-11
3 rdgs	*Romans 10*	*Genesis 24:1-27*
mass	Hebrews 10:19-25	2 Samuel 7:18-19,24-29
5 rdgs	*1 Corinthians 4*	*Genesis 44*
mass	Genesis 2:18-25	1 Kings 11:4-13
7 rdgs	*1 Corinthians 12:12-31a*	*2 Corinthians 4:5-18*
mass	Ben Sira 5:1-8	James 5:1-6
9 rdgs	*James 4:1-12*	*Galatians 4:8-31*
mass	Tobit 6:10-11;7:1,9-17;8:4-7	2 Timothy 2:8-15
11 rdgs	*Judges 7*	*Haggai 2*
mass	2 Corinthians 11:1-11	Ben Sira 48:1-15
13 rdgs	*1 Samuel 12*	*Nehemiah 9:22-37*
mass	Genesis 22:1-19	Amos 7:10-17
15 rdgs	*2 Samuel 7*	*Job 5*
mass	Exodus 3:13-20	Isaiah 26:7-9,12,16-19
17 rdgs	*1 Kings 12:20-33*	*Job 38 & 39*
mass	Exodus 40:16-21,34-38	Jeremiah 18:1-6
19 rdgs	*2 Kings 9 & 10*	*Zechariah 11*
mass	**Joshua** 3:7-10a,11,13-17	Ezekiel 12:1-12

THURSDAY MORNING

	Odd Years	**Even Years**
21 rdgs	*Ephesians 6:1-9*	*1 Timothy 2*
mass	1 Thessalonians 3:7-13	**1 Corinthians** 1:1-9
23 rdgs	*Hosea 2*	*2 Peter 3:1-10*
mass	Colossians 3:12-17	1 Corinthians 8:1b-7,11-13
25 rdgs	*Isaiah 10*	*Tobit 6*
mass	**Haggai** 1:1-8	**Ecclesiastes** 1:2-11
27 rdgs	*Isaiah 37*	*Sirach 5*
mass	**Malachi** 3:13-20a	Galatians 3:1-5
29 rdgs	*Habakuk 3*	*Sirach 38 & 39*
mass	Romans 6:19-23	Ephesians 3:14-21
31 rdgs	*Jeremiah 31*	*Wisdom 14 & 15*
mass	Romans 14:7-12	Philippians 3:3-8a
33 rdgs	*Ezekiel 24*	*Daniel 1*
mass	**1 Maccabees** 2:15-29	Revelation 5:1-10

READING   **ISAIAH 66:1-2**

This Adonai says, "The heavens are my throne and the earth is the footstool of my feet. Where is this house that you will build for me? Where is to be the place for my resting? Even all these my hand made, so all these came into being," declares Adonai.

"This I esteem: the one humble and contrite spirit, who trembles at my word."

RESPONSORY   Ps 130:1

Out of the depths I cry to you…
   …Lord, hear my voice!
My desire is to do your desire…
   …Lord, hear my voice!
Glory to the Father and to the Son and to the Holy Spirit:
   …Out of the depths I cry to you, Lord, hear my voice!

Gospel Canticle For Morning

Antiphon   *Lord, give us knowledge of salvation known in the forgiveness of our sins.*

Gospel Reading for Thursday of

Week			
1 Mark 1:40-45	**13** Matt 9:1-8	**25** Luke 9:7-9
3 Mark 4:21-25	**15** Matt 11:28-30	**27** Luke 11:5-13
5 Mark 7:24-30	**17** Matt 13:47-53	**29** Lk 12:49-53
7 Mark 9:41-50	**19** Matt 18:21-19:1	**31** Luke 15:1-10
9 Mark 12:28-34	**21** Matt 24:42-51	**33** Lk 19:41-44
11 Matt 6:7-15	**23** Luke 6:27-38	

CANTICLE of ZECHARIAH (The Benedictus)
LUKE 1:68-79

+ Blessed be the Lord the God of Israel
who chose a people to visit with redemption,
and raised salvation in the house of David,
saving strength from God's own servant,

speaking from the age of the prophets
through the mouth of the holy prophet:
Salvation out of enmity,
even out of those who hate us,

to show our ancestors how mercy works, -
and to remember the holy promise of the Lord,
the covenant made for our ancestor Abraham,
calming our fear and making us free
to serve with holy justice before God all our days.

And you also child -
will be called a prophet of the Most High
for you will go before the Lord to prepare his way
and give to people a knowledge of salvation
known in accepting forgiveness of their sins.

From the tender mercy of our God,
the sun rising from the height will visit with light
for those who sit in the dark or shadow of death
and to guide our feet into the way of peace.

Glory...

Antiphon

PETITIONS FOR THE CONSECRATION TO GOD
OF THE DAY AND ITS WORK

- For the Church and her ministry and apostolates…

- For secular authorities and all serving as stewards…

- For people who are poor or sick or in sorrow…

- For peace and the basic needs of each human being…

- For a culture of vocations all over the world…

TAKE LORD RECEIVE   Saint Ignatius of Loyola

Take, Lord, receive
all my liberty, my memory, my understanding,
and all my will, all I have and possess.
You have given all this to me;
to you, Lord, I return;
all is yours;
dispose of it wholly as you will.
Give me your love and your grace;
for me this is enough.

OUR FATHER…

Principles Toward
Harmony of Tensions:
1. Time is greater than space.
2. Unity prevails over conflict.
3. Realities are greater than ideas.
4. The whole is greater than the part.
See *The Joy of the Gospel* by Pope Francis

WEEK I
THURSDAY EVENING

+ *God, come to my assistance;* Psalm 70:2
  Lord, make haste to help me!

  Glory...

Beau-ti-ful Sa\-vior, King of Cre-a\-tion,
Son of\ Ma-ry\, Son of God!
Tru-ly I love\ you, Tru-ly I'll serve\ you,
Light of my soul, my Joy, my Crown.

Fair are the mea\-dows, Fair are the wood\-lands,
Robed in\ flow-ers of bloom-ing spring;
Je-sus is fair\-er, Je-sus is pur\-er;
He makes our sad-dest spir-it sing.

Fair is the sun\-shine, Fair is the moon\-light,
Bright are the spark-ling\ stars on high;
Je-sus shines bright\-er, Je-sus shines pur\-er,
Than all the an-gels in the sky.

Beau-ti-ful Sa\-vior, Lord of the na\-tions,
Full-y\ hu-man\, full-y God!
Praise, a-do-ra\-tion, Glo-ry and ho\-nor,
Now and for-ev-er-more, our Lord!

> 86, Text: based on Psalm 45:3; author unknown, 1677;
> translated by Joseph A. Seiss, 1873, altered
> Music: ST. ELIZABETH; Hoffman and Richter's
> Schleisische Volkslieder, 1842

PSALM 25

Antiphon *The time is full
and the reign of God has drawn near;
repent and believe in the gospel.* Mk 1:15

To you, Adonai, I lift up my soul;
in you, my God, I trust; let me not be shamed
and let enmity not triumph over me.
Indeed all who hope in you will not be shamed;
shamed will be those doing wanton treachery.

Show me your ways, Adonai; teach me your paths.
Guide me in your truth and teach me,
for you are my saving God;
you are my hope all the day.

Remember your mercies, Adonai,
and your loves, for they are from of old.
The sins of my youth and rebellious ways
you do not remember, as you are loving.

You do remember me, for you are good, Adonai.
Good and upright is Adonai,
who instructs sinners in the way,
guides humble ones in the right,
and teaches the way to the humble.

THURSDAY EVENING

All the ways of Adonai are loving and faithful
for those who keep the covenant demands.
For the sake of your name, Adonai,
now you forgive my iniquity, great as it is.

Who is the human who fears Adonai?
The one being instructed in the Lord's chosen way,
whose life will be days spent in prosperity,
whose descendants will inherit the land,
the confidence of Adonai is with those thus fearing;
the covenant is made known to them.

My eyes are ever on Adonai,
who will free my feet from the snare.
Turn to me! Be gracious to me!
For I am lonely and afflicted.

Troubles of my heart have multiplied;
free me from my anguish!
Look upon my affliction and distress!
Take away all of my sins!

See the enmity, the increase of fierce hate!
Guard my life! Rescue me!
Let me not be shamed, for I take refuge in you.
May integrity and honesty protect me
because I hope in you.

Redeem Israel, God, from all our troubles.

Glory...

Antiphon

PSALM 79:1-5,9-11,13

Antiphon

*If you only knew
what makes for peace.*   Lk 19:42a

God, the nations invaded into your inheritance,
they defiled your holy temple,
they reduced Jerusalem to rubbles.
They gave the bodies of your servants
as food to birds of the air,
the flesh of your saints to beasts of earth.

They poured out their blood
like the waters around Jerusalem
and no one is left to bury.
We are a reproach to our neighbors,
scorn and derision to those around us.
Until when, Adonai, will you be angry?
Will the fire of your jealousy burn to forever?...

Help us, God of our salvation,
for the glory of your name,
and deliver us and forgive our sins
for the sake of your name.

Why should the nations say,
"Where is their God?"
Let vengeance be known among the nations
before our eyes for your servants,
for their blood being poured out.

May the groan of prisoners come before you;
and by your strong arm
preserve the condemned...

We your people, the sheep of your pasture,
will praise you to forever.
Generation to generation
will recount your praise.

Glory...

Antiphon

A monk went to
Basil of Caesarea and
said, 'Speak a word, Father.'
Basil replied, 'You shall love the
Lord your God with all your heart.'
The monk went away at once. Coming
back twenty years later, the monk said, 'Abba,
I have kept the word; speak another word to me.'
Basil said, 'You shall love your neighbor as yourself.'
The monk returned in obedience to the cell to keep that also.

See *The Sayings of the Desert Fathers* by Benedicta Ward

PSALM 86

Antiphon *Leave both the weed and the wheat
to grow together until the harvest.* Mt 13:30

Hear in your ear, Adonai;
answer me for I am poor and needy.
Guard my life for I am devoted;
save your servant, my God,
the one trusting in you.

Have mercy on me, Lord,
for to you I call all the day.
Bring joy to your servant,
for to you, Lord, I lift up my soul.

Indeed, Lord, you are kind and forgiving
and abundant in love for all who call to you.
Hear my prayer, Adonai;
listen to the sound of my cries for mercy.

In the day of my trouble I will call to you
for you will answer me.
There is none like you among so-called "gods"
and there are no deeds like yours, Lord.

All the nations you made will come
and they will worship before you, Lord,
and they will bring glory to your name
for you are great and do marvelous deeds,
you, God, you yourself.

THURSDAY EVENING

Teach me, Adonai, your way
and I will walk in your truth.
Undivide my heart
that I may fear your name.

I will praise you, Lord my God, with all my heart
and I will glorify your name to forever
for great is your love of me
and you deliver my soul from the depth of Sheol.

Arrogant ones attack against me, God;
a band of ruthless people seek my life
and do not regard you before them.

But you, Lord El, Compassionate and Gracious,
are slow of anger and abundant in love and fidelity.
Turn to me! And have mercy on me!

Grant your strength to your servant
and save the child of your handservant!
Give to me a sign of goodness
that enmity may see and find shame,
for you, Adonai, help me and comfort me.

Glory…

Antiphon

Unless the
grain of wheat falling to
the ground dies, it remains one grain;
but if it dies, it bears much fruit.   Jn 12:24

PSALM 30

Antiphon　　　*Who touched my garments?*　　　Mk 5:30

I will exalt you, Adonai, for you lifted me
and did not let enmity gloat over me.

Adonai, my God, I cried to you for help
and you healed me.
Adonai, you brought my self up from Sheol;
you spared me from going into the pit.

Sing to Adonai, you saints!
Sing praise to the holy name!
One moment in anger,
lifetimes in the Lord's favor;
when through the night weeping abides,*
joy can rejoice in the morning.

I said in complacent security,
I will be unshaken to forever.
In your favor, Adonai,
you made me stand firm as a mountain;
you hid your faces and I was dismayed.

To you, Adonai, I called
and to you, Lord, I cried for mercy.
What would be the gain in my destruction?
What is gained if I go into the pit?

THURSDAY EVENING

Will the dust praise you?
Will the dust proclaim your fidelity?
Hear, Adonai! Be merciful to me!
Be my one helper, Adonai!

You turned my wailing into dancing;
you removed my sackcloth and clothed me in joy
so that my heart may sing to you,
and not be silent.
My God Adonai, I will thank you to forever.

Glory...

Antiphon

---

*Some of the Fathers
and Mothers of the Desert
recited all 150 psalms daily.
Saint Benedict (d. 547 AD)
in his monastic Rule laid out a
pattern of praying all the psalms
over each week. Different religious
orders used different versions, including
Saint Francis of Assisi who developed a shorter
breviary of psalm fragments designed to be easy to
carry and Saint Ignatius of Loyola who wanted the
Jesuits to be more free when working with the poor.
The Roman Breviary promulgated in 1568 had many
revisions. The Second Vatican Council led to a four-week
cycle, which is again being updated as this work is concluded.*
See *A Simple Family Breviary From the Psalms of Saint Francis*
by Stephen Joseph Wolf and *The Rule of Saint Benedict*

*weeping
spends the night
See *Being There*
by Peter Keese

PSALM 32

Antiphon
Do you see this woman?
Her many sins have been forgiven,
and so she has loved much.   Lk 7:44,47

Blessed is the one forgiven of faults,
no longer covered with sin.
Blessed is the human
against whom Adonai does not count sin,
and in whose spirit there is no deceit.

When I kept silent, my bones wasted away
through my groaning all day.
For by day and night
your hand was heavy upon me;
my strength withered as in dry summer heat.

I acknowledged my sin to you,
and did not cover up my iniquity;
I said I will confess my faults to Adonai
and you forgave the guilt of my sin.

For this let every godly one pray to you
at the time to find you.
Surely the rising of mighty waters
will not reach this one.
You are the hiding place for me;
you will protect me from trouble
and surround me with deliverance song.

I will instruct you and I will teach you
and counsel you in the way you should go,
keeping an eye on you.

Do not be like a horse
or like your mule with no understanding;
by bit and bridle and harness they are controlled
or else they will not even come to you.

Many woes have doers of the bad,
but the truster in Adonai
is surrounded in unfailing love.

Rejoice in Adonai!
Just ones, be glad!
And sing, all you upright of heart!

Glory...

Antiphon

Principle & Foundation:

Life is mostly about learning
to live with God so to love as God loves.
Things are God-gifts for knowing and loving God;
things clung to my center lose this God-given purpose.
In a balanced life every blessing and woe
can help me say a deeper 'Yes' to God.
May my one desire remain to choose each choice
that leads to me becoming God's mercy alive.

See *The Spiritual Exercises* (#23) of St. Ignatius of Loyola, d. 1556

PSALM 132

Antiphon   *To the one who has, more will be given;*
from the one who has not,
even what that one has
will be taken away.   Mk 4:25

Adonai, remember David
and all the hardships he endured,
the oath he swore to Adonai,
the vow he made to the Mighty One of Jacob.

I will not enter into the structure of my house;
I will not go to the mats of my bed;
I will not allow my eyes to sleep
nor let slumber come to my eyelids,
till I find a place for Adonai,
a dwelling for the Mighty One of Jacob.

See, we heard her in Ephrathah;
we came upon her in fields of Jaar.
"Let us go to the dwellings;
let us worship at the feet on the footstool."

Arise, Adonai, to your rest,
you and the ark of your might.
May your priests be clothed with justice
and may your saints sing for joy.

For the sake of your servant David
reject not the face of your anointed one.

Adonai swore an oath to David,
sure and not to be revoked.
"From the descendants of your body
I will place on your throne.

If your sons and daughters keep my covenant
and my statutes that I teach them
then their children to forever
will sit on your throne."

For Adonai chose Zion
and desired her as a dwelling:
"This is my resting place to forever;
here I will sit, for I desired her.

To bless I will bless her provisions;
her poor ones I will satisfy with food,
her priests I will clothe in salvation,
and her saints will sing; they will sing for joy.

Here I will sprout a horn for David;
I will set up a lamp for my anointed one.
Enmity will be clothed with shame.
The crown on David will be resplendent."

Glory... Antiphon

God has given us all these wonderful toys;
ought we not to play with them? Sister Wendy Beckett

REVELATION 11:17-18, 12:10-12a

Antiphon *I am the Alpha and the Omega, says the Lord God, the one who is and who was and who is to come, the Almighty.*   Rev 1:8

We thank you, Lord God Almighty,
the One who is and who was;
you have taken your great power and reign.

The nations raged and your anger came,
and the time to judge the dead
and to reward your servants and prophets,
the saints, and those fearing your name,
the small and the great...

Now have come the salvation and power
and reign of our God and the authority of Christ.
The accuser of our brothers and sisters was cast,
accusing them before our God day and night.

Their victory was because of the blood of the Lamb
and by the word of their witness.
They loved their life into their death,
and so be glad, you heavens,
and all you dwelling in them.

Glory...

Antiphon

THURSDAY EVENING

READING **1 PETER 1:3-9**

Blessed be the God and Father of our Lord Jesus Christ, in whose great mercy we are given rebirth to living hope through the resurrection of Jesus Christ from the dead, to the inheritance that is incorruptible, undefiled, and unfading, kept in heaven for you by the power of God, guarded through faith to a salvation ready to be revealed at the end time.

You exult in this, while yet you grieve if necessary for a little while by even many trials, for the proving of your faith, much more precious than gold that perishes even after being refined by fire, that you may be found giving praise and glory and honor at the revelation of Christ.

Without seeing him, you love him; still without seeing him you believe and exult with indescribable joy; and having been glorified, you are receiving the goal of your faith: the salvation of your souls.

RESPONSORY Ps 81:16b

The Lord our God feeds us…
   …and with finest of wheat.
Honey out of rock to satisfaction…
   …and with finest of wheat.
Glory to the Father and to the Son and to the Holy Spirit:
   …The Lord our God feeds us, and with finest of wheat.

CANTICLE of MARY (The Magnificat)
LUKE 1:46-55

Antiphon *God has exalted with dignity
the humble in need.*

+ My soul is stretched full with praise of the Lord,
and my spirit, beyond joy in God, my Savior,
who chose to lay eyes on this humble servant.

Behold, now and forward,
each and every age will call me blessed,
for the Mighty One did great things to me.

Holy is the name and the mercy
to generations and generations,
the ones fearing the One,

Who scattered the haughty of mind and heart,
pulled the powerful off their high place,
and lifted with dignity the humble in need.

The hungering are filled with good things,
the rich are sent away empty,
and servant Israel is given relief

with a memory of mercy to remember,
the promise spoken to our ancestors,
to Abraham and his descendants forever.

Glory...

Antiphon

INTERCESSIONS

- For learning and teaching what makes for peace…
- For all who have died…

- In gratitude for blessings…; Abba thank you.
- For the sins of this day…; Lord Jesus have mercy.
- With concerns over tomorrow…; Holy Spirit help.

VINCENTIAN MISSION PRAYER St John Gabriel Perboyre, C.M.

> Divine Savior,
> transform me into yourself.
> May my hands be your hands.
> May my tongue be your tongue.
> Grant that every faculty of my body
> may serve only to glorify you.
> Above all, transform my soul and all its powers,
> that my memory, my will and my affections may be
> the memory the will and the affections of you.
> I pray you destroy in me all that is not of you.
> Grant that I may live
> but in you, and by you, and for you,
> and that I may truly say with St. Paul,
> *I live now, not I, but Christ lives in me.*

OUR FATHER…

SHANTI, by Marty Haugen,
© GIA Publications, 1984,
is the current familiar tune

WEEK I
FRIDAY MORNING

+ *God, come to my assistance;*   Psalm 70:2
  Lord, make haste to help me!

  Glory...

A   **We walk by faith**, and not by sight;
No gra-cious words we hear
From him who spoke as none e'er spoke;
But we be-lieve him near.

We may not touch his hands and side,
Nor fol-low where he trod;
But in his prom-ise we re-joice,
And cry, "My Lord and God!"

Help then, O Lord, our un-be-lief;
And may our faith a-bound,
To call on you when you are near
And seek where you are found.

That, when our life of faith is done,
In realms of clear-er light
We may be-hold you as you are,
With full and end-less sight.

125, Text: CM, based on 2 Cor. 5:7 and John 20:24-29; Henry Alford,
1844, altered. Music: ST. AGNES, CM; John B. Dykes, 1866
Popular melody for: *Shepherd of Souls*

B "Take/ up your\ cross," the/ Sa-vior said,
"If you would my dis-ci-ple be;
De-ny your/-self\, the world\ for-sake,
And hum-bly fol-low af-ter me."

Take/ up your\ cross, let/ not its weight
Fill your weak spir-it with a-larm;
His strength s hall/ bear\ your spir\-it up,
And brace your heart and nerve your arm.

Take/ up your\ cross and/ fol-low Christ,
Nor think til death to lay it down;
In faith-ful/ bear\-ing of\ our cross
We hope to wear his glo-rious crown.

To/ you, great\ Lord, the/ One in Three,
All praise for-ev-er-more as-cend:
O grant us/ in\ our home\ to see
The heav'n-ly life that knows no end.

57, Text: Charles W. Everest,
Visions of Death and Other Poems, 1833, altered
Music option: ERHALT UNS HERR, LM;
Klug's *Geistliche Lieder*, 1543;
Popular melody for: *The Glory Of These Forty Days*

*If fear must be my primary or
only motivator, then let my fear be only
of God, whose Son has told us to 'be not afraid.'*

PSALM 69:2-22,30-37

Antiphon *Be not afraid of ones who can kill the body*
  but are unable to kill the soul;
  fear only the One able to destroy
  both soul and body in gehenna.   Mt 10:28

Save me, Adonai,
for waters have come to my neck.

I sink into the deep mire; there is no foothold.
I have come into deep waters; floods engulf me.

I am worn out from calling out;
my throat is parched and my eyes fail,
looking for my God.

Those hating me for no reason
are more numerous than the hairs of my head.
Many are the ones destroying me
in enmity for no reason.

What I did not steal, must I now restore?
You, God, you know my folly
and my guilts are not hidden from you.

May those who hope in you, God of Israel,
not be disgraced because of me.
For your sake I endure scorn
and shame covers my face.

Psalm 69, continued

I am a stranger to my brothers and sisters,
an alien to the children of my mother.
Zeal for your house consumes me
and insults of your insulters fall on me.

When I weep and fast, my self is a scorn to me.
When I put on my clothing of sackcloth
then I am as sport to them.
Those sitting at the gate mock at me
and drinkers of strong drink in their songs.

But I pray to you, Adonai, in the time of favor;
in the greatness of your love, God,
answer me with your sure salvation.

Rescue me from the mire and let me not sink;
let me be delivered from those who hate
and from the depths of the waters.
Let not the flood of waters engulf me,
nor the deep swallow me
nor the pit close its mouth over me.

Answer me, Adonai, for good is your love!
In your great mercies, turn to me!
Hide not your faces from your servant;
to my trouble, be quick! Answer me!
Come near because of the adversity;
rescue my self and redeem me!

You know my scorn and shame and disgrace;
all in enmity stand before you.
Scorn broke my heart and I became helpless
and I looked for compassion but there was none,
and for comforters, but found none.

They put gall in my food
and for my thirst gave me vinegar to drink…
I am in pain and suffering;
may your salvation protect me, God.

I will praise God's name in song and glory
with a thanksgiving more pleasing to Adonai
than ox or bull with horn and hoof.

The poor ones will see and be glad;
may your hearts now live, you seekers of God,
for Adonai hears the needy ones
and despises not the captives.

Let heaven and earth give praise
with the seas and all moving in them.
For God will save Zion
and rebuild the cities of Judah;

then they will settle there and be her steward
and the children of the servants will inherit her
and lovers of the Name will dwell in her.

Glory…

Antiphon *Be not afraid of ones who can kill the body but*
Mt 10:28 *are unable to kill the soul; fear only the One*
able to destroy both soul and body in gehenna.

PSALM 35:1-2c,3c,9-19,22-23,27-28

Antiphon   *The tax collector standing far off*
would not lift his eyes to heaven,
but beat his breast saying,
'God, be merciful to me, a sinner.'   Lk 18:13

Contend, Adonai, with my contenders!
Restrain those who would attack!
Take up shield and buckler and arise to my aid!...
Say to my soul, "I am your salvation."...

Then my soul will rejoice in Adonai
and take delight in salvation.
All of my bones will exclaim, "Adonai!
Who, like you, rescues the poor from the strong?
or the poor and the needy from robbers?"

Ruthless witnesses come forward;
on things I do not know they question me.
They repay me bad for the good; forlorn is my soul.

Yet when they were ill I clothed myself in sackcloth
and humbled myself with fasting when
my prayer had returned to my breast unanswered.
As a friend and a sibling I went about weeping,
bowing down like a grieving mother.

But at my stumbling they took glee
and gathered and gathered attackers
and did not cease to slander me unaware,
an ungodly circle of mockers
gnashing their teeth against me.

Until when, Lord? How long will you look on?
Rescue my life from the ravages,
my precious life from the lions.
I will give you thanks in the great assembly;
among people thronging I will praise you.

Let enmity neither gloat without cause or reason
nor wink the eye at me…

You have seen, Adonai; be not silent.
Be not far from me, Lord.
Awake!, my God and Lord,
and rise to my defense.
Vindicate me, Adonai, in your justice…

May those who delight in my vindication
shout and be glad and always say,
"May Adonai be exalted,
who delights in the well being of a servant."
My tongue will tell of your justice
and speak praise of you all the day.

Glory… Antiphon

Luke 18:13 is the source of the popular Jesus Prayer.

PSALM 51

Antiphon   *If anyone serves me,*
           that one the Abba will honor.   Jn 12:26b

Have mercy on me, God,
in accord with your unfailing love;
in accord with your great compassion
blot out my transgressions.

Wash me of my many iniquities
and cleanse me from my sin,
for I know my transgressions
and my sin is before me always.

Against you yourself I sinned,
doing what is bad in your eyes.
You are proven right when you speak
and justified when you judge.
Surely we are sinners from birth,
from conception in a mother's womb.

Surely you desire truth in our inner parts;
in my inmost place you teach me wisdom.
You cleanse me with hyssop and I will be clean;
you wash me and I will be whiter than snow…

You let me hear joy and gladness;
let the bones you let be crushed now rejoice.
Hide your faces from my sins
and blot out all my iniquities.

FRIDAY MORNING

A clean heart create in me, God!
Renew inside me a spirit to be steadfast.
Do not cast me from your presences,
nor take from me your Holy Spirit.

Restore to me the joy of your salvation
and sustain in me a willing spirit.
I will teach transgressors your ways
and sinners will turn back to you.

Save me from bloodguilt, God,
God of my salvation;
my tongue will sing of your justice.
Lord, open my lips
and my mouth will proclaim your praise.

Sacrifices give you no delight;
I could bring a burnt offering,
but it would give you no pleasure.
The sacrifices, God, you will not despise
are a broken spirit and a contrite heart.

Make Zion prosper in your pleasure,
and build up the walls of Jerusalem.
Then you will delight in the sacrifice of the just,
burnt offerings and whole offerings,
bulls offered on your altar.

Glory...

Antiphon

ISAIAH 45:15-25

Antiphon *The reign of God
is justice and peace
and joy in the Holy Spirit.* Rom 14:17

Truly, God, you hide yourself,
Saving God of Israel.
Makers of idols will know shame and disgrace,
all going off together in disgrace.

Israel will be saved by Adonai,
salvation everlasting.
You will not know shame or disgrace to the ages.

For this says Adonai, creating the heavens,
who fashioned and made and formed the earth,
creating it to be not an empty waste,
but formed to be inhabited,

"I am Adonai, and there is no other.
Not in secret did I speak,
from some place in a dark land,
saying to descendants of Jacob, 'seek me in vain.'
I, Adonai, speak truth and delare right things.

Gather together and come!
Assemble together, fugitives of the nations.
Those who carry idols of wood do not know:
they are praying to no-gods that cannot save.

Declare and present! Let them counsel together!
Who foretold this from long ago?
Who declared this from the distant past?
Not I, Adonai? There is no god apart from me,
God just and Saving; there is none but me.

Turn to me and be saved,
all you ends of the earth,
for I am God and there is no other.

By myself I swore integrity out of my mouth,
the word that will not be revoked.

Indeed, in front of me every knee will bow,
and every tongue will swear, and say,
'In Adonai alone are justice and strength,'

to whom will come and be shamed
all who have raged otherwise."
In Adonai they will be found just
and all the descendants of Israel will exult.

Glory...

Antiphon

---

*If someone is gay
and searches for the Lord
and has good will, who am I to judge?*
Pope Francis, July 29, 2013

JEREMIAH 14:17b-22

Antiphon *Before I formed you in the womb*
I knew you.

Jer 1:5

On sin,
a pondering:
Lord, when I examine
my conscience, every day
I am aware of sin, and it seems
always to be that in that moment of
sinning I was not aware of your love for
me. Why do I forget that you love me? How
can I stay aware of your love? Is it even possible?

A Consciousness Examen in Three Minutes (an aware prayer)

1st – *Replay your day. Pick out a high point in it – a good thing*
you did, like going out of your way to help someone…
Give God thanks for the opportunity.

2nd – *Replay your day again. This time pick out a low point*
– a bad thing you did, like putting down someone who
really needs to be lifted up… Ask Jesus for forgiveness.

3rd – *Look ahead to tomorrow to a critical point – a hard thing*
you must do, like dealing with a personal problem…
Ask the Holy Spirit for help with it.

See *Challenge 2000: A Daily Meditation Program based on*
the Spiritual Exercises of Saint Ignatius by Mark Link, Jesuit

FRIDAY MORNING

Let my eyes overflow with tears
by night, by day, without cease,
for the grievous wounds suffered
by the virgin daughter of my people,
a very crushing blow.

If I go out in the country, see: ones slain by sword!
If I go in the city, see: the ravages of famine!
Indeed, both prophet and priest
have gone to a land they do not know.

To reject you rejected Judah?
Is Zion despised by your self?
Why have you afflicted us so we have no healing?

Our hope is for peace, but no good happens;
for a time of healing, but see: the terror!
We are aware, Adonai, of our no-good ways
and the guilt of our ancestors;
indeed we ourselves sin against you.

For the sake of your Name, neither despise us
nor dishonor the throne of your glory.
Remember, and break not your covenant with us!

Is there one among the worthless nations
that can bring rain or send showers from the skies?
Is that One not you, our God Adonai?
And so we hope in you, for you do all these things.

Glory...

Antiphon

PSALM 95

Antiphon *Where two or three
are gathered in my name,
there am I in the midst of them.* Mt 18:20

Come, let us sing to Adonai;
let us shout to our saving Rock.
Let us come before the faces with gratitude
and make a joyful noise with song.

Adonai is the great El,
the great Ruler above all those little "g" gods,
holding in hand the depths of earth
and peaks of mountains,
the sea and dry land formed by the hand.

Come, let us worship and bow and kneel
before Adonai who made us.
For God is our God, and we are the people
of the pasture and flock and care of our God.

"If today you hear this voice
do not harden your heart,
as at Meribah and the desert day at Massah
where your ancestors tested me;
they tried me though they saw my work.

For forty years was my anger on that generation,
the people straying in their heart;
and so they did not know my ways,
and so were unable to enter my rest."

Glory...

Antiphon

PSALM 100

Antiphon
*Go to the lost sheep
of the house of Israel.* Mt 10:6

Shout for joy to Adonai, all you earth!
Serve Adonai with gladness!
Come into the presence with joyful song.

Know that Adonai is God, who made us,
whose people we are,
in whose pasture we are the sheep.

Enter the gates with thanksgiving,
go into the courts with praise!
Give thanks and give praise to the Name!

Good is Adonai, and loving to forever,
and faithful through generations and generation.

Glory...

Antiphon

OFFICE OF READINGS and FIRST READING AT MASS

	Odd Years	**Even Years**
1 readings	*Romans 3:1-20*	*Genesis 6 & 7*
mass	Hebrews 4:1-5,11	1 Samuel 8:4-7,10-22a
3 rdgs	*Romans 7:1-13*	*Genesis 16*
mass	Hebrews 10:32-39	2 Samuel 11:1-4a,5-10a
5 rdgs	*1 Corinthians 5*	*Genesis 45 & 46*
mass	Genesis 3:1-8	1 Kings 11:29-32;12:19
7 rdgs	*1 Corinth 12:31b-13:13*	*2 Corinthians 5*
mass	Ben Sira 6:5-17	James 5:9-12
9 rdgs	*James 4:13-5:11*	*Galatians 5*
mass	Tobit 11:5-17	2 Timothy 3:10-17
11 rdgs	*Judges 8 & 9*	*Zechariah 1*
mass	2 Corinth 11:18,21b-30	**2 Kings** 11:1-4,9-18,20
13 rdgs	*1 Samuel 15*	*Nehemiah 12*
mass	Gen 23:1-4,19;24:1-8,62-67	Amos 8:4-6,9-12
15 rdgs	*2 Samuel 11*	*Job 6*
mass	Exodus 11:10-12,14	Isaiah 38:1-6,21-22,7-8
17 rdgs	*1 Kings 17*	*Job 40 & 41*
mass	**Lev** 23:1,4-11,15-16,27,34b-37	Jeremiah 26:1-9
19 rdgs	*2 Kings 11 & 12*	*Zechariah 12 & 13*
mass	Joshua 24:1-13	Ezekiel 16:1-15,60,63

	Odd Years	**Even Years**
21 rdgs	*Ephesians 6:10-24*	*1 Timothy 3*
mass	1 Thessalonians 4:1-18	1 Corinthians 1:17-25
23 rdgs	*Hosea 4 & 5*	*2 Peter 3:11-18*
mass	**1 Timothy** 1:1-2,12-14	1 Corinth 9:16-19,22b-27
25 rdgs	*Isaiah 28*	*Tobit 7 & 8*
mass	Haggai 1:15b-2:9	Ecclesiastes 3:1-11
27 rdgs	*2 Kings 21*	*Sirach 6*
mass	**Joel** 1:13-15;2:1-2	Galatians 3:7-14
29 rdgs	*Jeremiah 22:10-30*	*Sirach 42 & 43*
mass	Romans 7:18-25a	Ephesians 4:1-6
31 rdgs	*Jeremiah 42 & 43*	*Wisdom 16 & 17*
mass	Romans 15:14-21	Philippians 3:17-4:1
33 rdgs	*Ezekiel 28*	*Daniel 2*
mass	1 Maccabees 4:36-37,52-59	Revelation 10:8-11

READING **EPHESIANS 4:25-32**

Put off the lie, and speak the truth to each neighbor, for we are members of one another.

If you become angry, do not sin; do not let the sun set on provocation, and do not give a place for the diabolo.

Let the thief steal no more, but rather let the former stealer labor working with his or her own hands, the good thing, to share with the one who has need.

Ephesians 4, continued

Keep every corrupt word from coming out of your mouth, but let the word be heard that gives grace to the hearer who needs building up.

And do not grieve the Holy Spirit of God, by whom you were sealed for the day of redemption.

Let all bitterness and rage and anger and fighting and blasphemy be removed from you with all evil.

Be kind to one another, tenderhearted, and forgive yourselves as also God in Christ has forgiven you.

RESPONSORY   Ps 143:8

Bring word at break of day…
…in your unfailing love.
Show the way for me to go…
…in your unfailing love.
Glory to the Father and to the Son and to the Holy Spirit:
…Bring word at break of day in your unfailing love.

Gospel Canticle For Morning

Antiphon: *God chose to visit God's people and brought redemption.*

Gospel Reading for Friday of
Week 1 Mark 2:1-12	13 Matt 9:9-13	25 Luke 9:18-22
3 Mark 4:26-34	15 Matt 12:1-8	27 Lk 11:15-26
5 Mark 7:31-37	17 Matt 13:54-58	29 Lk 12:54-59
7 Mark 10:1-12	19 Matt 19:3-12	31 Luke 16:1-8
9 Mark 12:35-37	21 Matt 25:1-13	33 Lk 19:45-48
11 Matt 6:19-23	23 Luke 6:39-42	

CANTICLE of ZECHARIAH (The Benedictus)
LUKE 1:68-79

+ **Blessed be** the Lord the God of Israel
who chose a people to visit with redemption,
and raised salvation in the house of David,
saving strength from God's own servant,

speaking from the age of the prophets
through the mouth of the holy prophet:
Salvation out of enmity,
even out of those who hate us,

to show our ancestors how mercy works, -
and to remember the holy promise of the Lord,
the covenant made for our ancestor Abraham,
calming our fear and making us free
to serve with holy justice before God all our days.

And you also child -
will be called a prophet of the Most High
for you will go before the Lord to prepare his way
and give to people a knowledge of salvation
known in accepting forgiveness of their sins.

From the tender mercy of our God,
the sun rising from the height will visit with light
for those who sit in the dark or shadow of death
and to guide our feet into the way of peace.

Glory...

Antiphon

PETITIONS FOR THE CONSECRATION TO GOD
OF THE DAY AND ITS WORK

- For the Church and her ministry and apostolates…

- For secular authorities and all serving as stewards…

- For people who are poor or sick or in sorrow…

- For peace and the basic needs of each human being…

- For guardian angel intercession for those considering use of violence…

- For any elders or children who feel abandoned…

- In gratitude for blessings and grace…

MORNING OFFERING   Apostleship of Prayer*

God, our Father, I offer you my day.
I offer you my prayers, thoughts, words, actions,
joys, and sufferings in union with the Heart of Jesus,
who continues to offer himself in the Eucharist
for the salvation of the world.
May the Holy Spirit, who guided Jesus,
be my guide and my strength today
so that I may witness to your love.
With Mary, the mother of our Lord and the church,
I pray for all Apostles of Prayer
and for the prayer intentions
proposed by the Pope this month.

OUR FATHER…

* https://popesprayerusa.net/

WEEK I
FRIDAY EVENING

+ *God, come to my assistance;*   Psalm 70:2
Lord, make haste to help me!

Glory...

A

When I sur-vey the/ won-drous\ cross
On which the Prince of\ glo-ry/ died,
My rich-est gain I/ count as\ loss,
And pour con-tempt on all my\ pride.

For-bid it, Lord, that/ I should\ boast,
Save in the death of\ Christ my/ God!
May all vain things that/ charm me\ most,
Be sac-ri-ficed as with his\ blood.

Were the whole realm of/ na-ture\ mine,
That trea-sure would be\ far too/ small;
Love so a-ma-zing/, so div\-ine,
Claims my_ soul, my life, my\ all.

55, Text: Isaac Watts, *Hymns and Spiritual Songs*, 1707, altered
Music: HAMBURG, Lowel Mason, 1824;
The Boston Handel and Haydn Society Collection of Church Music, 1825

B   **O God, grant me ser-en-i-ty**
to'ac-cept the things I can-not change,
The cour'ge to change the things I can,
And wisd'm to know the diff-er-ence.

Take, Lord, re-ceive my lib-er-ty,
My will en-tire and mem-o-ry,
My un-der-stand-ing, ev-'ry-thing,
Pos-ses-sions all, my off-er-ing.

The giv'n by you I do re-turn;
Con-form my life as is your will.
Suf-fic-ient now, no more to own:
E-nough are love and grace a-lone.

Lord A-do-nai, give love and grace,
Suf-fic-ient these in time and space,
Your love and grace, un-earned and free,
This true a-bun-dance may we see.

Love show-ing more in deed than word,
Love sha-ring in the com-mon good,
I pon-der with a-ffec-tion great
What God has done and does of late.

130, Text: Verse 1: *The Serenity Prayer*,
attributed to Reinhold Niebuhr, d. 1071
Text: Suscipe from *The Spiritual Exercises*, St. IgnatiusLoyola,#234,d.1556,
inspired by *Veneremur*, Jesuit Spirituality Center, Grand Coteau, LA, 1957
Music: TALLIS CANON, LM, Thomas Tallis, d. 1585
An alternate melody: *Praise God From Whom All Blessings Flow*

C **My life flows on in end-less song**
   A-bove earth's lam-en-ta-tion.
   I hear that near and far-off hymn,
   It hails a new cre-a-tion:
   Thru all the tu-mult and the strife
   I hear that mu-sic ring-ing;
   It finds an ech-o\ in my soul;
   How can I keep from sing-ing?

   What though my joys and com-forts fade
   The Lord my Sa-vior liv-eth;
   What though the shad-ows gath-er round
   Songs in the night he giv-eth:
   No storm can shake my in-most calm,
   While to that ref-uge cling-ing;
   Since Christ is Lord of\ heav'n and earth,
   How can I keep from sing-ing?

   I lift my eyes; the clouds grow thin;
   I see the blue a-bove it;
   And day by day clears way the path
   Since first I learned to love it:
   The peace of Christ makes fresh my heart,
   A foun-tain ev-er spring-ing;
   All things are mine since\ I am his;
   How can I keep from sing-ing?

98, Text: Robert Lowry, 1860, altered
Music: 87 87, ENDLESS SONG, Quaker Hymn; Robert Lowry, 1860

D   **All glo-ry, laud, and hon-or,**
to you, re-deem-er, King,
To whom the lips of chil-dren
make sweet ho-san-nas ring.
The King you are of Is-ra-el,
and Da-vid's roy-al Son,
Be-lov-ed of the Fa\-ther,
our Roy-al Bless-ed One.

The com-pa-ny of an-gels
are prais-ing you on high,
With hu-man be-ings too all
cre-a-tion makes re-ply.
The Cho-sen of the Cov-e-nant
with psalms be-fore you went;
So too our praise and an\-thems
be-fore you we pre-sent.

To you, be-fore your pass-ion,
a-pos-tles sang your praise;
To you, now high ex-al-ted,
our mel-o-dy we raise.
Ac-cep-ta-ble their voi\-ces;
hear too the praise we bring:
De-light in your be-lov\-ed,
our Sa-vior and our King.

42, Text: St. Theodulph of Orleans, c. 821, for Palm Sunday;
translated by John M. Neal, 1854, altered
Music: 76 76 D, ST. THEODULPH, Melchior Teschner, 1613

PSALM 22

Antiphon   *I am the true vine*
and my Abba is the vinegrower.   Jn 15:1

My God, my God, why have you forsaken me?
Far from my salvation are the words of my groan.
My God, I cry out by day, but you do not answer,
and at night with no relief.

Yet you Holy One are enthroned, praises Israel.
In you our ancestors trusted and were delivered.
To you they cried and they were saved.
In you they trusted and were not disappointed.

But I am a worm and a no-human,
the scorn of humanity and despised by people.
All those seeing me mock at me;
they shake their heads in insult:
"In the one you trust, let your Adonai rescue you;
let the one who 'delights' in you deliver you!"

You brought me out from the womb,
to trust in you at the breasts of my mother.
From the womb I was cast upon you;
from the womb of my mother, you are my God.
Be not far from me,
for trouble is near with no one to help.

Psalm 22, continued

Many bulls surround me;
the strong of Bashan encircle me.
They open wide their mouths against me,
lions tearing up prey and roaring.

Like the waters I am poured out
and my bones are all out of joint.
My heart like wax melts away within my insides.

Like a broken clay pot, my strength is dried up,
and my tongue is stuck in the roof of my mouth;
you lay me in the dust of death.
Dogs indeed surround around me,
a band of doers of the bad encircles me as a lion
ready to tear into my hands and my feet.

I can count all of my bones;
they stare and they gloat over me.
They divide my garments among them
and for my clothing they cast lots.

But you, Adonai, be not far off;
come quickly to help me, my Strength!
Deliver my precious life from the sword
and from the power of the dog.
Rescue me from the mouth of the lion
and from the horns of wild oxen.

I will declare your name to my siblings
and praise you within the assembly.

You fearing Adonai, give praise!
All you descendants of Jacob, give honor!
All you descendants of Israel, give reverence
before Adonai, who despised not, nor disdained,
nor hid the holy face from those suffering affliction,
but heard their cry for help.

From you comes my praise in the great assembly;
my vows will I fulfill before those who fear you.
The poor ones will eat to satisfaction,
and the seekers will praise Adonai;
may your heart live to forever.

All the ends of the earth
will remember and turn to Adonai,
and all the families of nations will bow down,
for to Adonai is the dominion, ruling over nations.
All those rich on the earth will feast and worship
and kneel, all will go down to the dust,
all who cannot keep their own self alive.

Those to come will be served by being told,
and in the same way serve generations to come.
They will come and they will proclaim
the deeds of the fidelity of the Lord,
the story, to people yet to be born.

Glory…

Antiphon *I am the true vine
and my Abba is the vinegrower.* Jn 15:1

PSALM 26

Antiphon   *The tax collectors and prostitutes*
are going into the reign of God
before you.   Mt 21:31

Vindicate me, Adonai,
for I have walked blameless in my life
and in Adonai I trusted without waver.

Test me, Adonai! And try me!
Examine my heart and my mind!
For your love is before my eyes
and I walk in your truth.

I do not sit with humans of deceit
nor consort with hypocrites.
I abhor the assembly of those who do the bad,
and do not sit with them.

I wash my hands in innocence
and go about your altar, Adonai,
to proclaim a voice of praise
and to tell of all your wonderful deeds.

Adonai, I love the living place of your house,
the dwelling place of your glory.

Take not my soul away with sinners
nor my life with people doing bloody things,
those who scheme in their hands
with their right hand full of bribes.

But I walk blameless in my life.
Redeem me! Be merciful to me!
My foot stands on level ground;
in great assemblies I will praise Adonai.

Glory...

Antiphon

As the psalms
serve well for private
prayer, they are even more
a prayer for the people of God
and for the whole world. But when a
psalm seems to not apply to my life today,
I can simply step in another's shoes and pray in
the stead of someone who is feeling so strongly these
very emotions that they cannot bring themselves to pray.

PSALM 88

Antiphon *Leave the dead to bury their own dead;*
you go proclaim the reign of God. Lk 9:60

Adonai, **Elohay**, my Savior,
I cry out day and night before you.
May my prayer come before you;
turn your ear to my cry.

My soul is full of troubles
and my life draws near to Sheol.
I am counted among those
going down to the pit,
like a human with no strength,

set apart with the dead ones
like slain ones lying in the grave,
whom you no longer remember,
whom are cut off from your care.

You put me in the pit of the lowest,
in the darkest deep.
Your anger lies heavy upon me
and all your waves overwhelm.

You took friends away from me
and made me repulsive to them;
in confinement I cannot escape.
My eye is dim from grief;
I call to you, Adonai,
and in every day spread my hands to you.

Is it to the dead ones you show wonder?
Do the dead rise up and praise you?
Is your love declared in the grave
or your fidelity in the no-more?
Is your wonder known in the darkness
or your righteous deeds in the land of oblivion?

But to you, Adonai, I cry for help;
in the morning my prayer comes before you.
Why do you reject my self, Adonai?
Why hide your faces from me?

Afflicted and coming close to death
and despairing from youth,
I have suffered your terrors.
Your anger has swept over me
and your terrors destroy me.

They surround me all the day like the floods,
engulfing over me completely.
You took far away my loving companion;
my one friend is darkness.

Glory... Antiphon

PSALM 41

Antiphon *Is it easier to say to the paralytic,*
your sins are forgiven,
or to say, rise and walk?
That you may know
that the Son of Humanity
has authority to forgive sins on earth,
to you paralyzed I say,
'rise; take your mat
and go to your house.' Mk 2:9-11

Blessed are they
who give regard to the weak.
In the time of trouble Adonai will deliver.
Adonai will protect their life,
preserve it blessed in the land,
and give no surrender to the desire of enmity.
Adonai will sustain on the sickbed,
and restore on the bed from all illness.

Adonai, have mercy on me!
Heal my self for I have sinned against you!
Enmity asks in malice:
"When will that one die and be forgotten?"
When they come to see me,
they speak with false hearts, gather slander,
and then go out to the outside to speak.

Together against me they whisper,
imagining the worst for me:
"A vile disease has set in;
that one will not recover."
Even my close friend
has lifted the heel against me,
the human being I trusted,
who ate of my own bread.

But you, Adonai, have mercy on me
and raise me up that I may repay them.
In this I know that you are pleased with me,
for enmity does not triumph over me;
in my integrity you hold me up
and set me in your presences to forever.

Blessed be Adonai, God of Israel,
from everlasting to the everlasting.
Amen and amen.

Glory...

Antiphon

---

*If sometimes people
have had to die of starvation, it is not
because God didn't care for them, but because
you and I were not instruments of love in the hands
of God,to give them bread, because we did not recognize
when once more the hungry Christ came in distressing disguise.*
Saint Teresa of Kolkata, d. 1997

PSALM 46

Antiphon *Do you want to be whole?* Jn 5:6

God is our refuge and strength,
our help in troubles, ever present.
And so we will not fear,
even if earth were to give way,
even if mountains were to fall
into the heart of the sea,
even if sea waters foam
or mountains quake with their surging.

River streams make glad the city of God,
the holy dwelling place of the Most High.
God is inside her and she will not fall.
God will help her at break of day.
Nations are in uproar and realms fall;
the earth melts at the voice of God.

Adonai Sabaoth is with us;
the God of Jacob is our fortress.

Come and see the works of Adonai,
the desolations brought on the earth:
making wars to cease to the ends of the earth,
breaking the bow and shattering the spear
and burning with fire the chariot and shield.

"Be still! And know that I am God.
I will be exalted among the nations;
I will be exalted on the earth."

Adonai Sabaoth is with us;
the God of Jacob is our fortress.

Glory... Antiphon

PSALM 135

Antiphon *What is the profit for a human to gain
the whole world but lose their life?* Mt 16:26

Hallelujah! Praise the name of Adonai!
Servants of Adonai, give praise!
You who minister in the house of Adonai,
in the courts of the house of our God,

praise Adonai, for good is Adonai!
Sing praise to the Name, for it is pleasant!
Adonai has chosen Jacob, Israel the chosen treasure.

For I know that great is our Lord;
greater than all the "gods" is Adonai,
who does as Adonai pleases
in the heavens and on earth and in the deep sea,

making clouds rise from the ends of the earth,
sending lightning with the rain,
and bringing wind from the storehouses,

who struck down the firstborn of Egypt,
from human to animals,
sending signs and wonders to the midst of Egypt
against Pharaoh and against all of his servants,

having struck down
many nations and mighty rulers:
Sihon, rulers of the Amorites, and Og of Bashan,
and all the rulers of Canaan,
who gave their land as an inheritance,
an inheritance to Israel, the people of Adonai.

Your name, Adonai, is to forever,
your renown to generation and generation,
for you, Adonai, will vindicate your people
and will have compassion on your servants.

Idols of the nations are silver and gold,
the work of human hands.
A mouth to them but they cannot speak.
Eyes to them but they cannot see.

Ears to them but they cannot hear,
and there is no breath in their mouth.
Like them will be their makers
and all who trust in them.

House of Israel, praise Adonai!
House of Aaron, praise Adonai!
House of Levi, praise Adonai!
You who fear Adonai, praise Adonai!

Praised be Adonai from Zion,
dwelling in Jerusalem.
Hallelujah!

FRIDAY EVENING

Glory...

Antiphon *What is the profit for a human to gain the whole world but lose his or her life?* Mt 16:26

REVELATION 15:3b-4

Antiphon *They sang the song of Moses,*
the servant of God,
and the song of the Lamb. Rev 15:3a

Great and wonderful are your works,
Lord God Almighty.
Just and true are your ways,
Ruler of the nations.

Who will not fear, O Lord,
or glorify your name?

Only you are holy.
All the nations will come
and worship before you;
your ordinances are shown to all.

Glory...

Antiphon

Behold God
beholding you
 ...and smiling.

Anthony de Mello, Jesuit

READING **ROMANS 15:1-6**

We who are strong ought to bear the weaknesses of those who are not strong, and not to please ourselves. Let each one of us please his or her neighbor for good and for building up, for even Christ pleased not himself. As it has been written, *The reproaches of those reproaching you fell on me.* What was written for our teaching was written that through patience and through the comfort of the writings we may have hope. May the God of patience and comfort give to you the same mind among yourselves in accord with Christ Jesus.

RESPONSORY Rev 1:5,6

Loving us, Christ washed away our sins…
   …*in his own blood;*
Making us to our God a realm of royals and priests…
   …*in his own blood;*
Glory to the Father and to the Son and to the Holy Spirit:
   …*Loving us, Christ washed away our sins*
   in his own blood;

The traditional doxology (*Father, Son, and Holy Spirit*) is from the Matthew 28:19 baptism instructions. These may also be helpful in private prayer; if not, ignore them:

In the name of the Abba and of the Son and of their Holy Breath.
Ruler, Prophet, and Ruah   *Intimate Friend, Brother, and Sister*
All-Knowing, Teacher, and Guide   *Creator, Redeemer, and Sanctifier*
Almighty, Savior, and Advocate

CANTICLE of MARY (The Magnificat)
LUKE 1:46-55

Antiphon *God has given relief to servant Israel*
with a memory of mercy to remember.

+ **My soul** is stretched full with praise of the Lord,
and my spirit, beyond joy in God, my Savior,
who chose to lay eyes on this humble servant.

Behold, now and forward,
each and every age will call me blessed,
for the Mighty One did great things to me.

Holy is the name and the mercy
to generations and generations,
the ones fearing the One,

Who scattered the haughty of mind and heart,
pulled the powerful off their high place,
and lifted with dignity the humble in need.

The hungering are filled with good things,
the rich are sent away empty,
and servant Israel is given relief

with a memory of mercy to remember,
the promise spoken to our ancestors,
to Abraham and his descendants forever.

Glory…

Antiphon

INTERCESSIONS

- For all who have died…

- In gratitude for blessings…; Abba thank you.
- For the sins of this day…; Lord Jesus have mercy.
- With concerns over tomorrow…; Holy Spirit help.

SERENITY PRAYER *attributed to Reinhold Niebuhr*

God, grant me serenity
to accept the things I cannot change,
courage to change the things I can,
and wisdom to know the difference,
living one day at a time,
enjoying one moment at a time,
accepting hardships as a pathway to peace,
taking as Jesus did
this sinful world as it is, not as I would have it,
trusting that you will make all things right
if I surrender to your will,
that I may be reasonably happy in this life
and supremely happy with you forever in the next.

OUR FATHER…

---

*We call God 'Father' (Abba,
Papa, Daddy) because Jesus asks us to,
and in asking us to call his Abba Our Father,
he is asking us to know ourselves as his siblings.*

WEEK I
SATURDAY MORNING

+ *God, come to my assistance;*   Psalm 70:2
Lord, make haste to help me!

Glory…

    O sanc-tis-si-ma/, O pi-is-si-ma/,
    Dul-cis vir-go Ma-ri\-a!
    Ma/-ter a-ma/-ta, In/ te-me-ra/-ta,
    O\-ra\, O\-ra\ pro-no\-bis.

    Ho-ly, ho-ly Ma-ry,
    Strong and hum-ble Ma-ry,
    Sweet-ness, vir-gin Ma-ri\-a!
    Moth-er of our Sa/-vior,
    In your fi-at "yes" and more,
    O\-ra\, O\-ra\, pray\ for us.

    138, Text: *Stimmen der Volker in Liedern*, 1807
        Music: 55 7 55 7, O DU FROLICHE;
        Tattersall's *Improved Psalmody*, 1704

Jesus is not half-God and half-
human, but fully God and fully human.
As Mary is the mother of Jesus, and Jesus is God,
we rightly call Mary the Mother of God or God-bearer,
in Greek Theotokos. *We think of her as the First Disciple.*

PSALM 105

Antiphon *Simeon sang in the temple
of seeing salvation,
a light for revelation to the nations.* Lk 2:29-32

Give thanks to Adonai; call on the Name.
Make known among the nations the Lord's deeds!

Glory be to the holy Name;
let the heart of the seeker of Adonai rejoice.
Look to Adonai, to the strength;
seek always the faces of the Lord.

Remember the deeds of wonder done,
the miracles and the judgments mouthed,
you descendants and servants of Abraham,
you chosen ones of Jacob.

Adonai is our God, judge in all the earth,
remembering the covenant to forever
commanded for a thousand generations,
the word made with Abraham,
the oath to Isaac,

confirmed to Jacob as a decree,
to Israel as an everlasting covenant:
"I will give to you land of Canaan,
a portion of your inheritance."

When they were few, few in numbers,
with strangers in their midst,
then they wandered from nation to nation,
from one people to another.

No one was allowed to oppress them
and for their sake rulers were rebuked:
"Do not touch my anointed ones;
do no harm to my prophets."

Famine was allowed onto the land
and the ruler's food supply was destroyed.
A man Joseph was sent before them,
sold as a slave;
they bruised his foot with the shackle

and his neck entered the irons
till the time foretold of him came to pass.
The word of Adonai proved him true.
The ruler sent for him and released him;

the ruler of the peoples set him free
and made him master of his household
and ruler over all his possessions
to instruct the royals as was his pleasure
and to teach the elders.

Then Israel entered Egypt;
Jacob lived as an alien in the land of Ham.

Psalm 105, continued

This people became very numerous,
more fruitful than their others.
The hearts of the rulers were turned to hate
and conspired against this servant people.

Moses was sent as servant of the Lord
and Aaron as chosen of the Lord.
They performed the deeds of the Lord,
signs and wonders in the land of Ham.

The Lord sent darkness and it was dark;
for they rebelled against the word.
Their waters were turned into blood
which caused their fish to die.

Their land was teemed with frogs,
even the bedrooms of their rulers.
Swarms of flies were sent at a word,
gnats through all of their country.

Their rains were turned into hail
and lightning flamed through their land.
Their vine and fig tree were struck down
and the trees of their country were shattered.

Locusts came at the word
and grasshoppers without number.
Every green thing in their land was eaten up,
eaten up with the produce of their soil.

Then their firstborn were struck down, all of them,
the firstfruit of their humanity in all of their land.

The Lord brought them out with silver and gold
and no one faltered among the tribes.
Egypt was glad when they left, glad with dread.

A cloud as a cover was spread out
and fire to give them light at night.
They asked for quail and the Lord brought it
and satisfied them with bread from heaven.

The rock was opened and waters gushed out
flowing in the desert as a river,
for the holy promise was remembered,
the promise made to servant Abraham,
and the people were brought out rejoicing,
the chosen ones with shouts of joy.

They received the lands of nations
and inherited the toil of peoples
so that they might keep the precepts
and observe the laws of the Lord.

Hallelujah!

Glory…

Antiphon *Simeon sang in the temple
of seeing salvation,
a light for revelation to the nations.* Lk 2:29-32

PSALM 107

Antiphon *In awe, the disciples asked,
who then is this, whom
both the wind and the sea obey?*   Mk 4:41

"**Give thanks** to Adonai, who is good,
whose love is to forever."

Let this be said by the redeemed of Adonai,
who redeemed them from the hand of enmity
and gathered them from the lands,
from east and west, from north and the south sea.

Some wandered in the desert wasteland,
finding no way to a city for settling.
Hungry and thirsty,
their life ebbed away in them.

Then they cried out to Adonai in their trouble,
who delivered them from their distresses
and led them by a direct way
to go to a city for settling.

Let them give thanks to Adonai for unfailing love,
for deeds of wonder done
for sons and daughters of Adam and Eve,
for satisfying the throats of the thirsty
and filling the hungry with good things.

Some sit in the dark and deep gloom,
prisoners of suffering and iron,
for they rebelled against the word of El
and despised the counsel of the Most High
who subjected their heart to the bitter labor,
and no one was there to help.

Then they cried in their trouble to Adonai,
who saved them from their distresses,
brought them out from the dark and deep gloom,
and broke away their chains.

Let them give thanks to Adonai for unfailing love,
for deeds of wonder done
for sons and daughters of Adam and Eve,
for breaking down gates of bronze
and cutting through bars of iron.

Some were fools through their rebellious ways,
afflicted because of their iniquities.
Loathing all food, they drew themselves
near to the gates of death.

Then they cried in their trouble to Adonai,
who saved them from their distresses,
sending forth the word to heal them
and rescue them from their graves.

Psalm 107, continued

Let them give thanks to Adonai for unfailing love,
for deeds of wonder done
for sons and daughters of Adam and Eve,
and let them sacrifice offerings of thanksgiving
and tell of the works with songs of joy.

Some went to the sea in ships
to do trade on the mighty waters.
They saw the works in the deep,
the wonderful deeds of Adonai,
who spoke and stirred up the tempest wind
and lifted up the waves.

They mounted up to the heavens
and went down to the deep;
in peril their courage melted away.
They reeled and staggered like drunkards,
all of them at their wits end.

Then they cried in their trouble to Adonai,
who brought them out from their distresses,
stilling the storm to a whisper
and hushing the waves.
They were glad when it grew calm
and they were guided to the haven they desired.

Let them give thanks to Adonai for unfailing love,
for deeds of wonder done
for sons and daughters of Adam and Eve,
and let them exalt in the assembly of the people,
and in the council of elders give praise.

Adonai turned rivers into desert,
springs of waters into thirsty ground,
and land of fruit into a salt waste
because of bad ways of those living there.

Adonai then turned desert into pools of waters,
parched ground into springs of waters,
and brought hungry ones to live there.

They founded and settled a city,
sowed fields and planted vineyards,
and yielded the fruit of harvest.
They were blessed and they increased greatly,
and their herds were not allowed to diminish.

Then they decreased and were humbled
by oppression, calamity and sorrow.
With contempt poured on them,
nobles were made to wander in a trackless waste.

But the needy were lifted from affliction
and their families increased like a flock.
The upright see this and rejoice,
but doers of the bad shut their mouth.

Whoever is wise, heed these things
and ponder the unfailing love of Adonai.

Glory…

Antiphon *In awe, the disciples asked,
who then is this, whom
both the wind and the sea obey?*   Mk 4:41

EXODUS 15:1b-4,8-13,17-18

Antiphon   *By faith they passed
through the Red Sea
as if it were dry land.*   Heb 11:29a

I will sing to Adonai, exalting exaltation,
who hurled horse and rider into the sea.

My strength and my song,
Yah has become to me salvation.
I will praise my God
and exalt the God of my ancestors.

Adonai the warrior, named Adonai,
hurled Pharaoh's army of chariots into the sea...
By the blast of your nostrils the waters piled up;
like a wall they stood firm in the heart of the sea,
raging deep waters congealed.

The enemy boasted, "I will pursue and overtake,
divide the spoils and gorge on them myself;
I will draw my sword;
my hand will destroy them."

You blew with your breath
and the sea covered them;
they sank like lead in the mighty waters.

Who is like you among "gods," Adonai?
Who like you is majestic and holy,
awesome in glory and working wonders?
You stretched your right hand
and the earth swallowed them.

You will lead in your love
the people you redeemed.
You will guide them in strength
to your holy dwelling…

You will bring them in and you will plant them
on the mountain of your inheritance,
the dwelling place you made, Adonai,
the sanctuary, Lord, that your hands established.
Adonai will reign forever and ever.

Glory…

                                                     Antiphon

---

Big Stories of
Hebrew Scripture:
1 Creation
2 The Great Flood
3 Covenant with Abraham
4 Exodus out of Slavery in Egypt
5 Desert Wandering & the Promised Land
6 Judges, Prophets, Royals & Temple Priesthood
7 The Babylonian Exile & then Return from the Exile

WISDOM 9:1-6,9-11

Antiphon

*And Jesus advanced
in wisdom and age and favor
before God and humans.*

Lk 2:52

God of my ancestors, Lord of mercy,
who made all things by your word
and through your wisdom framed humanity
to be master of the creatures you have created,
and to govern the world in holiness and justice
and judge justly and with an upright heart,

give me Wisdom, your companion at your throne,
and do not reject me from among your children,
for I am your servant, born of your handmaid,
a feeble human with a short life
and a weak understanding of justice and laws.

Though a human be
ever so perfect in human eyes,
without your Wisdom that same one
will be of no account…

With you is Wisdom,* who knows your works
and was present when you created the world,
who knows what is pleasing in your eyes
and what is right in accord with your ordinances.

* *Sophia, Lady Wisdom*

Send her forth from the holy heavens
and dispatch her from your majestic throne,
that she may labor beside me
and I may learn what pleases you.

For she knows and understands all things
and will guide me to prudence in my actions
and guard me in her magnificence.

Glory...

Antiphon

Sometime when you are in the presence of
what Thomas Merton called 'children in a moment
when they are really children,' ponder that there was a day
when God was exactly that tall and weighed exactly that much.

PSALM 119:145-152

Antiphon
*Ask and it will be given you,
seek and you will find,
knock and it will be opened to you.*   Lk 11:9

I call with all my heart: answer me, Adonai;
your decrees I will obey.
I call to you: save me,
and I will keep your statutes.

I rise before dawn and I cry for help;
in your word I put my hope.
My eyes stay open in the night watch
to meditate on your promise.

Hear my voice, as you are loving, Adonai,
as your law makes me alive.
Scheming devisers are near,
but they are far from your law.

You are near, Adonai,
and all your commands are true.
I learned long ago from your statutes
that you established them to forever.

Glory...   Antiphon

---

*God does not ask us to be worthy but to be
willing; it is the mercy of God that makes us worthy.*
Anthony Zoghby, Our Lady of the Gulf, Gulf Shores Alabama

PSALM 117

Antiphon *As the centurion responded:*
I am not worthy
for you to enter under my roof,
but only say the word
and let your servant be healed.   Lk 7:6,7

Praise Adonai, all you nations;
and give glory, all you peoples.

Great is this steadfast love toward us;
the fidelity of Adonai to forever.

Hallelujah!

Glory…

Antiphon

There is an old joke that Jesus
walking around heaven asks Peter how some
folks got in, and Peter says, 'I'm doing my job boss,
but they go to the back door and your mother lets them in.'

OFFICE OF READINGS and FIRST READING AT MASS

	Odd Years	**Even Years**
1 readings	*Romans 3:21-31*	*Genesis 8*
mass	Hebrews 4:12-16	1 Sam 9:1-14,17-19;10:1a
3 rdgs	*Romans 11:13-24*	*Genesis 25*
mass	Hebrews 11:1-2,8-9	2 Samuel 12:1-7a,10-17
5 rdgs	*1 Corinthians 6:1-11*	*Genesis 49*
mass	Genesis 3:9-24	1 Kings 12:26-32;13:33-34
7 rdgs	*1 Corinthians 14:1-19*	*2 Corinthians 6*
mass	Ben Sira 17:1-15	James 5:13-20
9 rdgs	*James 5:12-20*	*Galatians 6*
mass	Tobit 12:1,5-15,20	2 Timothy 4:1-8
11 rdgs	*Judges 11*	*Zechariah 2*
mass	2 Corinthians 12:1-10	2 Chronicles 24:17-25
13 rdgs	*1 Samuel 16*	*Isaiah 59:1-14*
mass	Genesis 27:1-5,15-29	Amos 9:11-15
15 rdgs	*2 Samuel 12*	*Job 7*
mass	Exodus 12:37-42	**Micah** 2:1-5
17 rdgs	*1 Kings 18*	*Job 42*
mass	Leviticus 25:1,8-17	Jeremiah 26:11-16,24
19 rdgs	*2 Kings 13*	*Zechariah 14*
mass	Joshua 24:14-29	Ezekiel 18:1-10,13b,30-32
21 rdgs	*Philemon*	*1 Timothy 4*
mass	1 Thessalonians 4:9-12	1 Corinthians 1:26-31

I SATURDAY MORNING

	Odd Years	**Even Years**
23 rdgs	*Hosea 6 & 7*	*Jude*
mass	1 Timothy 1:15-17	1 Corinthians 10:14-22a
25 rdgs	*Micah 1 & 2*	*Tobit 10 & 11*
mass	**Zechariah** 2:5-9a,14-15a	Ecclesiastes 11:9-12:8
27 rdgs	*Zephaniah 1 & 2*	*Sirach 7*
mass	Joel 4:12-21	Galatians 3:22-29
29 rdgs	*Jeremiah 19 & 20*	*Sirach 51*
mass	Romans 8:1-11	Ephesians 4:7-16
31 rdgs	*Ezekiel 1*	*Wisdom 18 & 19*
mass	Romans 16:3-9,16,22-27	Philippians 4:10-19
33 rdgs	*Ezekiel 34*	*Daniel 3*
mass	1 Maccabees 6:1-13	Revelation 11:4-12

READING **2 PETER 1:3-11**

The divine power has given us all things that go with life and piety through the full knowledge of the one who called us to this glory and virtue, through which the precious things and the very great promises have been given to us, so that through these you might come to share in the divine nature and escape from the corruption of worldly desire. Also for this very thing bring all your diligence to supply your faith with virtue, virtue with knowledge, knowledge with self-control, self-control with endurance, endurance with piety, piety with filial friendship (*philadelphia*), and filial friendship with love (*agape*).

2 Peter 1, continued

If these things abound in you, this will keep you from being barren and unfruitful in full knowledge of our Lord Jesus Christ. Blind and short-sighted is the one who lacks these things, and forgetful of how his or her sins were cleansed.

And so, brothers and sisters, be diligent in your call and firm in your choice, and you will not fail in what you do. Richly supplied will be your entry into the eternal kingdom of our Lord and Savior Jesus Christ.

RESPONSORY   Ps 142:6,7a

I cry to you, my Lord,…
   …*you are my refuge.*
My portion in the land of the living,…
   …*you are my refuge.*
Glory to the Father and to the Son and to the Holy Spirit:
   …*I cry to you, my Lord, you are my refuge.*

Gospel Canticle For Morning

Antiphon   *Lord, shine on those hidden in the shadows.*

Gospel Reading for Saturday of

Week			
1 Mark 2:13-17	**13** Matt 9:14-17	**25** Lk 9:43b-45
3 Mark 4:35-41	**15** Matt 12:14-21	**27** Lk 11:27-28
5 Mark 8:1-10	**17** Matt 14:1-12	**29** Luke 13:1-9
7 Mark 10:13-16	**19** Matt 19:13-15	**31** Luke 16:9-15
9 Mark 12:38-44	**21** Matt 25:14-30	**33** Lk 20:27-40
11 Matt 6:24-34	**23** Luke 6:43-49	

CANTICLE of ZECHARIAH (The Benedictus)
LUKE 1:68-79

+ Blessed be the Lord the God of Israel
who chose a people to visit with redemption,
and raised salvation in the house of David,
saving strength from God's own servant,

speaking from the age of the prophets
through the mouth of the holy prophet:
Salvation out of enmity,
even out of those who hate us,

to show our ancestors how mercy works, -
and to remember the holy promise of the Lord,
the covenant made for our ancestor Abraham,
calming our fear and making us free
to serve with holy justice before God all our days.

And you also child -
will be called a prophet of the Most High
for you will go before the Lord to prepare his way
and give to people a knowledge of salvation
known in accepting forgiveness of their sins.

From the tender mercy of our God,
the sun rising from the height will visit with light
for those who sit in the dark or shadow of death
and to guide our feet into the way of peace.

Glory...

Antiphon

PETITIONS FOR THE CONSECRATION TO GOD
OF THE DAY AND ITS WORK

- For the Church and her ministry and apostolates...
- For secular authorities and all serving as stewards...
- For people who are poor or sick or in sorrow...
- For the basic needs of each human being...
- For awareness of being created in the image of God...
- For discovery and discernment of our charisms...
- For consensus on both rights and responsibilities...
- For loving respect for folks who think differently...
- For God's healing of the core wounds of enemies...
- For the world peace that only God can give...
- For elders who feel abandoned...
- For just treatment of migrant workers and refugees...
- For the starving child awakening our conscience...
- For those suffering physical and mental torture...
- For people living in subhuman conditions...
- For human beings enslaved or unjustly imprisoned...
- For workers in degrading or unsafe conditions...
- For laborers where treated as mere tools for profit...
- For rejection of judging the inner guilt of others...
- For a culture of vocations all over the world...
- For those who have asked for my prayer...
- For those for whom I have promised to pray...
- For those who weigh on my heart...

OUR FATHER...

WEEK II
VIGIL of SUNDAY
(Saturday Evening)

+ *God, come to my assistance;*   Psalm 70:2
Lord, make haste to help me!

Glory...

Praise to the Lord, the Al-migh-ty,
the King of cre-a-tion! O my soul, praise the Lord,
who is our health and sal-va-tion!
Join the full throng;
Wake, harp and psal-ter and song;
Sound forth in glad ad-o-ra-tion!

Praise to the Lord, the on-ly One,
the Ma-ker of heav-en,
It is the Lord who made the earth,
the seas and all in them.
Can we yet see How our de-sire\ and need
Meet in our Lord's will and un-ion.

Praise to the Lord, who brings our work
to pros-per be-fore us; Who from the heav-ens
sent the mer-cy riv-er in-to us.
Pon-der a-new What the Al-migh-ty can do,
Who in div-ine love be-friends us.

> 123, Text: from Nehemiah 9:6, Joachim Neander, 1679;
> translated by Catherine Winkworth, 1863, altered;
> verse 2 by Stephen J. Wolf, 2009   Music: 14 14 4 7 8
> LOBE DEN HERREN; Straslund Gesangbuch, 1665

PSALM 34

Antiphon *The bread that I will give*
is my flesh for the life of the cosmos. Jn 6:51b

I will extol Adonai at all times,
praise always on my lips.
My soul she will boast in Adonai,
let afflicted ones hear and let them rejoice.

Glorify Adonai with me!
Let us exalt the name together.
I sought Adonai, who answered me
and delivered me from all my fears.

They look to the Name and are radiant;
their faces are never covered with shame.
Adonai heard this poor human call
and saved me from all the troubles.

An angel encamps around
and delivers all who fear Adonai.
Taste and see that Adonai is good!
Blessed is the one who takes this refuge.

Fear Adonai, you saints;
for those who do so there is no lack.
Lions may grow weak and may grow hungry,
but seekers of Adonai lack no good thing.

VIGIL of SUNDAY (Saturday Evening)

Come, children! Listen to me!
I will teach you the fear of Adonai.
Who is the human who loves living?
Who desires days to see the good?

Keep your tongue from evil
and your lips from speaking the lie.
Turn from the bad and do the good.
Seek and pursue peace.

The eyes of Adonai are on the just
with ears open to their cry.
The faces of Adonai turn from doers of the bad
to cut off from the earth their memory.

They cry and Adonai hears
and delivers them from all their troubles.
Close is Adonai to the brokenhearted,
saving those whose spirit is crushed.

Many are the troubles of the just
but Adonai delivers them from all of them,
protecting all of their bones;
not one of them will be broken.

The bad will slay the bad
and condemned will be those who hate the just.
The servants of Adonai are being redeemed
and the lives of any who take refuge in God
will not be condemned.

Glory...   Antiphon

PSALM 134

Antiphon — *Be not afraid.* — Mt 10:26, 14:27, 17:17, 28:10,…; Mk 6:50,…; Lk 5:10, 12:4,…; Jn 6:20,…

See Adonai and give praise,
all you servants of Adonai,
and ministers at night in the house of Adonai.

Lift up your hands in the sanctuary
and praise Adonai!

May Adonai bless you from Zion,
the One Maker of heavens and the earth.

Glory…

Antiphon

Somebody went to the bother of counting the number of times that "be not afraid" is found in the Bible. How many? Once for each day of the year: 365

VIGIL of SUNDAY (Saturday Evening)

PSALM 119:105-112

Antiphon *Every scribe discipled to the reign of heaven*
is like a head of a household
who puts forth from the treasure
things both new and old. Mt 13:52

Your word is the lamp to my foot
and the light for my path.
I have made an oath and confirmation
to follow your just laws.

I have suffered much, Adonai;
make me alive as is your word.
Accept the willing praise of my mouth!
And now, Adonai, teach me your laws!

My life is constantly in my hand,
but I will not forget your law.
Doers of the bad set a snare for me,
but I did not stray from your precepts.

I have your statutes as a heritage to forever,
they are indeed the joy of my heart.
I set my heart to keep your decrees
to forever, the very end.

Glory...

Antiphon

PSALM 16

Antiphon *Heaven and earth will pass away,*
but my words will not pass away. Mk 13:31

VIGIL of SUNDAY (Saturday Evening)

Keep me safe, **El**, for I take refuge in you.
I said to Adonai, "You are my Lord;
I have no good apart from you."

Worthless are the false gods in the land,
even though some delight in them.
Those who run after other gods
will increase their sorrows;
I will not pour out their blood libations,
nor let their names pass my lips.

Adonai, you assign my portion and my cup;
you make my lot secure.
Boundary lines fall for me in the pleasant places;
surely this inheritance is my delight.

I will praise Adonai who counsels me,
even in the night instructing my heart.
With Adonai before me, always by my side,
I will not be shaken.

And so my heart is glad and my tongue rejoices.
My body will rest in security
because you will not abandon my self to Sheol;
you will not let your faithful one see decay.

You will show me the path of living,
fullness of joy in your presences,
eternal pleasures at your right hand.

Glory...

Antiphon

PSALM 122

Antiphon *Amen, you will be with me*
in paradise. Lk 23:43

I rejoiced with those saying to me,
"Let us go to the house of Adonai."
Our feet stand in your gates, Jerusalem.

Jerusalem is built like a city
formed together, a compact.
There the tribes go up, the tribes of Adonai.

Make it in Israel a statute
to praise the name of Adonai,
for there stand the thrones of justice,
the thrones of the house of David.

Pray for the peace of Jerusalem!
May those who love you be secure.
May peace be within your walls,
security within your citadels.

For the sake of my sisters and brothers and friends
I will say, "Now, peace be within you."
For the sake of the house of our God Adonai
I will seek your prosperity.

Glory…

Antiphon

VIGIL of SUNDAY (Saturday Evening)

PSALM 130

Antiphon   *Whoever does the will of God
is my brother and sister and mother.*   Mk 3:35

Out of the depths I cry to you, Adonai.
Lord, hear my voice.
Let your ears be attentive to my cries for mercy.

If you kept a record of sins, Adonai,
Lord, who could stand?
But with you is the forgiveness,
and so you are revered in awe.

I wait, my soul waits for Adonai,
in whose word I put hope.
My soul waits for the Lord
more than watchers for the morning,
even watchers for the morning.

Put hope, Israel, in Adonai!
For unfailing love is from Adonai,
in whom is full redemption,
who will redeem Israel from all their sins.

Glory…

Antiphon

---

*The glory of God is
the human person fully alive.*
Saint Irenaeus, d. 202

PHILIPPIANS 2:6-11

Antiphon
*Do nothing out of selfishness
or for vainglory,
but humbly deem others
as greater than yourselves.*   Phil 2:3

Christ Jesus, subsisting in the form of God,
did not deem equality with God
something to grab,
but emptied himself,
taking the form of a slave,
becoming in human likeness.

And being found in human fashion,
he humbled himself,
becoming obedient until death,
and death on a cross.

And so God highly exalted him,
and gave to him the name above every name,
that in the name of Jesus
every knee should bend,
of heavenly beings and earthly beings,
and beings under the earth;

And every tongue acknowledge
to the glory of God the Father
that Jesus Christ is Lord.

Glory...   Antiphon

VIGIL of SUNDAY (Saturday Evening)

READING   **COLOSSIANS 1:3-6**

We give thanks always to God the Father of our Lord Jesus Christ praying concerning you, having heard of your faith in Christ Jesus and the love you have toward all the saints because of the hope being laid up for you in the heavens, which you heard previously in the word of the truth of the gospel coming to you, as it is also bearing fruit and growing in all the world as also in you, from the day you heard and fully knew in truth the grace of God.

RESPONSORY   Ps 113:3,4

From the rising of the sun to its setting…
   …praised be the name of the Lord.
The glory above the heavens,…
   …praised be the name of the Lord.
Glory to the Father and to the Son and to the Holy Spirit:
   …From the rising of the sun to its setting,
   praised be the name of the Lord.

The
primary
addiction is
addiction to self,
plain old selfishness.
Fr Phillip Breen

Gospel Canticle For Evening
Antiphons

Ordinary Time		YEAR A Responsorial
Wk 2	Here am I, Lord; I come to do your will.	Ps 40
4	Blessed are the poor in spirit.	Ps 146
6	Blessed are they who follow the law of the Lord!	Ps 119
8	Rest in God alone, my soul.	Ps 62
10	The upright will see God's saving power.	Ps 50
12	Lord, in your great love, answer me.	Ps 69
14	I will praise your name forever, my God.	Ps 145
16	Lord, you are good and forgiving.	Ps 86
18	The hand of the Lord feeds us.	Ps 145
20	O God, let all the nations praise you!	Ps 67
22	My soul is thirsting for you, O Lord my God.	Ps 63
24	The Lord is kind and merciful.	Ps 103
26	Remember your mercies, O Lord.	Ps 25
28	I shall live in the house of the Lord.	Ps 23
30	I love you, Lord, my strength.	Ps 18
32	My soul is thirsting for you O Lord my God.	Ps 63

34   The Lord is my shepherd;
     there is nothing I shall want.   Ps 23

CANTICLE of MARY (The Magnificat)
LUKE 1:46-55

+ **My soul** is stretched full with praise of the Lord,
and my spirit, beyond joy in God, my Savior,
who chose to lay eyes on this humble servant.

Behold, now and forward,
each and every age will call me blessed,
for the Mighty One did great things to me.

Holy is the name and the mercy
to generations and generations,
the ones fearing the One,

Who scattered the haughty of mind and heart,
pulled the powerful off their high place,
and lifted with dignity the humble in need.

The hungering are filled with good things,
the rich are sent away empty,
and servant Israel is given relief

with a memory of mercy to remember,
the promise spoken to our ancestors,
to Abraham and his descendants forever.

Glory…

                                               Antiphon

INTERCESSIONS

- Lord, make your Church ever new…
- Watch over our pope and bishops…
- Keep us united in our diversity…
- Inspire leaders with your justice…
- Keep married couples in love…
- For respect for the dignity of the human person…
- For a culture of vocations all over the world…
- For all who have died…

- In gratitude for blessings, Abba thank you…
- For the sins of this day, Lord Jesus have mercy…
- With concerns over tomorrow, Holy Spirit help…

CLOSING PRAYER FOR MORNING AND EVENING

Our Fath-er, who art in heav-en;
hal-lowed be thy name.
Thy king dom come, thy will be done
on earth as it is in heav-en.
Give us this day our dai-ly bread
and for-give us our tres-pass-es
as we for-give those who tres-pass a-gainst/ us
and lead us not in-to temp-ta/-tion
but de-liv-er us from e\-vil.
A-men.

WEEK II
SUNDAY MORNING

+ *God, come to my assistance;*   Psalm 70:2
 Lord, make haste to help me!

Glory…

Ho-ly, ho-ly, ho-ly, Lord God Al-migh-ty!
Ear-ly in the morn-ing our song shall rise to thee;
Ho-ly, ho-ly, ho-ly, mer-ci-ful and migh-ty!
God in Three Per-sons, bless-ed Trin-i-ty!

Ho-ly, ho-ly, ho-ly! All the saints a-dore thee,
Cast-ing down their gold-en crowns
                  a-round the glass-y sea;
Cher-u-bim and ser-a-phim fall-ing down be-fore thee,
Who was, and is, and ev-er-more shall be.

Ho-ly, ho-ly, ho-ly! Though con-fu-sion hide you,
Glo-ry shin-ing through the blurr
                  of cloud-ed hu-man view;
Ho-ly a-lone are you; there is none be-side you:
Per-fect and pure, your love in all you do.

Ho-ly, ho-ly, ho-ly! Lord God Al-migh-ty!
All cre-a-tion praise your name in earth & sky & sea.
Ho-ly, ho-ly, ho-ly, mer-ci-ful and migh-ty!
God in Three Persons, bless-ed Trin-i-ty!

97, Text: From Revelation 4:8; by Reginald Heber, 1827, altered
Music: 11 12 12 10, NICAEA; John B. Dykes, 1861

PSALM 104

Antiphon *Peace to you;*
as the Abba has sent me, so I send you;
receive the Holy Spirit.   Jn 20:21

Soul of me, praise Adonai!
My God, Adonai, you are beyond measure.
Splendor and majesty clothe you,
wrapped in light as a garment,

stretching out over the heavens like a tent,
laying beams on the waters of the upper chambers.
You make a chariot of the clouds,
riding on wings of wind,
making messengers of the winds
and servants of flaming fire.

You have set foundations on earth,
unmoveable for ever and ever.
Deep is your garment, covering the earth;
above the mountains the waters stood.

At your rebuke, they then fled;
at the sound of your thunder they took flight.
They flowed over mountains
and went down into valleys
to the places you assigned for them.
You set a boundary they are not to cross;
never again are they to cover the earth.

You make springs of water pour into ravines;
between the mountains they flow.
They give drink to all beasts of the field;
they quench the thirst of donkeys.
Birds of the air nest in branches beside them;
they give you their song.

You water mountains from your upper chambers;
by the fruit of your works the earth is satisfied.
You make grass grow for the cattle
and plants for human beings to cultivate

to bring forth food from the earth,
wine to make glad the human heart,
oil to make faces shine,
and bread to sustain the human heart.

They are all Adonai's well watered trees,
cedars of Lebanon planted
where birds make their nests,
and the pine tree where the stork makes a home,
mountains, the high ones, for wild goats,
and crags, a refuge for rock badgers.

You made the moon to mark off seasons
and the sun that knows when to set.
You bring darkness
and all beasts of the forest prowl in the night.
The lions roar for prey
seeking their food from God.

Psalm 104, continued

The sun rises, they steal away,
and into their dens they lie down.
Human beings go out to do their work
and labor until the evening.

How varied are your works, Adonai!
All of them in wisdom you made.
The earth is full of your creatures.

There is the sea, vast and spacious;
living creatures countless there,
small ones and large ones.
There ships go about
and leviathan which you formed for frolic.

All of them look to you
to give them food at their time.
You give to them and they gather,
you open your hands
and they are goodly satisfied.

You hide your face and they are lost,
you take away their breath and they die
and to their dust they return.
You breathe your Spirit, and they are created,
and you renew the faces of earth.

May the glory of Adonai endure to forever.
May Adonai rejoice in these works:
looking at the earth, she trembles,
touching the mountains, they smoke.

I will sing to Adonai during my life
and sing praise to my God while I still am.
May my meditation be found pleasing.
I rejoice in Adonai.
May sin vanish from the earth
and the bad be done no more.

Praise Adonai, my soul!
Hallelujah!

Glory…

Antiphon   *Peace to you;*
as the Abba has sent me, so I send you;
receive the Holy Spirit.   Jn 20:21
Jesus' words
on that first
Easter Sunday

Hallelujah!
It means, "Praise God"!
Can you now and then raise your
hands in the air and say, even quietly,
"God, I praise you"? It's OK that some of us
must go to our inner room and close the door to do this.

When you pray, enter your room and close your door
and pray to your Abba in secret.   Mt 6:6

PSALM 66

Antiphon *The harvest is plenty but workers are few;*
ask the Lord of the harvest
to cast workers into the harvest. Lk 10:2

Shout joy to God all you earth!
Sing the glory of the name!
Offer glory and praise to God!
Say to God, "How awesome are you;
how great are your deeds."

Enmity cringes before you and your power.
All of the earth bow down to you,
they sing praise to you,
they sing praise to your name.

Come and see the deeds of God who is awesome,
the works on behalf of all sons and daughters.
God turned the sea into dry land;
through the river they passed on foot.

Let us rejoice in God,
who rules forever with power
with eyes watching the nations.
Let no rebels rise up.

Peoples, make heard the praise of our God
who preserves our life among the living,
and lets not our feet to slip.

God, you tested us, refined us as silver is refined.
You let us be brought into prison,
you let burdens be put on our backs,
you let human beings set foot on our neck.

We went through the fire and through the waters
and you brought us to a spacious place.

I will come to your temple with burnt offerings,
I will fulfill to you my vows, promised on my lips,
spoken in a time of trouble.

Sacrifices of fat animals I will sacrifice to you;
with offerings of rams I will offer bull and goats.

Come! Listen! Let me tell all who fear God
what God has done for my very self.
To God my mouth cried out
with praise on my tongue.

If I cherished sin in my heart
the Lord would not have listened.
Surely God listened and heard my voice of prayer.

God, be praised, who rejected not my prayer
nor took from within me
the Lord's own *hesed* love.

Glory...

Antiphon

---

*In a culture of vocations, all of us would be helping each
other discern what God's call is for our life, this year, this day.*

PSALM 118

Antiphon *I am the good shepherd,*
and I know mine and mine know me.   Jn 10:14

Give thanks to Adonai who is good,
whose love is to forever.

Let Israel now declare:
the love of the Lord to forever.
Let the house of Aaron declare:
the love of the Lord to forever.
Let those who fear Adonai declare:
the love of the Lord to forever.

In anguish I cried to Adonai
who answered me with freedom.
Adonai is with me, I will not be afraid.
What can any human do to me?
Before enmity I keep this in mind:
Adonai is with me, ready to help me.

Better to take refuge in Adonai
than to trust in the human;
Better to take refuge in Adonai
than to trust in a prince.

All of the nations surrounded me,
indeed did they surround me;
in the name of Adonai indeed I cut them.
They swarmed around me like bees,
they crackled like thorns in a fire;
in the name of Adonai indeed I cut them.

To push back they pushed me back to fall
but Adonai came to my help.
Adonai became my strength and my song
and became to me salvation.
Shout joy and victory in your tents, you just.

Adonai's right hand does a mighty thing,
Adonai's right hand lifted high.
Adonai's right hand does a mighty thing.
I will not die; I will live
and proclaim these deeds indeed.
To chasten, Adonai let me be chastened,
but did not give me to death.

Open for me the gates of the just;
I will enter through them
and give thanks to Adonai.
This is Adonai's gate,
where just ones may enter.
I will give thanks to you for you answered me
and you became to me salvation.

Psalm 118, continued

The stone the builders rejected
became the cornerstone.
With Adonai this happened
and it is marvelous in our eyes.
This is the day Adonai has made;
let us rejoice and be glad in it.

Adonai, save us now!
Adonai, grant success now!
Blessed is the one coming in the name of Adonai;
We bless you from the house of Adonai.
Our El Adonai has shined light onto us.

Join with leaf branches in the festal procession
up to the horns of the altar.
To you, my God, I will give thanks.
You, my God, I will give glory.
Give thanks to Adonai who is good,
whose love is to forever.

Glory…

Antiphon *I am the good shepherd,
and I know mine and mine know me.* Jn 10:14

---

*Hallel Psalms (after Hebrew for 'to praise') are
113-118, sung on major feasts such as Passover
(see Mk 14:26). Ps 136 is called the Grand Hallel.*

DANIEL 3:52-57

Antiphon *God sent the Son into the cosmos*
not to condemn, but that the cosmos
might be saved through him.   Jn 3:17

Blessed are you, O Lord, God of our ancestors,
praiseworthy and exalted above all forever.

Blessed is your glorious and holy name,
praiseworthy and exalted above all forever.

Blessed are you in the temple of your sacred glory,
praiseworthy and exalted above all forever.

Blessed are you who sit high on the cherubim
and look into the depths,
praiseworthy and exalted above all forever.

Blessed are you on your royal throne,
praiseworthy and exalted above all forever.

Blessed are you in the dome of heaven,
to be hymned and glorified forever.

Bless the Lord, all you works of the Lord,
sing praise and high exaltation forever.

Glory...   Antiphon

My book, sir philosopher, is the nature of created things,
and it is always at hand when I wish to read the words of God.
Anthony of Egypt, see *Praktikos* (#92) by Evagrius Ponticus

PSALM 150

Antiphon *Be merciful
as your Abba is merciful.* Lk 6:36

Hallelujah!

To El in the sanctuary, give praise.
In the mighty heavens, give praise.
For the works of power, give praise.
For surpassing greatness, give praise.

With sounding of trumpet, give praise.
With harp and lyre, give praise.
With tambourine and dance, give praise.
With flute and string, give praise.

With cymbals clashing, give praise.
With cymbals resounding, give praise.
Let all that has breath praise Adonai!

Hallelujah!

Glory...

Antiphon

The psalms are properly called
tehillim *(songs of praise) in Hebrew
and* psalmoi *(songs to be sung to the lyre)
in Greek; all the psalms have a musical quality.*
See *Introduction to the Liturgy of the Hours*, 103

OFFICE of READINGS

	Odd-Numbered Years	Even-Numbered Years
Wk 2	Romans 4	Genesis 9
4	Romans 11:25-36	Genesis 27:1-29
6	1 Corinthians 6:12-20	1 Thessalonians 1:1-2:12
8	1 Corinthians 14:20-40	2 Corinthians 7
10	Sirach 46	Philipians 1:1-11
12	Judges 13	Zechariah 3 & 4
14	1 Samuel 17	Proverbs 1 & 2
16	2 Samuel 15 & 16	Job 11
18	1 Kings 19	Obediah
20	Ephesians 1:1-14	Ecclesiastes 1
22	2 Kings 14	1 Timothy 5:3-25
24	Hosea 8	Esther 1 & 2
26	Micah 3	Judith 1 & 2 & 3
28	Zephaniah 3	Sirach 10
30	Jeremiah 23	Wisdom 1
32	Ezekiel 2 & 3	1 Macabees 1:1-25
34	Daniel 7	Daniel 7

MASS READINGS

	Year A	Year B	Year C
Wk 2	Isaiah 49:3,5-6 1 Corin 1:1-3	1 Sam 3:3b-10,19 1 Cor 6:13c-15a,17-20	Isaiah 62:1-5 1 Corin 12:4-11
4	Zeph 2:3; 3:12-13 1 Corin 1:26-31	Deut 18:15-20 1 Corinth 7:32-35	Jer 1:4-5,17-19 1Cor 12:31-13:13
6	Sirach 15:15-20 1 Corin 2:6-10	Lev 13:1-2,44-46 1 Cor 10:31-11:1	Jeremiah 17:5-8 1 Cor 15:12,16-20

DAWN & DUSK WEEK II
Mass Readings, continued

	Year A	Year B	Year C
Wk 8	Isaiah 49:14-15 1 Corin 4:1-5	Hos 2:16b,17b,21-22 2 Corin 3:1b-6	Sirach 27:4-7 1 Corin 15:54-58
10	Hosea 6:3-6 Romans 4:18-25	Genesis 3:9-15 2 Corin 4:13-5:1	1 Kings 17:17-24 Galatians 1:11-19
12	Jeremiah 20:10-13 Romans 5:12-15	Job 38:1,8-11 2 Corin 5:14-17	Zec 12:10-11;13:1 Gal 3:26-29
14	Zechariah 9:9-10 Romans 8:9,11-13	Ezekiel 2:2-5 2 Corin 12:7-10	Isaiah 66:10-14c Gal 6:14-18
16	Wis 12:13,16-19 Romans 8:26-27	Jeremiah 23:1-6 Ephesians 2:13-18	Gen 18:1-10a Coloss 1:24-28
18	Isaiah 55:1-3 Romans 8:35,37-39	Exod 16:2-4,12-15 Eph 4:17,20-24	Eccl 1:2; 2:21-23 Col 3:1-5,9-11
20	Isaiah 56:1,6-7 Rom 11:13-15,29-32	Proverbs 9:1-6 Ephesians 5:15-20	Jer 38:4-6,8-10 Hebrews 12:1-4
22	Jeremiah 20:7-9 Romans 12:1-2	Deut 4:1-2,6-8 Jam 1:17-18,21b-22,27	Sir 3:17-18,20,28-29 Heb 12:18-19,22-24a
24	Sirach 27:30-28:9 Romans 14:7-9	Isaiah 50:5-9a James 2:14-18	Ex 21:7-11,13-14 1 Tim 1:12-17
26	Ezekiel 18:25-28 Philippians 2:1-11	Numb 11:25-29 James 5:1-6	Amos 6:1a,4-7 1 Tim 6:11-16
28	Isaiah 25:6-10a Phil 4:12-14,19-20	Wisdom 7:7-11 Hebrews 4:12-13	2 Kings 5:14-17 2 Tim 2:8-13

SUNDAY MORNING

	Year A	**Year B**	**Year C**
30	Exodus 22:20-26 1 Thess 1:5c-10	Jeremiah 31:7-9 Hebrews 5:1-6	Sir 35:12-14,16-18 2 Tim 4:6-8,16-18
32	Wisdom 6:12-16 1 Thess 4:13-18	1 Kings 17:10-16 Hebrews 9:24-28	2 Mac 7:1-2,9-14 2 Thess 2:16-3:5
34 *Christ the King*	Ez 34:11-12,15-17 1 Cor 15:20-26,28	Daniel 7:13-14 Revelation 1:5-8	2 Samuel 5:1-3 Coloss 1:12-20

READING — **EZEKIEL 36:22-26**

Say to the house of Israel: Sovereign Adonai says that not for your sake do I act, house of Israel, but rather for my holy name which you profaned among the nations where you went. And I will show my great holy name, profaned by you among the nations. Then the nations will know that I am Adonai, declares Sovereign Adonai, when through you I show my holy self before their eyes.

For I will take you out of the nations and I will gather you from all of the countries, and I will bring you back into your land. I will sprinkle on you clean waters, and you will be clean from all of your impurities, and from all of your idols I will cleanse you. I will give to you a new heart and I will put inside of you a new spirit, and I will remove the heart of stone from your flesh and I will give to you a heart of flesh.

RESPONSORY — Is 12:4,5

We give thanks to you, Adonai,…
   …*calling on your name.*
We proclaim and make known your deeds…
   …*calling on your name.*
Glory to the Father and to the Son and to the Holy Spirit:
   …*We give thanks to you, Adonai, calling on your name.*

Gospel Canticle For Morning
Antiphons

YEAR B
Responsorial

Ordinary Time

| Trinity Sunday | Blessed the people the Lord has chosen. | Ps 33 |

A- John 3:16-18 **B-** Mt 28:16-20 **C-** Jn 16:12-15

| Corpus Christi | I will take the cup of salvation, and call on the name of the Lord. | Ps 116 |

A- John 6:51-58 **B-** Mk 14:12-16,22-26 **C-** Lk 9:11b-17

Week

2   Here am I, Lord; I come to do your will.   40
    A- John 1:29-34   **B-** John 1:35-42   **C-** John 2:1-11

4   If today you hear his voice,
    harden not your hearts.   95
    A- Matt 5:1-12a   **B-** Mark 1:21-28   **C-** Luke 4:21-30

6   I turn to you, Lord, in time of trouble.   32
    A- Matt 5:17-37   **B-** Mark 1:40-45   **C-** Lk 6:17,20-26

8   The Lord is kind and merciful.   103
    A- Matt 6:24-34   **B-** Mark 2:18-22   **C-** Luke 6:39-45

10 With the Lord there is mercy.   130
    A- Matt 9:9-13   **B-** Mark 3:20-35   **C-** Luke 7:11-17

12 The love of the Lord is everlasting.   107
    A- Matt 10:26-33   **B-** Mark 4:35-41   **C-** Luke 9:18-24

14 Our eyes are fixed on the Lord.   123
    A- Matt 11:25-30   **B-** Mark 6:1-6   **C-** Lk 10:1-12,17-20

Gospel Canticle For Morning

	Antiphons	YEAR B
Ordinary Time		Responsorial

16 The Lord is my shepherd. Ps 23
   A- Matt 13:24-43   **B-** Mark 6:30-34   **C-** Lk 10:38-42

18 The Lord gave them bread from heaven. Ps 78
   A- Matt 14:13-21   **B-** John 6:24-35   **C-** Lk 12:13-21

20 Taste and see the goodness of the Lord. Ps 34
   A- Matt 15:21-28   **B-** John 6:51-58   **C-** Lk 12:49-53

22 One who does justice lives in
   the presence of the Lord. Ps 15
   A- Matt 16:21-27   **B-** Mk 7:1-8,14-15,21-23   **C-** Lk 14:1,7-14

24 I will walk before the Lord. Ps 116
   A- Matt 18:21-35   **B-** Mark 8:27-35   **C-** Luke 15:1-32

26 The precepts of the Lord
   give joy to the heart. Ps 19
   A- Matt 21:28-32   **B-** Mk 9:38-43,45,47-48   **C-** Lk 16:19-31

28 Fill us with your love, O Lord. Ps 90
   A- Matt 22:1-14   **B-** Mark 10:17-30   **C-** Lk 17:11-19

30 The Lord has done great things for us,
   we are filled with joy! Ps 126
   A- Matt 22:34-40   **B-** Mark 10:46-52   **C-** Luke 18:9-14

32 Praise the Lord, my soul! Ps 146
   A- Matt 25:1-13   **B-** Mark 12:38-44   **C-** Lk 20:27-38

34 The Lord our ruler is robed in majesty. Ps 93
   A- Matt 25:31-46   **B-** John 18:33b-37   **C-** Lk 23:35-43

CANTICLE of ZECHARIAH (The Benedictus)
LUKE 1:68-79

+ Blessed be the Lord the God of Israel
who chose a people to visit with redemption,
and raised salvation in the house of David,
saving strength from God's own servant,

speaking from the age of the prophets
through the mouth of the holy prophet:
Salvation out of enmity,
even out of those who hate us,

to show our ancestors how mercy works, -
and to remember the holy promise of the Lord,
the covenant made for our ancestor Abraham,
calming our fear and making us free
to serve with holy justice before God all our days.

And you also child -
will be called a prophet of the Most High
for you will go before the Lord to prepare his way
and give to people a knowledge of salvation
known in accepting forgiveness of their sins.

From the tender mercy of our God,
the sun rising from the height will visit with light
for those who sit in the dark or shadow of death
and to guide our feet into the way of peace.

Glory...

Antiphon

PETITIONS FOR THE CONSECRATION TO GOD
OF THE DAY AND ITS REST

- For the Church and her ministry and apostolates…
- For secular authorities and all serving as stewards…
- For people who are poor or sick or in sorrow…
- For peace and the basic needs of each human being…
- For acceptance of the gift of the infinite love of God…
- For the blessings of faithful Sabbath rest…
- In gratitude for blessings and grace…
- For those who have asked for my prayer…
- For those for whom I have promised to pray…
- For those who weigh on my heart…

CLOSING PRAYER FOR MORNING AND EVENING

Our Fath-er, who art in heav-en;
hal-lowed be thy name.
Thy king dom come, thy will be done
on earth as it is in heav-en.
Give us this day our dai-ly bread
and for-give us our tres-pass-es
as we for-give those who tres-pass a-gainst/ us
and lead us not in-to temp-ta/-tion
but de-liv-er us from e\-vil.
A-men.

HYMN, TE DEUM

You are God: we praise you;
You are the Lord; we acclaim you;
You are the eternal Father: all creation worships you.

To you all angels, all the powers of heaven,
Cherubim and Seraphim, sing in endless praise:
Holy, holy, holy, Lord, God of power and might,
heaven and earth are full of your glory.

The glorious company of apostles praise you.
The noble assembly of prophets praise you.
The white-robed army of martyrs praise you.

All over the world the holy church acclaims you:
Father, of majesty unbounded,
your true and only Son, worthy of all worship,
and the Holy Spirit, advocate and guide.

You, Christ, are the royal of glory,
the eternal Son of the Father.

When you became human to set us free
you did not spurn the Virgin's womb.

You overcame the sting of death,
and opened the reign of heaven to all believers.

You are seated at God's right hand in glory.
We believe that you will come and be our judge.

Come then, Lord, and help your people,
bought with the price of your own blood,
and bring us with your saints
to glory everlasting. Amen.

WEEK II
SUNDAY EVENING

+ *God, come to my assistance;*   Psalm 70:2
  Lord, make haste to help me!

  Glory…

A **Joy-ful, joy-ful, we a-dore you**,
God of glo-ry, Lord of love;
Hearts un-fold like flow'rs be-fore you,
Op'n-ing to the sun a-bove.
Melt the clouds of sin and/ sad-ness;
Drive the/ dark of doubt a-way;
Giv-er of e-ter-nal glad-ness,
Fill us with the light of day.

You are giv-ing and for-giv-ing,
Ev-er bless-ing, ev-er blest,
Well-spring of the joy of liv-ing,
O-cean depth of hap-py rest!
You our Fa-ther, Christ our/ bro-ther,
All who/ live in love are thine;
Teach us how to love each oth-er,
Ho-ly Spir-it, joy div-ine.

85, Text: Henry Van Dyke, 1907, altered
Music: 8787D, HYMN TO JOY, Ludwig van Beethoven, d.1827;
ad. by Edward Hodges, 1824

B **Love Div-ine/, all love ex-cell\-ing,**
Joy of heav'n, to earth\ come down,
Fix in us/ your hum-ble dwell-ing,
All your faith-ful mer\-cies crown.
Je-sus, you\ are true com-pass\-ion,
Pure, un-bound/-ed love\ you are;
Vis\-it us\ with your\ sal-va//\-tion,
En-ter-ing\ the trem-bling heart.

Breathe, oh breathe/, your lov-ing Spir\-it
In-to ev-'ry troub\-led breast;
Let us all/ in you in-her\-it,
Let us find the prom\-ised rest.
Take a-way\ the love of sin\-ning;
Al-pha and/ O-me\-ga be;
End\ of faith\ as its be-gin//\-ning,
Set our hearts\ at lib-er-ty.

Fin-ish, then/, your new cre-a\-tion;
Pure and spot-less let\ us be.
Let us see/ your great sal-va\-tion
Per-fect-ly re-stored\ and free,
Changed from glo\-ry into glo\-ry,
Till in heav'n/ we find\ our place,
Till\ we cast\ our cares\ be-fore//\ you,
Lost in won\-der, love, and grace.

112, Text: from Psalm 106:4; by Charles Wesley, 1747, altered
Music: 87 87 D, HYFRYDOL, Rowland H. Prichard, 1811-1887

PSALM 23

Antiphon *For I was hungry and you gave me to eat,*
thirsty and you gave me drink,
a stranger and you welcomed me,
naked and you clothed me,
ill and you cared for me,
in prison and you visited me.   Mt 25:35,36

Adonai is my shepherd; nothing do I lack.
My Lord lays me down in green pastures
and leads me beside still quiet waters,
restoring my soul and guiding me
in paths of justice for the Lord's own namesake.

So when I walk in the deep dark valley
I will not fear for you are with me,
your rod and staff a comfort to me.

A table you prepare before me
in the presence even of enmity.
My head you anoint with oil
and my cup is overflowing.

Surely goodness and love will follow me
all the days of my life
and I will dwell in the Lord's own house
for length of days.

Glory…

Antiphon

PSALM 76

Antiphon   *The Son of Humanity*
                is Lord also of the sabbath.   Mk 2:28

God is known in Judah;
great in Israel is the Name.
In Salem is God's tent,
in Zion the dwelling place.
There flashes broke the arrow,
shield and sword, and weapons of war.

Giver of Light, you are,
more majestic than mountains of game.
Human beings of valiant heart lie plundered;
they sleep their sleep
and warriors can no more lift up their hands.
At your rebuke, God of Jacob,
both chariot and horse lie still.

You are feared, you.
Who can stand before you when you are angry?
From the heavens you pronounced judgment;
the land feared and she was quiet
when you rose, God, for the judgment
to save all the afflicted of the land.

Psalm 76, continued

Even the angry humans come to praise you,
and you hold close the survivor of anger.
Make vows! Fulfill vows to your God Adonai!
Let all the neighbors of God bring their gift
to the One rightly feared,
who breaks the spirit of rulers,
the One rightly feared by kings and queens.

Glory…

Antiphon *The Son of Humanity
is Lord also of the sabbath.*   Mt 2:28

Son of Humanity, **ben adam**
in Hebrew, is usually translated *Son
of Man,* perhaps *Son of Human* would also
work. As Jesus applies the phrase to himself,
it is generally understood as a combination of the
vision of the glorified Just Judge at the end times in
Daniel 7, with the image of the *Servant of the Lord* (or the
Suffering Servant from four canticles of the Prophet Isaiah:
Isaiah 42:1-4 – *A bruised reed he will not break.*
Isaiah 49:1-7 – *I will make you a light to the nations.*
Isaiah 50:4-11 – *I gave my back to those who beat me.*
Isaiah 52:13-53:12 – *By his wounds we were healed.*
Folks who pray the Stations of the Cross will recognize some of this,
and so the phrase *Son of Humility* might be suggested.
Ben adam could also refer to the mystery of the incarnation,
so the phrase *Son of Woman* could also be appropriate.

PSALM 110:1-6a,7

Antiphon　　*Get the people to recline in groups of about fifty.*　　Lk 9:14

Adonai said to my Lord:
"Sit at my right hand
until I make enmity
as a footstool for your feet."

A scepter of your might
Adonai will extend from Zion,
and rule in the midst of enmity!

Your troops are willing on the day of your battle.
In holy majesty from the womb of the dawn,
to you is the dew of your youth.
Adonai pledged in a mind unchanging,
"You are a priest to forever
in the order of Melchizedek."

The Lord is at your right hand
and will crush rulers on the day of wrath,
will judge the nations…
and will drink from a brook on the way
with head lifted up in it all.

Glory…

　　　　　　　　　　　　　　　　　　　　　Antiphon

PSALM 112

Antiphon *Blessed are those hungering
and thirsting for justice;
they will be satisfied.* Mt 5:6

Hallelujah!

Blessed are the ones who fear Adonai,
and delight greatly in the commandments.
Mighty in the land will they be,
blessed with generations of upright children,

wealth and riches in their houses,
and justice enduring to forever.
Light dawns in the darkness
for the upright, gracious,
compassionate and just.

The good human, generous and lending,
conducts affairs with justice.
Surely to forever the good one will not be shaken;
remembered forever will the just one be.

The good will have no fear of bad news,
being steadfast of heart and trusting Adonai
with heart secure, no fear to the end,
when face to face with enmity.

The good one scatters, giving to the poor,
with justice enduring to forever;
the dignity of the good one will be lifted in honor.

Doers of the bad will see this and be vexed
with gnashing of teeth and a wasting away,
longings for the bad coming to nothing.

Glory…

                                                            Antiphon

---

Four Ways to Pray Deeper:

↓ Talking <u>at</u> God, using memorized prayers to simply pray,
or throwing up on God today's urgency;
↓ Talking <u>to</u> God, sharing joys that are lifting my heart
and sorrows that are weighing me down;
↓ <u>Listen</u>ing to God, willing to be surprised by God who is
always saying, *I made you, I know you, I love you*;
↓ <u>Being with</u> God, contemplation, beatific vision, we can
choose to do the first three, but this is always a gift.

See *Armchair Mystic* by Mark E. Thibodeaux, S.J.

PSALM 115

Antiphon *Anyone who loves me will keep my word;*
my Abba will love that one,
within whom we will come
and make our dwelling. Jn 14:23

Not to us, **Adonai**, not to us,
but to your name give glory
because of your love, because of your fidelity.
Why say the nations, "Where now is their God?"

Our God now is in the heavens
and does all that God pleases.
Their idols are silver and gold,
made of human hands.

Made with a mouth, they cannot speak;
made with eyes, they cannot see;
made with ears, they cannot hear;
made with a nose, they cannot smell;

made with hands, they cannot feel;
made with feet, they cannot walk,
and they make not a sound in their throat.
Like them will become those who make them,
and all who trust in them.

SUNDAY EVENING

Israel, trust Adonai, your help and your shield.
Aaron, trust Adonai, your help and your shield.
You who fear Adonai, trust Adonai,
your help and your shield.

Adonai remembers us and will bless us,
will bless the house of Israel,
will bless the house of Aaron,
will bless ones who fear Adonai,
the small ones with the great ones.

May Adonai make an increase to you,
to you and to your children.
May you be blessed by Adonai,
Maker of heavens and earth.

All the heavens are the heavens of Adonai,
but earth is given to humanity.
The dead ones do not praise Adonai,
and not all those who go down in silence.

But we, we give glory to Adonai,
from now and to forevermore.
Hallelujah!

Glory...

Antiphon

Given ten words to tell what his Mr. Jesus is about:
We are all bastards, and God loves us anyway.

See *Brother to a Dragonfly* by Will D. Campbell,
preacher, civil rights activist

REVELATION 19:1b,2a,5b,6b,7

Antiphon
*We are an Easter people
and **alleluia** is our song.*   St. Augustine

Alleluia!
Salvation and glory and power are to our God,
whose judgments are true and just.

Alleluia!
Praise our God, all you servants of the Lord,
you small and you great, who hold God in awe.

Alleluia!
The Lord is reigning, our God, the Almighty.
Let us rejoice and let us exult,
and we will give the glory to the Lord.

Alleluia!
The day has come
for the marriage of the Lamb,
and the bride has prepared herself.

Glory…

Antiphon

---

*Evangelization
is one beggar telling
another beggar where to
find bread.*   D.T. Niles

READING **2 THESSALONIANS 2:13-17**

We ought to thank God always concerning you, brothers and sisters loved by the Lord, because God chose you as the firstfruit to salvation by sanctification of spirit and faith in the truth, and called you through our gospel to obtain the glory of our Lord Jesus Christ.

So then, brothers and sisters, stand and hold the traditions which you were taught either through speech or through our letter.

And may our Lord Jesus Christ and God our Father, the one who has loved us and given us eternal comfort and a good hope by grace, comfort your hearts and confirm every good work and word.

RESPONSORY Ps 147:5

Great is our Lord…
 …and mighty in power.
Unlimited in understanding…
 …and mighty in power.
Glory to the Father and to the Son and to the Holy Spirit:
 …Great is our Lord, and mighty in power.

Gospel Canticle For Evening

	Antiphons	YEAR C Responsorial
Wk 2	Proclaim the marvelous deeds of the Lord.	Ps 96
4	I will sing of your salvation.	Ps 71
6	Blessed are they who hope in the Lord.	Ps 1
8	Lord, it is good to give thanks to you.	Ps 92
10	I will praise you, Lord, who rescued me.	Ps 30
12	My soul is thirsting for you, O Lord my God.	Ps 63
14	Let all the earth cry out to God with joy.	Ps 66
16	One who does justice will live in the presence of the Lord.	Ps 15
18	If today you hear God's voice harden not your hearts.	Ps 90
20	Lord, come to my aid!	Ps 40
22	God, in your goodness, you have made a home for the poor.	Ps 68
24	I will rise and go to my Father. (Lk 15:18)	Ps 51
26	Praise the Lord, my soul!	Ps 146
28	The Lord has revealed to the nations the saving power of God.	Ps 98
30	The Lord hears the cry of the poor.	Ps 34
32	Lord when your glory appears my joy will be full.	Ps 17

34 Let us go rejoicing to the house of the Lord. Ps 122

CANTICLE of MARY (The Magnificat)
LUKE 1:46-55

+ **My soul** is stretched full with praise of the Lord,
and my spirit, beyond joy in God, my Savior,
who chose to lay eyes on this humble servant.

Behold, now and forward,
each and every age will call me blessed,
for the Mighty One did great things to me.

Holy is the name and the mercy
to generations and generations,
the ones fearing the One,

Who scattered the haughty of mind and heart,
pulled the powerful off their high place,
and lifted with dignity the humble in need.

The hungering are filled with good things,
the rich are sent away empty,
and servant Israel is given relief

with a memory of mercy to remember,
the promise spoken to our ancestors,
to Abraham and his descendants forever.

Glory...

Antiphon

INTERCESSIONS

- For respect for conscience and religious freedom…
- For all who are not yet ready for this week…
- For those who have gone before us marked with the sign of faith…

- In gratitude for blessings…;   Abba thank you.
- For the sins of this day…;   Lord Jesus have mercy.
- With concerns over tomorrow…;   Holy Spirit help.

AN EASTER PRAYER for VOCATIONS

Come, Holy Spirit,
fill the hearts of your faithful;
set fire in us your confirming love.
Give us wisdom to seek the face of God,
understanding of our baptism in Christ, and
right judgment to discern his call in freedom.
Give us courage to say yes to our vocations,
knowledge of what Jesus teaches,
and reverence for the ways of the Father.
Give us wonder and awe in your presence,
that the witness we give
to the resurrection of the Son
may be pleasing to the Father
and help you, Holy Spirit,
renew the face of the earth.

OUR FATHER…

WEEK II
MONDAY MORNING

+ *God, come to my assistance;*   Psalm 70:2
  Lord, make haste to help me!

Glory...

I know that my Re/-deem-er\ lives;
What com-fort this sweet sen-tence gives!
Liv-ing\ Proph/-et/, Priest\, and\ King;
Liv-ing and as he lives I'll sing.

He lives/ hun-gry/ souls to\ feed,
Liv-ing to help in time of need.
Liv-ing to grant/ us/ rich\ sup\-ply,
Liv-ing to guide us with his eye.

He lives/ qui-et/ing our\ fears,
Liv-ing to wipe a-way our tears,
Liv-ing to calm/ our/ troubl\-ed\ heart,
Liv-ing all bless-ings to im-part.

He lives/, glo-ry/ to his\ Name!
Liv-ing, my Je-sus, still the same.
Oh, sweet the joy/ this/ sen\-tence\ gives:
"I know that my Re-deem-er lives!"

93, Text: from Job 19:25-27, Samuel Medley, 1775, altered
Music: DUKE STREET, LM, John Hatton, 1793
Popular melody for: *From All That Dwells Below The Skies*

PSALM 31:1-17,20-25

Antiphon *Everyone who hears my words and does them
will be like a wise human
who built the house on rock.*   Mt 7:24

In you, **Adonai**, I take refuge;
let me never be shamed.
Deliver me in your justice.
Quickly turn to me your ear! Rescue me!

Be for me a rock of refuge,
a fortress house to save me.
Since you are my rock and my fortress,
for the sake of your name
you lead me and guide me.

You free me from the trap they set for me,
for you are my refuge.
Into your hands I commend my spirit;
you redeem me, Adonai God of truth.

I hate when humans cling to worthless idols,
and I trust in Adonai.
I will rejoice in your love and be glad
for you saw my affliction;
you knew the anguishes of my soul.

You do not put me into hands of enmity;
you set my feet in the spacious place.

Be merciful to me, Adonai, in my distress;
my eyes and my soul and my body
grow weak with sorrow.

My life is consumed by anguish
and my years with groaning.
My strength fails because of my guilt
and my bones grow weak.

Because of enmity I am
the utter contempt of even my neighbors
and a dread to my friends
who see me on the street and flee.

I am forgotten as though dead;
my heart became like broken pottery,
for I hear the slander of many
and terror on every side
when they conspire together against me
and plot to take my life.

But I trust in you, Adonai;
I say you are my God;
my times are in your hand.
Deliver me from the hands
of enmity and pursuers.

Shine your faces on your servant!
Save me in your unfailing love!...

Psalm 31, continued

How great is the goodness
you store up for ones who fear you
and bestow on those taking refuge in you
in the sight of the children of humanity.

You hide them in the shelter of your presence;
from human intrigues you keep them
in a dwelling safe from the strife of tongues.

Adonai is praised for showing wonderful love
to me in the city besieged, and I said in my alarm,
"I am cut off from before your eyes."
Yet you heard the sound of my cries for mercy
when I called to you for help.

Love Adonai, all you saints,
Adonai faithful and preserving,
but paying back in full the arrogant.

Be strong and strengthen your heart,
all you hoping in Adonai!

Glory…

Antiphon *Everyone who hears my words and does them
will be like a wise human
who built the house on rock.* Mt 7:24

---

*God calls…where your deep
gladness meets the world's deep hunger.*

Frederick Buechner

PSALM 73

Antiphon   *Any of you who do not detach
from all your possessions
cannot be my disciple.*   Lk 14:33

Surely good to Israel is El,
to those pure of heart.
But my feet almost slipped,
as nearly lost were my footholds,
for I envied the arrogant
and the prosperity of doers of the bad.

None of them struggle with death
and healthy are their bodies.
Human burdens are not theirs,
nor human plagues.

And so pride wraps them as a necklace
clothing violence on them.
Their eyes bulge with fat;
their conceits pass the limits of the mind.

They scoff and they speak with malice
and threaten arrogant oppression.
Their mouths lay claim to the heavens,
and their tongues to possession of the earth.

Psalm 73, continued

And so people turn to them for themselves
as they drink all the waters of abundance.
They say, "How does El know?"
and, "Does the Most High know about this?"
See these doers of the bad:
even carefree of Always they increase their wealth.

Surely in vain have I kept my heart clean
and washed my hands in innocence.
But I am plagued all the day
and punished in the mornings.

If I said that I would speak as they do,
see the generation of your children I would betray!

My efforts to understand this
are oppressive to my eyes.
Until! I entered into sanctuaries of God
and understood about their final destiny.

Surely you place them on slippery ground
and cast them down to ruins.
How sudden is their destruction,
swept away complete by terrors.
As with a dream when waking up, Lord,
their fantasy you will despise when you arise.

When my heart was grieved,
and my spirits bitter
and senseless and unknowing,
I was but a brute beast before you.

MONDAY MORNING

Yet I am always with you;
you hold me by my right hand.
With your counsel you guide me
and will take me after the glory.

Who in the heavens is to me?
And with you, nothing on earth do I desire.
My flesh and my heart may fail,
but Elohim is the strength of my heart
and my portion to forever.

For see! Those far from you will perish…
But the nearness of Elohim is my good.
I have made you my refuge, Lord Adonai,
to tell of all your deeds.

Glory…

Antiphon	*Any of you who do not detach from all your possessions cannot be my disciple.*	Lk 14:33

If we had any possessions, we should need weapons and laws to defend them.

Saint Francis of Assisi, d. 1221

PSALM 42

Antiphon *When the shepherd sends them forth
and goes before them, the sheep follow
because they know this voice.* Jn 10:4

As a deer breathes heavy for streams of water,
so my soul throbs for you, God.

My soul she thirsts for God, the living God.
When can I go and meet the faces of God?

My tears were food for me by day and by night,
while all day they said to me,
"Where is your God?"

These things I remember
as my soul pours out before me:
How I would go with the multitude
to lead them to the house of God
sounding shouts of joy and thanksgiving,
a festive throng!

Why are you downcast, my soul?
Why are you disturbed within me?
Put hope in God, whom I will yet praise,
the saving help and presence.

My God, within me my soul she is downcast.
For this I will remember you
from the land of Jordan and heights of Hermon,
from the Mount of Mizar:

Deep calls to deep in the roar of your waterfalls.
All your waves and breakers are swept over me.

By day Adonai directs love
and at night the song within me
is a prayer to the God of my life.

I say to El my Rock, "why do you forget me?
Why must I go about mourning,
oppressed by enmity?"

With mortal agony in my bones,
taunted by adversity,
while all day they say to me,
"Where is your God?"

Why are you downcast, my soul?
Why are you disturbed within me?
Put hope in God, whom I will yet praise,
my saving help and God.

Glory...

                                                            Antiphon

---

On the original Easter Sunday Jesus
breathed in, then onto them, and said, 'Receive
the holy breath, whose sins you forgive are forgiven...,'
breathing onto them and us the power to forgive.   John 20.23

SIRACH 36:1-6,13-22

Antiphon *The Lord hears the cry of the poor;*
blessed be the Lord.   Ps 34

Come to our aid, God of all;
let all the nations be in fear of you.
Raise your hand to the foreign nations,
that they may see your might.

As you have used us to show them your holiness,
so now use them to show us your glory.
They will know as we know
that there is no God but you.

Give new signs and work new wonders;
show the splendor of your right hand and arm...

Gather all the tribes of Jacob,
that they may inherit the land as at the beginning.
Show mercy to the people called by your name:
Israel, whom you named your firstborn.

Have pity on your holy city, Jerusalem,
the foundation for your throne.
Fill Zion with your majesty,
and your temple with your glory.

Give witness of your deeds of old;
fulfill the prophecies spoken in your name.
Reward those who have hoped in you,
and let your prophets be proven true.

Hear the prayers of your servants,
as you are good to your people.
Thus all will know to the ends of the earth
that you are God eternal.

Glory…

                                                         Antiphon

---

Perhaps
the basic sin in
the psalms is idolatry,
letting anything have priority
over God. Perhaps the clearest sign
that I am serving a lifeless idol is when
I am no longer able to hear the cry of the poor.

ISAIAH 42:10-16

Antiphon *I, your Lord,*
have called you for justice.   Is 42:6a

Sing to Adonai a new song,
praise from the ends of the earth!

Ones going down to the sea and all in it,
and the islands, the ones living in them,
and the desert and its towns
and settlements where Kedar lives,
let them arise, let them sing for joy,

and the people of Sela
let them shout from the top of mountains.
Let them give to Adonai the glory
and proclaim praise in the islands.

Adonai will march out like the mighty human
and stir up zeal like a warrior,
and shouting and raising a cry
will triumph over enmity.

I was silent for a long time
and held back in quiet;
like a woman bearing a child,
I cry out and gasp and pant.

MONDAY MORNING

I will lay waste mountains and hills
letting all their vegetation dry up;
I will turn rivers into islands
and dry up pools.

I will lead blind ones by ways they did not know;
along paths they did not know I will guide them.
I will turn what is dark before them into light
and rough places into smooth.

These things I will do
and I will not forsake them.

Glory...

Antiphon

a cosmology of the ancients

PSALM 19

Antiphon   *The Samaritan did mercy*
to the beaten man;
you go and do likewise.   Lk 10:37

The heavens declare the glory of God,
and the sky proclaims the work of God's hands.
Day after day, speech pouring forth,
knowledge is on display night after night.

There is no speech, there is no language,
and no sound is heard.
Yet into all the earth their line goes out
and their words to the ends of the world.

There God has pitched a tent for the sun,
and like a bridegroom coming forth,
and like an athlete running the course, rejoices.

At the end of the heavens is the rising of the sun,
to their furthest ends is the circuit,
and nothing is hidden from its heat.

The law of Adonai is perfect, reviving the soul;
statutes of Adonai are trustworthy,
making wise of the simple;
precepts of Adonai are right ones,
giving joy of heart;

the command of Adonai is radiant,
giving light to eyes;
the fear of Adonai is pure, enduring to forever;
ordinances of Adonai are sure and altogether just;

more precious than gold,
much more than pure gold,
sweeter than honey,
the honey of honeycombs.

Your servant is warned by them;
to keep them is a great reward.
Who can discern errors?
From those hidden from me, forgive me!

And keep your servant from willful sins!
May they not control me;
then will I be blameless
and innocent of great transgression.

May the words of my mouth be as pleasing
and the meditation of my heart be as pleasing
before you, Adonai,
my Rock and my Redeemer.

Glory…

                                                          Antiphon

---

*And who is my neighbor? The family
living next door to me are neighbors, and the family
next door to them. How far away does someone have to live
to no longer be my neighbor? Jesus says there is no such distance.*

PSALM 90

Antiphon *Be wary and on guard against all greed*
for life is not about possessions.   Lk 12:15

You, Lord, you have been our refuge
from generation to generation.
Before the mountains were born,
before you brought forth earth,
from eternity to eternity, you are God.

You turn humans back to dust and say,
"Return, sons and daughters of humanity."
A thousand years in your eyes
are like the day yesterday that went by,
like one watch of the night.

You sweep humans into the sleep
like new grass in the morning that sprouts:
in the morning it springs up and sprouts
and then by the evening is withered and dry.

Indeed we can be consumed in your anger
and terrified by your indignation.
You set our iniquities before you,
our secrets in the light of your presences.

Indeed all our days pass away under your anger;
we finish our years like a sigh.
Our days last for seventy years
or eighty if given the strength.

MONDAY MORNING

The best part of them are trouble and sorrow,
passing quickly, and we fly away.
Who knows the power of your anger,
who fears your wrath?

Number our days aright;
teach, that we may gain hearts of wisdom.
How long, Adonai, until you relent?
Have compassion on your servants.

Satisfy our morning hunger
with your unfailing love
that we may sing for joy and be glad all our days.
Make us glad, equal to our affliction,
the years of trouble we have seen.

May your deeds be shown to your servants
and your splendor to their children.
May the favor of the Lord our God rest upon us
and the work of our hands be made good;
yes, make good the work of our hands.

Glory…

Antiphon

Psalm 90
is used in the
ritual for blessing
of a place of business.

OFFICE OF READINGS and FIRST READING AT MASS

	Odd Years	**Even Years**
2 readings	*Romans 5:1-11*	*Genesis 11*
mass	Hebrews 5:1-10	1 Samuel 15:16-23
4 rdgs	*Romans 12*	*Genesis 27:30-46*
mass	Hebrews 11:32-40	2 Samuel 15:13-14,30
6 rdgs	*1 Corinthians 7:1-24*	*1 Thessalonians 2:13-3:13*
mass	Genesis 4:1-15,25	**James** 1:1-11
8 rdgs	*1 Corinthians 15:1-19*	*2 Corinthians 8*
mass	Ben Sira 17:19-27	**1 Peter** 1:3-9
10 rdgs	*Joshua 1*	*Philippians 1:12-26*
mass	**2 Corinthians** 1:1-7	**1 Kings** 17:1-6
12 rdgs	*Judges 16*	*Zechariah 8*
mass	**Genesis** 12:1-9	2 Kings 17:5-8,13-15a
14 rdgs	*1 Samuel 18*	*Proverbs 3*
mass	Genesis 28:10-22a	**Hosea** 2:16,17b-18,21-22
16 rdgs	*2 Samuel 18 & 19*	*Job 12*
mass	Exodus 14:5-18	Micah 6:1-4,6-8
18 rdgs	*1 Kings 21*	*Joel 1*
mass	**Numbers** 11:4b-15	Jeremiah 28:1-17
20 rdgs	*Ephesians 1:15-23*	*Ecclesiastes 2*
mass	**Judges** 2:11-19	Ezekiel 24:15-24

MONDAY MORNING

	Odd Years	**Even Years**
22 rdgs	*Amos 1*	*1 Timothy 6:1-10*
mass	1 Thessalonians 4:13-18	1 Corinthians 2:1-5
24 rdgs	*Hosea 9*	*Esther 3*
mass	1 Timothy 2:1-8	1 Corinthians 11:17-26,33
26 rdgs	*Micah 6*	*Judith 4 & 5*
mass	Zechariah 8:1-8	**Job** 1:6-22
28 rdgs	*Jeremiah 1*	*Sirach 11*
mass	**Romans** 1:1-7	Galatians 4:22-24,26-27
30 rdgs	*Jeremiah 25*	*Wisdom 2*
mass	Romans 8:12-17	Ephesians 4:32-5:8
32 rdgs	*Ezekiel 4 & 5*	*1 Macabees 1:26-63*
mass	**Wisdom** 1:1-17	**Titus** 1:1-19
34 rdgs	*Ezekiel 36*	*Daniel 5*
mass	**Daniel** 1:1-6,8-20	Revelation 14:1-3,4b-5

READING **JEREMIAH 15:16**

Your words came and I ate them, and your word was my joy and the delight of my heart, for your name, Adonai God Sabaoth, called to me.

RESPONSORY Ps 147:2

How good to sing praise to our God,...
 ...and give God the praise that is fitting.
How pleasant to sing a new song,...
 ...and give God the praise that is fitting.
Glory to the Father and to the Son and to the Holy Spirit:
 ...How good to sing praise to our God
 and give God the praise that is fitting.

Gospel Canticle For Morning

Antiphon   *Blessed be the Lord our God.*

Gospel Reading for Monday of
Week **2** Mark 2:18-22   **14** Matt 9:18-26   **26** Luke 9:46-50
     4 Mark 5:1-20   **16** Matt 12:38-42 **28** Lk 11:29-32
     6 Mark 8:11-13   **18** Matt 14:22-36 **30** Lk 13:10-17
     8 Mark 10:17-27 **20** Matt 19:16-22 **32** Luke 17:1-6
    10 Matt 5:1-12   **22** Luke 4:16-30   **34** Luke 21:1-4
    12 Matt 7:1-5   **24** Luke 7:1-10

CANTICLE of ZECHARIAH (The Benedictus)
LUKE 1:68-79

✢ **Blessed be** the Lord the God of Israel
who chose a people to visit with redemption,
and raised salvation in the house of David,
saving strength from God's own servant,

speaking from the age of the prophets
through the mouth of the holy prophet:
Salvation out of enmity,
even out of those who hate us,

to show our ancestors how mercy works, -
and to remember the holy promise of the Lord,
the covenant made for our ancestor Abraham,
calming our fear and making us free
to serve with holy justice before God all our days.

And you also child -
will be called a prophet of the Most High
for you will go before the Lord to prepare his way
and give to people a knowledge of salvation
known in accepting forgiveness of their sins.

From the tender mercy of our God,
the sun rising from the height will visit with light
for those who sit in the dark or shadow of death
and to guide our feet into the way of peace.

Glory…

Antiphon

PETITIONS FOR THE CONSECRATION TO GOD
OF THE DAY AND ITS WORK

- For the Church and her ministry and apostolates...

- For secular authorities and all serving as stewards...

- For people who are poor or sick or in sorrow...

- For peace and the basic needs of each human being...

- For people caught in the crossfires of war...

- For justice for migrant workers and refugees...

- For starving children awakening our conscience...

- For people living in subhuman conditions...

- For human beings enslaved or unjustly imprisoned...

- For laborers where treated as mere tools for profit...

- For good work for all to do in dignity...

- In gratitude for blessings and grace...

- For those who have asked for my prayer...

- For those for whom I have promised to pray...

- For those who weigh on my heart...

LORD TAKE ME   Mychal Judge, OFM

Lord, take me where you want me to go;
let me meet who you want me to meet;
tell me what you want me to say;
and keep me out of your way.

OUR FATHER...

WEEK II
MONDAY EVENING

+ *God, come to my assistance;* Psalm 70:2
  Lord, make haste to help me!

  Glory...

A **The Church's one foun-da-tion**
Is Je-sus Christ, her Lord;
She is his new cre-a-tion
By wa-ter and the Word.
From heav'n he came and sought her
To be his ho-ly bride;
By blood re-deem-ing bought her,
And for her life he died.

E-lect from ev-'ry na-tion,
Yet one o'er all the earth,
Her char-ter of sal-va-tion
One Lord, one faith, one birth.
One ho-ly name she bless-es,
Par-takes one ho-ly food,
And to one hope she press-es,
With ev-'ry grace en-dued.

126, Text: see Ephesians 2:20; Samuel J. Stone, 1866, altered
Music: 76 76 D, AURELIA, Samuel S. Wesley, 1864

B

I sing the\ migh-ty pow'r of God,
that made/ the moun-tains rise,
That spread the\ flow-ing seas a-broad,
and built/ the loft-y skies.
I/ sing the wis-dom that or/-dained
the/ sun to rule the day;
The moon shines\ full at God's com-mand,
and all/ the stars o-bey.

I sing the\ good-ness of the Lord,
who filled/ the earth with food,
Who formed the\ crea-tures through the Word,
and then/ pro-nounced them good.
Lord/, how your won-ders are dis/-played,
wher/-e'er I turn my eye,
If I sur\-vey the ground or tread,
or gaze/ up-on the sky.

There's not a\ plant or flow'r be-low,
but makes/ your glo-ries known,
And clouds a\-rise, and temp-ests blow,
by or/-der of your throne;
While/ all that bor-rows life from/ you
is/ ev-er in your care;
And ev-'ry\-where that we can be,
you, God/, are pres-ent there.

101, Text: Isaac Watts, *Divine and Moral Songs for Children*, 1715
Music: 76 76 D, ELLACOMBE; *Gesangbuch der Herzogl*, Wirtemberg, 1784

PSALM 12

| Antiphon | *A cloud came overshadowing them and a voice came out of the cloud: this is my Beloved Son; hear him.* | Mk 9:7 |

Help, Adonai, for the godly are no more;
the faithful vanish from humanity's children.
They speak the lie to each of their neighbors,
lips flattering with a double heart.

May Adonai close all flattering lips
and tongues speaking the boast that say:
"With our tongues we will triumph,
our lips are our own; who is our master?"

But because of oppression of the weak,
because of groaning of the needy,
now Adonai says, "I will arise and protect them."

Words of Adonai are flawless words,
like silver refined in the furnace of clay,
and being purified seven times over.

You, Adonai, you will keep them safe;
you are our protection to forever.
But doers of the bad will still strut about
when vileness is honored among human beings.

Glory... Antiphon

In contrast with the Transfiguration, at the Baptism in Mark and Luke the voice says You *are my Beloved Son.*

PSALM 40:2-14,17-18

Antiphon   *I have come to throw fire on the earth
and how I wish it was ablaze.*   Lk 12:49

Waiting, I waited for Adonai,
who turned to me and heard my cry,

who lifted me from the slime pit
and from the muddy mire,
and set my feet on rock,
making firm my standing place,

and put in my mouth a new song,
a hymn of praise to our God.
Many will see and fear and trust Adonai.

Blessed is the one who trusts in Adonai
and looks not to the proud
or those turning to false "gods."

Adonai, my God, many are your deeds of wonder
and your plans cannot be equaled.
Should I speak and tell of them
they would be too many to declare.

Sacrifice and offerings you did not desire,
but my ears you keep open for me.
Burnt offering and sin offering you did not require.
Then I said, "Here, I have come;

in the scroll, in the book, it is written of me.
To do your will, my God, is my desire,
and your law is within my heart."

Your deed I proclaim in the great assembly.
See my lips unsealed; you, Adonai, you know!

I do not hide in my heart what you do;
your faithfulness and your salvation I speak.
I do not conceal your love and your truth
from the great assembly.

Adonai, withhold not your mercies from me,
may your love and your truth protect me always
for countless troubles surround around me.

My sins overtake me and I cannot see.
They are more than the hairs of my head
and my heart fails me.

Be pleased, Adonai, to save me;
Adonai, come quickly to help me!...

May all who seek you rejoice in you and be glad
and may lovers of your salvation say always,
"Let God be exalted."

Yet I am poor and needy.
May the Lord think of me and not delay,
my help and my deliverer, my God.

Glory...

Antiphon

PSALM 82

Antiphon
*One is the lawgiver and judge,
the one able to save and destroy;
who are you
to be judging your neighbor?*   James 4:12

God Elohim, presiding in the assembly of El,
gives judgment among little "g" gods:

"Until when will you defend the unjust
and show partiality to the faces of bad doers?
Defend the weak and the orphans!
Maintain justice for the poor and oppressed!
Rescue the weak and the needy!
Deliver them from the hands of doers of the bad!"

They know nothing and they understand nothing.
They walk in darkness
and all the foundations of earth are shaken.

"I said, 'you are gods, all of you,
sons and daughters of Elyon Most High,'
but like all humans you too will die
and like other rulers you too will fall."

Rise up, Elohim, and judge the earth!
For to you belong all the nations!

Glory…

                                                                     Antiphon

PSALM 120

Antiphon

*The Son of Humanity
did not come to be served
but to serve,
to give his life
in ransom for the many.*   Mk 10:45

In my distress I call on Adonai who answers me.
Adonai, save my self from lips of the lie
and from the deceitful tongue.

What will be done to you and what more
will be done to you, deceitful tongue?
Arrows of war made sharp
with coals of broom trees.

Woe to me, an alien in Meshech,
living among tents of Kedar.

Too long has my self lived
among haters of peace.
I am of peace, but when I speak
they are for war.

Glory…

Antiphon

PSALM 45

Antiphon *Rejoice on that day and leap for joy,*
for great is your reward in heaven. Lk 6:23

My heart is stirred with a noble theme;
I recite my verses for the ruler;
my tongue is a pen of a skillful scribe.

You were anointed with grace on your lips,
more excellent among children of humanity.
For thus has God blessed you to forever.

Gird your sword upon your side, mighty one,
your splendor and your majesty.
Your majesty, be victorious!
Ride forth on behalf of truth and justice;
let your right hand display awesome deeds.

Your arrows are sharp;
let nations fall beneath you into the heart
of ones who choose enmity with the royal
on God's throne forever and ever.
The scepter of the realm is a scepter of justice.

You love justice
and hate when people do the bad;
for this your God anointed you
above your companions with oil of gladness,
with myrrh and aloes and cassia on your robes,
and from ivory palaces strings make you glad.

MONDAY EVENING

Children of royalty are honored among you
and the royal spouse stands at your right hand,
honored in gold of Ophir.

Listen, child, and consider!
Give your ear and forget your people
and the house of your parents.
The ruler enthralled for your beauty
is your lord, so give honor!
With the gift of your face, child of Tyre,
wealthy people will seek you.

The all-glorious offspring of the ruler
is in a gown with interweavings of gold,
led to the ruler in embroidered garments
with virgin companions following.
They are led in with joy and gladness;
they enter the royal palace.

In the place of your parents will your children be,
as royals through all the land.
I will make perpetual the memory of your name
through all generations and generation.
For this the nations will praise you
ever and to forever.

Glory... Antiphon

Nothing in life is to be feared, it is only to be understood.
Now is the time to understand more, so that we may fear less.
Maria Sktodowska-Curie

PSALM 136

Antiphon   *My food is that I may do the will*
            of the one who sent me.   Jn 4:34

Give thanks to Adonai who is good,
loving to forever.
Give thanks to the One who is El of the "els,"
loving to forever.
Give thanks to the One who is Lord of the lords,
loving to forever,

to the One who has alone done great wonders,
loving to forever,
who made the heavens by understanding,
loving to forever,
who spread out the earth upon the waters,
loving to forever,

who made the great lights,
loving to forever,
the sun to govern the day,
loving to forever,
the moon and stars to govern the night,
loving to forever,

who struck down Egypt in their firstborn,
loving to forever,
who brought Israel out from among them,
loving to forever,   --

MONDAY EVENING

with mighty hand and outstretched arm,
loving to forever,

who divided the Reed Sea in half,
loving to forever,
and brought Israel through its midst,
loving to forever,
but swept Pharoah and the army into the Reed Sea,
loving to forever,

who then led the people through the desert,
loving to forever,
who struck down great rulers, loving to forever,
and killed mighty rulers, loving to forever,

Sihon, king of the Amorites, loving to forever,
and Og, the king of Bashan, loving to forever,

who gave the land as an inheritance,
loving to forever,
an inheritance to servant Israel,
loving to forever,
who remembered us in our low estate,
loving to forever,

and freed us from enmity, loving to forever,
who gives food to every creature, loving to forever.
Give thanks to El of the heavens,
who indeed is loving to forever!

Glory...

Antiphon

EPHESIANS 1:3-10

Antiphon *Come yourselves privately to a desert place and rest a little.* Mk 6:31

Blessed be the God and Abba
of our Lord Jesus Christ,
who has blessed us in Christ
with every spiritual blessing in the heavens.

God chose us in Christ
before the foundation of the world,
to be holy and free of blemish before him.

In love, God gave us a destiny:
as parents adopt, through Jesus Christ himself,
in accord with the good pleasure of God's will
to the praise of the glory of grace
by which we are favored as God's beloved.

In Christ we have the redemption
through his blood, the forgiveness of sins,
in accord with the riches of his grace
which he made abound to us.

In all wisdom and intelligence
the mystery of God's will is made known to us
in accord with God's good pleasure and purpose:

A stewardship of the fullness of time,
heading up all things in Christ,
the things in the heavens and the things on earth.

Glory…

                                                Antiphon

READING **1 THESSALONIANS 2:13**

And so we give thanks to God unceasingly, that having received the word of God, hearing it from us, you welcomed it not as a word of humans but as it truly is, the word of God, which is at work in you who believe.

RESPONSORY Ps 141:2

When I call, Lord, hear my voice…
…which rises up to you.
Like incense set before you…
…which rises up to you.
Glory to the Father and to the Son and to the Holy Spirit:
…When I call, Lord, hear my voice
which rises up to you.

CANTICLE of MARY (The Magnificat)
LUKE 1:46-55

Antiphon   *My soul is stretched full*
                    with praise of the Lord.

+ **My soul** is stretched full with praise of the Lord,
and my spirit, beyond joy in God, my Savior,
who chose to lay eyes on this humble servant.

Behold, now and forward,
each and every age will call me blessed,
for the Mighty One did great things to me.

Holy is the name and the mercy
to generations and generations,
the ones fearing the One,

Who scattered the haughty of mind and heart,
pulled the powerful off their high place,
and lifted with dignity the humble in need.

The hungering are filled with good things,
the rich are sent away empty,
and servant Israel is given relief

with a memory of mercy to remember,
the promise spoken to our ancestors,
to Abraham and his descendants forever.

Glory…

                                                    Antiphon

INTERCESSIONS

- Lord, keep married couples in love…
- Grow our youth in wisdom and grace…
- For respect for the dignity of the human person…
- For all who have died…

- In gratitude for blessings, Abba thank you…
- For the sins of this day, Lord Jesus have mercy…
- With concerns over tomorrow, Holy Spirit help…

RESTLESS HEART *Confessions*, Saint Augustine

> To praise you, Lord,
> is the desire of the human,
> a little piece of your creation.
> You stir us to take pleasure in praising you,
> for you have made us for yourself,
> and our heart is restless until it rests in you.

OUR FATHER…

102, Text: see Galatians 3:8, William A. Dunkerley, 1908,
under the pseudonym of John Oxenham, altered
Music: MCKEE, CM; African American Spiritual,
arranged by Harry T. Burleigh, 1866-1949

WEEK II
TUESDAY MORNING

+ *God, come to my assistance;* Psalm 70:2
  Lord, make haste to help me!

  Glory...

A **In/ Christ there is no/ East or West**,
In him no South\ or/ North;
But/ one com-mu-nion of God's love
Through/-out/ the whole\ wide earth.

In/ Christ shall true hearts/ ev-'ry-where
Their high vo-ca\-tion/ find;
His/ ser-vice is the gold-en cord,
Close/ bind/-ing hu\-man-kind.

Join/ hands, then, mem-bers/ of the faith,
What-e'r your race\ may/ be!
Who/ serves my Fa-ther as his child
Is/ sure/-ly kin\ to me.

In/ Christ now meet both/ East and West,
In him meet South\ and/ North;
All/ souls of Christ are one in him
Through/-out/ the whole\ wide earth.

DAWN & DUSK WEEK II

additional verses to
In Christ There Is No East or West

B

In/ God's eye all are/ black and white,
All shades, pink, yell-ow and/ brown,
For to live, all sis-ters, bro-thers free,
Let our love for each fam-'ly a-stound.

Un-til ev-'ry-bo-dy/ matters to me
As much as my\ own/ tribe,
Un-til all the lives of our one race
Are/ cher-ished with-out\ div-ide,

Whe-ther Jew-ish, Chris-tian/, Mus-lim, Hin-du,
Bud-dhist, Sikh, Ba-hai or None,
Let us yet a-gree that dig-ni-ty
Is the birth-right of ev\-'ry-one.

102, Text: Stephen J. Wolf, 2022
Music: MCKEE, CM; African American Spiritual,
arranged by Harry T. Burleigh, 1866-1949

113, Text: Zechariah 7:9-10 & Matthew 25, Stephen J. Wolf, 2017,
tribute to the priesthood of Michael Johnston
Music: 87 87 D, HYFRYDOL, Rowland H. Prichard, 1811-1887
Popular melody for: *Love Divine All Love Excelling*

C **Proph-ets out/ of an-cient times\ to**
Je-sus out of Naz\-a-reth
and his saints by the Ho-ly Spir\-it
tell the truth to peo-ple of wealth:
If we want to live by our Lord's\ Way
we will watch for the mar-gin-al-ized.
Their\ wel-fare\ is our\ best mea/-sure\ of
our o-be-dience to God's de-signs.

Judge with hum-ble and faith-ful jus\-tice
know-ing who is Judge of us all
for your Lord/ a-lone knows ev-'ry thought
in the heart of each of us all.
To each o-ther show kind com-pass\-ion
as to wid-ows and or-phans, the poor,
with\ the res-i-dent strang\-er
    liv-ing in your midst;
keep your heart clean of self-ish store.

I was hung/-ry so you fed\ me,
thirst-y and you gave me to drink,
a-lien strang/-er and you wel-comed me,
nak-ed and you gave me to wear,
ill_ and\ you gave me tend-er care,
locked in pris-on, you vis-it-ed there;
when\ my peo-ple were griev-ing you
    bur/-ied their dead;
Christ your King is for you pre-pared.

PSALM 37

Antiphon *There is nothing entering from outside
that can defile a human;
rather things that defile
come from within.*   Mk 7:15

Fret not over those who do the bad;
envy not those who do wrong.
For like grass their efforts will soon wither,
and like the green plant they wilt away.

Trust in Adonai and do good!
Dwell in the land and enjoy safe pasture!
Delight in Adonai
who will give the desires of your heart.

Commit your way and your trust
to Adonai who will do it:
making your integrity shine like the dawn
and your justice like the noonday sun.

Be still before Adonai and wait with patience.
Fret not over the ways of the successful,
over schemes carried out by human beings.

Refrain from anger and turn from wrath!
Fret not; it brings only the bad,
for humans doing the bad will be cut off;
those who hope in Adonai will inherit the land.

A little while and bad doings will be no more;
you will look and not find them in their places.
But the meek will inherit the land
and they will enjoy greatness of peace.

Plotters of bad things to do to the just
gnash their teeth at them.
But the Lord laughs at them,
knowing their day is coming.

They draw their sword and bend their bow
to bring down the poor and the needy,
to slay those of the honest way.
Their sword will pierce into their own heart
and their bows will be broken.

Better the little bit of the just
than the wealth of many who do the bad,
for the powers of bad doers will be broken
while Adonai upholds the just.

Adonai knows the days of the blameless
and their inheritance will endure to forever.
They will not wither in times of disaster
and in days of famine they will enjoy plenty.

But bad ways will perish
and those who choose enmity with Adonai
will vanish like the beauty of fields;
like smoke they will vanish.

Psalm 37, continued

A doer of the bad borrows and does not repay,
but the just are generous and giving.
Their blessing is to live in the land;
but the curse of doing the bad is to be cut off.

The steps of human beings are made firm
by Adonai who delights in their way.
Though we stumble, we will not fall
for Adonai upholds us by the hand.

I was young and now I am old,
yet never have I seen the just forsaken
or their children begging bread.
Generous and lending all the day,
their children are a blessing.

Turn from the bad and do the good!
Then live to always!
For Adonai loves justice
and will not forsake the faithful…
The just will inherit the land
and they will dwell in her to forever.

The mouth of the just he utters wisdom
and the tongue she speaks justice.
The law of their God is in their heart
and their feet do not slip.

Bad ways lie in wait for the just,
seeking to kill them;
Adonai will not leave them under this power
nor let them be condemned when on trial.

Wait for Adonai and keep to the way
of the one who will exalt you to possess the land,
and you will see bad ways cut off.

I saw a ruthless human flourishing
like a native green tree,
but passing away is seen no more;
though I looked he was not to be found.

Consider the honest and observe the upright
for the future is for the person of peace.
But sinners sinning will be destroyed together;
the future of bad ways will be cut off.

The salvation of the just is from Adonai,
their stronghold in times of trouble.
Their help and deliverance and salvation,
their deliverance from ways that are bad,
is Adonai in whom they take refuge.

Glory…

Antiphon *There is nothing entering from outside
that can defile a human;
rather things that defile
come from within.* Mk 7:15

---

*'Out from within the human heart come bad thoughts, unchastities,
thefts, murders, adulteries, greeds, bad deeds, deceits, lewdness,
envies, blasphemy, arrogance and folly.' (Mk 7:21,22) So this
saying could also be called the parable of the latrine, as
our collective selfishness craps all over creation.*

PSALM 102

Antiphon *Whoever is not against you
is for you.* Lk 9:50

Adonai, hear my prayer
and let my cry for help come to you.
Hide not your faces from me
on the day of my distress.
Turn your ear to me on the day I call!
Quickly! Answer me!

My days vanish like smoke
and my bones burn like a glowing ember.
My heart is blighted like the grass
and so withered that I forget to eat my food.
Because of my loud groaning
my bones cling to my skin.

I am like a desert owl;
like an owl of the ruins lying awake,
I became like a bird alone on the housetop.
Enmity taunts me all the day,
railing against me, cursing by me.

I eat ash as food and mingle my drink with tears
because of your anger and your wrath,
for you took me up and threw me aside.
My days are like the long shadow,
and like the grass I wither away.

But you, Adonai, sit enthroned to forever;
your renown is to generation and generation.
You will arise.
You will have compassion on Zion,
for the time to show favor to her,
the appointed time, has come,
for her stones are dear to your servants
and her dust moves them to pity.

The nations will fear your name, Adonai,
and all the rulers of the earth your glory.
Adonai will rebuild Zion and appear in glory
and respond to the prayers of the destitute
and not despise their plea.

Let this be written for future generations
that people yet to be created may praise Yah.
Adonai looked down
from the high sanctuary place
viewing from heavens to earth,
to hear the groans of prisoners
and release those doomed to death

Declare in Zion the name of Adonai
and give praise in Jerusalem
when peoples assemble together,
and nations, to give worship.

Psalm 102, continued

Adonai broke my strength in mid-course
and cut short my days, and I said, "My El,
take me not away in the midst of my days.
Your years are through generation of generations.

In the beginning you founded the earth
and the heavens, the work of your hands.
They will perish, but you remain;
they will all wear out like a garment;
like clothing you will change them
and they will be discarded.

But you: the same; your years will never end.
Children of your servants will live
and their descendants
will be established before you."

Glory…

Antiphon   *Whoever is not against you*
               is for you.   Lk 9:50

Let us not look back
to the past with anger
nor to the future with fear
but around with awareness.

James Thurber, cartoonist d. 1961

PSALM 43

| Antiphon | *Blessed are those mourning,* | |
| | *for they will be comforted.* | Mt 5:4 |

God, vindicate me;
plead my cause against an ungodly nation;
rescue me from humans deceitful doing the bad.

God, my strength, why am I rejected?
Why must I go about mourning,
oppressed by enmity?

Send forth your light and your fidelity;
let them guide me to your dwellings
and bring me to your holy mountain.

Then I will go to the altar of God,
to El, my joy and delight,
and I will praise you with harp, God, my God.

Why are you downcast, my soul?
Why are you disturbed within me?
Put hope in God, whom I will yet praise,
the saving help of my face, my God.

Glory...

Antiphon

PSALM 101

Antiphon *A great prophet is risen among us,
and God has visited the people of God.* Lk 7:16

I will sing of *hesed* love and justice;
to you, Adonai, I will sing praise.
I will take care to act with integrity in life.
When will you come to me?

I will walk with integrity of heart
in the midst of my house.
I hate and will not set before my eyes
vile things that faithless people do;
they will not cling to me.

The corrupt heart will be far from me;
I will know nothing of the bad.
I will silence the secret slandering of a neighbor;
haughty eyes and proud hearts I will not endure.

My eyes are on the faithful of the land,
to dwell with me;
one who walks in a way of integrity
can be in my service.

Anyone practicing deceit
will not dwell in the midst of my house;
nor will one speaking falsehoods
stand before my eyes.

Each morning I will silence bad doers in the land
to cut off doings of bad things
from the city of Adonai.

Glory…

                                               Antiphon

ISAIAH 38:10-14,17b-20

Antiphon *The living alive praise Adonai.*

I asked, "Must I go in the prime of my days
through the gates of Sheol;
must I be robbed of the rest of my years?"

I said, "I will no longer see Adonai,
Adonai in the land of the living.
As a dweller of the place of cessation
I will look on humanity no longer."

My house was pulled down
and taken from me
like the tent of my shepherd;
I rolled up my life,
as a weaver cuts off from a loom.

From day to night you made an end of me.
I waited till dawn;
all my bones are broken as by a lion.
From day to night you made an end of me.

Like a swift or thrush I cried;
I moaned like the dove.
My eyes to the heavens grew weak.
Lord, troubles are at me; come to my aid…

In your love you have kept my self
out of the pit of destruction;
indeed you put behind your back all my sins.

Sheol cannot praise you
and death cannot sing to you praise,
nor can those going down the pit
hope for your faithfulness.

The living alive praise you, as I do this day.
Fathers and mothers tell the children
all about your faithfulness.

Adonai saves us;
we will play our stringed instruments
and sing in the temple of Adonai
all the days of our lives.

Glory...

                                                          Antiphon

---

For the Christian,
Easter makes all the difference,
and Easter is not just about our earthly
death. By the time we get to heaven, we will have
let go of everything unhealed about us, mainly through
forgiving enemies, family, friends, ourselves, even God. Jesus
is inviting us to the extent made possible by grace to live right
now today as if all this has happened, to be fully alive right now.

DANIEL 3:26-27,29,34-41b

Antiphon   *Lord, do not withhold your mercy.*

Blessed be you, Lord, God of our ancestors,
your name worthy of praise and glory forever.

For you are just in all you do;
all your deeds are true and your ways upright,
and all your judgments are true…

We have sinned and broken your law
in turning from you;
in all ways possible we have sinned…

For the sake of your name,
do not give us up to forever
and do not void your covenant.

Do not take your mercy from us
for the sake of Abraham your beloved,
for the sake of Isaac your servant,
and Israel, your holy one,

to whom you promised to multiply
descendants like the stars of heaven
and like the sand on the shore of the sea.

For we, Lord, have become
least of the other nations
and are brought low in the world this day
because of our sins.

We have in our day no ruler, prophet, or leader,
no burnt offering, sacrifice, oblation or incense,
no place to make an offering before you
and so find your favor.

But with a contrite heart and a humble spirit
may we be accepted
as if they were burnt offerings of rams and bulls
or thousands of fat lambs.

As such may our sacrifice be seen by you today
and may we follow you without reserve,
for no shame will come to those who trust you.

And so we follow you with all our heart;
we fear you and seek your face.

Glory…

Antiphon

Let nothing trouble.
Let nothing frighten.
Everything passes.
God never changes.
Patience obtains.
Whoever has God
wants for nothing.
God alone is enough.

Saint Teresa of Avila, d. 1582
written in the margin of her breviary

PSALM 65

Antiphon   *And that sown on the good soil*
is the one hearing
and understanding the word,
who indeed bears fruit.   Mt 13:23

For you, O God, praise we owe in Zion,
and to you will our vow be fulfilled.

You hear our prayer.
To you all humanity will come.
When my sins overwhelm me
you forgive them.

Blessed are the ones you choose
and bring near to live in your courts.
We are filled with the goodness of your house
and the holiness of your temple.

Deeds awesome and just are your answer,
God of our salvation,
hope of all the ends of the earth
and of the far seas.

You form mountains by your power,
arming yourself with strength.
You still the roar of the seas,
the roar of their waves,
and the turmoil of nations.

TUESDAY MORNING

Those who live in far away places
fear your wonders;
in dawns of morning and in the evening
you call forth songs of joy.

You care for the land and water her;
with an abundance you enrich her.
God's stream is as you ordain the earth:
filled with waters, providing grain.
You drench its furrows and level its ridges;
you soften her with showers and bless the crops.

You crown the year with your bounty;
paths overflow with your abundance.
The desert grasslands are overflowing
and the hills are clothed with gladness.

The meadows are covered with the flock
and valleys are coated with grain.
They shout for joy; for joy they sing.

Glory…

Antiphon

You do not have to change for God to love you.

Be grateful for your sins; they are carriers of grace.

Say goodbye to golden yesterdays
or your heart will never learn to love the present.

Anthoney de Mello, Jesuit
See *Hearts on Fire: Praying with Jesuits* by Michael Harter, S.J.

OFFICE OF READINGS and FIRST READING AT MASS

	Odd Years	**Even Years**
2 readings	*Romans 5:12-21*	*Genesis 12 & 13*
mass	Hebrews 6:10-20	1 Samuel 16:1-13
4 rdgs	*Romans 13*	*Genesis 28 & 29*
mass	Hebrews 12:1-4	2 Samuel 18:9-10,14b
6 rdgs	*1 Corinthians 7:25-40*	*1 Thessalonians 4*
mass	Genesis 6:5-8;7:1-5,10	James 1:12-18
8 rdgs	*1 Corinthians 15:20-34*	*2 Corinthians 9*
mass	Ben Sira 35:1-12	1 Peter 1:10-16
10 rdgs	*Joshua 2*	*Philippians 1:27-2:11*
mass	2 Corinthians 1:18-22	1 Kings 17:7-16
12 rdgs	*1 Samuel 1:1-19*	*Ezra 6*
mass	Genesis 13:2,5-8	2 Kings 19:9b-11,14-21
14 rdgs	*1 Samuel 19 & 20*	*Proverbs 8*
mass	Genesis 32:22-33	Hosea 8:4-7,11-13
16 rdgs	*2 Samuel 24*	*Job 13 & 14*
mass	Exodus 14:21-15:1	Micah 7:14-15,18-20
18 rdgs	*1 Kings 22*	*Joel 2*
mass	Numbers 12:1-13	Jeremiah 30:1-2,12-15,18-22
20 rdgs	*Ephesians 2:1-10*	*Ecclesiastes 3 & 4*
mass	Judges 6:11-24a	Ezekiel 28:1-10
22 rdgs	*Amos 2*	*1 Timothy 6:11-21*
mass	1 Thess 5:1-6,9-11	1 Corinthians 2:10b-16

	Odd Years	**Even Years**
24 rdgs	*Hosea 10*	*Esther 4*
mass	1 Timothy 3:1-13	1 Corinth 12:12-14,27-31a
26 rdgs	*2 Kings 17:1-8*	*Judith 6 & 7*
mass	Zechariah 8:20-23	Job 3:1-3,11-17,20-23
28 rdgs	*Jeremiah 2*	*Sirach 14*
mass	Romans 1:16-25	Galatians 5:1-6
30 rdgs	*Jeremiah 36*	*Wisdom 3*
mass	Romans 8:18-25	Ephesians 5:21-33
32 rdgs	*Ezekiel 8 & 9*	*2 Macabees 6*
mass	Wisdom 2:23-3:9	Titus 2:1-8,11-14
34 rdgs	*Ezekiel 37*	*Daniel 6*
mass	Daniel 2:31-45	Revelation 14:14-19

READING **1 THESSALONIANS 5:1-11**

Concerning the times and the seasons, brothers and sisters, you have no need to be written, for you know correctly that the day of the Lord comes as a thief in the night. Whenever they say, "peace and safety," then sudden destruction comes on them as the birth pang to a pregnant woman, and by no means may they escape. But you, brothers and sisters, are not in the darkness that the day should overtake you as a thief. For all of you are children of light and children of the day. We are not of the night nor of darkness.

1 Thessalonians 5, continued

And so let us not sleep as the rest, but let us watch and be sober. For those sleeping by night sleep, and those being drunk by night are drunk. But being of the day, let us be sober, putting on a breastplate of faith and of love and a helmet of hope in salvation because God did not appoint us to wrath but to come to salvation through our Lord Jesus Christ, the one who died for us, in order that whether we watch or we sleep, together with him we may live. And so, comfort one another and edify one another, as indeed you do.

RESPONSORY   Ps 119:147

Lord, hear my voice,…
   …my hope is in your word and promise.
Awake in the watch for dawn I cry for help,…
   …my hope is in your word and promise.
Glory to the Father and to the Son and to the Holy Spirit:
   …Lord, hear my voice; my hope is in your word
   and promise.

Gospel Canticle For Morning

Antiphon   *God raised salvation in the house of David.*

Gospel Reading for Tuesday of
Week **2** Mark 2:23-28 **14** Matt 9:32-38   **26** Luke 9:51-56
     4 Mark 5:21-30 **16** Matt 12:46-50   **28** Lk 11:37-41
     6 Mark 8:14-21 **18** Mt 15:1-2,10-14 **30** Lk 13:18-21
     8 Mark 10:28-31 **20** Matt 19:23-30   **32** Luke 17:7-10
    10 Matt 5:13-16 **22** Luke 4:31-37   **34** Luke 21:5-11
    12 Matt 7:6,12-14 **24** Luke 7:11-17

CANTICLE of ZECHARIAH (The Benedictus)
LUKE 1:68-79

+ **Blessed be** the Lord the God of Israel
who chose a people to visit with redemption,
and raised salvation in the house of David,
saving strength from God's own servant,

speaking from the age of the prophets
through the mouth of the holy prophet:
Salvation out of enmity,
even out of those who hate us,

to show our ancestors how mercy works, -
and to remember the holy promise of the Lord,
the covenant made for our ancestor Abraham,
calming our fear and making us free
to serve with holy justice before God all our days.

And you also child -
will be called a prophet of the Most High
for you will go before the Lord to prepare his way
and give to people a knowledge of salvation
known in accepting forgiveness of their sins.

From the tender mercy of our God,
the sun rising from the height will visit with light
for those who sit in the dark or shadow of death
and to guide our feet into the way of peace.

Glory...

Antiphon

PETITIONS FOR THE CONSECRATION OF THE DAY AND ITS WORK

- For the Church and her ministry and apostolates...

- For secular authorities and all serving as stewards...

- For people who are poor or sick or in sorrow...

- For peace and the basic needs of each human being...

- For those who weigh on my heart...

A FRANCISCAN BLESSING

adapted from a blessing by Sr. Ruth Fox, OSB

Bless us, O Lord, with discontent
at easy answers, half-truths, and superficiality,
that we may live out of the depths of our hearts.
Bless us, O Lord, with anger
at injustice, oppression, and exploitation of people,
that we may work for justice, freedom and peace.
Bless us, O Lord, with tears to shed
for those who suffer from pain, rejection,
starvation, and war,
that we may reach out
hands of Christ that bring comfort.
And bless us, O Lord, with enough foolishness
to believe that your way makes all the difference
so that your desire may be fulfilled.

OUR FATHER...

WEEK II
TUESDAY EVENING

+ *God, come to my assistance;* Psalm 70:2
  Lord, make haste to help me!

  Glory…

A

How love-ly is_ your dwell-ing place,
O Lord of hosts_! Be-lov-ed\ Lord!
My soul does yearn_ for the liv-ing God.
Bod-y and soul_ cry out, "my God!"

The spar-row finds_ a home to rest,
The swal-low too_ a set-tled\ nest,
The mock-ing-bird_ her\ place to sing:
"My home is with_ my God and King!"

Pass-ing through val_ -leys, hills and springs
And pools of wa_ -ter for the\ lost;
Hap-py in ref_ -uge\ pil-grims bring
Good news of God_, our Lord and King.

99 (first three verses), Text: Psalm 84, by Stephen J. Wolf, 2007,
tribute to Thomas Merton
Music: O WALY WALY, LM; traditional English
Popular melody for: *As The Deer Longs For Flowing Streams*

B

Be still, my soul, the Lord is at your side/!
Bear pa-tient-ly the cross of grief or pain;
Leave to your God to or-der and pro-vide/
In ev-'ry change, who faith-ful will re-main.
Be still, my soul, your best, your heav'n-ly friend/
Through thorn-y ways leads to a joy-ful end.

Be still, my soul, your God does un-der-take/
To guide the fu-ture as God has the past;
Your hope, your con-fi-dence let noth-ing shake/
All now mys-te-rious shall be bright at last.
Be still, my soul, the waves and winds still know/
His voice who ruled while dwell-ing here be-low.

Be still, my soul, the hour is has-t'ning on/
When we shall be for-ev-er with the Lord,
When dis-ap-point-ment, grief, and fear are gone/,
Sor-row for-got, love's pur-est joys re-stored.
Be still, my soul, when change and tears are past/,
All safe and bless-ed we shall meet at last.

135, Text: Katherina von Schlegel;
in *Neue Sammlung Geistlicher Lieder,* 1752;
translated by Jane Borthwick, 1813-1897
Music: 10 10 10 10 10 10 FINLANDIA; Jean Sibleius, 1865-1957

PSALM 13

Antiphon   *Emmanuel! God is with us!*   Mt 1:23

Until when, Adonai?
Will you forget me to forever?
Until when will you hide your faces from me?
Until when must I wrestle
with thoughts of my soul
and sorrow in my heart by day?
Until when will enmity triumph?

Look! Answer me, my God Adonai!
Give light to my eyes, or I will sleep the death!
Or enmity will say, "I overcame that one,"
and foes will rejoice when I fall.

But my trust is in your unfailing love;
my heart rejoices in your salvation.
I will sing to Adonai, who is good to me.

Glory...

Antiphon

---

*'Until When?' is also
translated 'How Long?'*

PSALM 53

Antiphon *Whoever does not receive the reign of God as a child by no means may enter into it.* Mk 10:15

In the heart of a fool is said, "There is no God."
The bad way is vile and corrupt;
there is no one doing good.

God looks from the heavens
on children of humanity
to see if there is one who understands,
one who is seeking God.

All of them turned away together;
they became corrupt;
there is no one doing good, not even one.

Will the ones doing the bad never learn?
Devouring my people, they eat bread;
they do not call on God.

There they dreaded as dread had not been,
for God scattered the bones of attackers
put to shame in God's rejection.

Who would be brought from Zion
for the salvation of Israel?
When God restores the people of God,
let Jacob rejoice, let Israel be glad.

Glory...

Antiphon

PSALM 54:1-6,8-9

Antiphon *The Son of Humanity will be betrayed*
into human hands and they will kill him,
and three days after being killed
he will rise up. Mk 9:31

God, save me by your name
and by your might vindicate me.
God, hear my prayer!
Listen to the words of my mouth!

For strangers attack me
and ruthless people seek my life
without regard for God before them.
See, God is helping me!
The Lord sustains my self…

With a freewill offering I will sacrifice to you;
I will praise, Adonai, your good name,
for my eyes have seen enmity
but you delivered me from every trouble.

Glory…

Antiphon

The opposite of war
isn't peace…; it's creation.

Jonathan Larson, d. 1996, composer/playwright

PSALM 49

Antiphon *You cannot serve God and mammon;*
where your treasure is
there also will your heart be. Mt 6:24b,21

Hear this all peoples! Listen, all alive in the world!
Men and women, all sons and daughters,
rich and poor alike:

My mouth will speak words of wisdom
and my heart utter understanding of things.
I will turn an ear to a proverb;
I will expound my riddle with harp music.

Why should I fear in days of the bad
the deceivers who surround me,
the trusters of wealth,
and the boasters of the greatness of their riches?

No human can redeem redemption of another,
nor for oneself give a ransom to God.
Ransom of a life is costly; no ransom can be enough
for one to live to forever and not see the decay.

For we see that even wise people die;
like the foolish and the senseless they perish,
and leave all their wealth to others.

Their thoughts are of their houses to forever
as their dwelling for generations and generation,
and so they call lands by their own names.

The human, despite riches, does not endure,
but perishes just like the beasts.

This is their fate who trust in themselves
and their followers who give them approval.
Like the sheep they are destined for Sheol,
and death will be their shepherd.

Upright ones will rule over them in the morning
and their form will decay in Sheol, their mansion.
But God will redeem my soul
and take me from the hand of Sheol.

Be not overawed when human beings grow rich,
when they increase the splendor of their houses.
For in death they will take none of it;
with none of their splendor will they descend.

Though during their lives they blessed themselves,
and people do praise you when you prosper,
they will go to the generation of their ancestors
and never see light to forever.

Like the beast that must perish
so is a human with riches
but still poor in understanding.

Glory...

Antiphon

PSALM 137:1-6

Antiphon *God so loved the cosmos,*
and so gave the only begotten Son that
everyone believing in him may not perish
but have eternal life.   Jn 3:16

By rivers of Babylon, there we sat and wept
as we remembered Zion;
On the poplars in their midst we hung our harps,

for there our captors asked us for words of song,
our tormentors for joy:
"Sing for us from the songs of Zion!"

How can we sing in a foreign land
a song of Adonai?
If I forget you, Jerusalem,
may my right hand forget its skill.

May my tongue cling to the roof of my mouth
if I remember you not,
if I consider any but Jerusalem
as the height of my joy.

Glory…

Antiphon

Scholars suggest that what we know as the Pentateuch, the first five books, the Torah, were edited 2,500 years ago in the Babylonian Exile, not knowing if they would return to Jerusalem.

PSALM 138

Antiphon *Put out into the deep*
and let down your nets for a catch.   Lk 5:4

I will praise you, **Adonai**, with all my heart.
Before those so-called "gods"
I will sing my praise of you.
I will bow toward your holy temple
and I will praise your name
for your love and your fidelity.

You are exalted above all,
your name and your word.
On the day I called, then you answered me.
You made me bold and stout in my heart.

May all the rulers of the earth praise you, Adonai,
when they hear the words of your mouth.
May they sing of the ways of Adonai,
for great is the glory of Adonai.

Though on high, Adonai looks upon the lowly
and knows the proud from afar.
Though I walk in the midst of trouble,
you keep me alive
against the anger of enmity.

Psalm 138, continued

You stretch out your hand, your right hand,
and you save me.
Adonai will fulfill me.
Your love, Adonai, is to forever.
Abandon not the works of your hands.

Glory…

Antiphon   *Put out into the deep
and let down your nets for a catch.*   Lk 5:4

REVELATION 4:8b,11; 5:9,10,12,13b

Antiphon *Holy, Holy, Holy,*
Lord God Almighty
who was and is and is to come.   Rev 4:8b

Worthy are you, our Lord and our God,
to receive the glory and honor and power,
for you have created all things,
and by your will all things were created and are.

Worthy are you to receive the scroll and unseal it
for you were sacrificed, and by your blood
ransomed for God those from every
tribe and tongue and people and nation.

You made of them for our God
a realm of royals and priests,
and thus will they reign over the earth.

Worthy is the Lamb, sacrificed to receive
the power and riches and wisdom and strength
and honor and glory and blessing.

Glory...   Antiphon

READING **ROMANS 3:21-31**

Now without law a righteousness of God has shown forth, witnessed by the law and the prophets, a righteousness of God through faith in Jesus Christ for all who believe.

Romans 3, continued

There is no difference, for all have sinned and come short of the glory of God, and are justified freely by God's grace through the redemption in Christ Jesus, in whom God set forth an expiation through faith by his blood, for a showing forth of his righteousness because of the passing by of the sins previously committed, in the forebearance of God, for the showing forth of righteousness in the present time, that God should be just and justifying those of faith in Jesus.

And so, where is the boasting? It was shut out. Through what law? Of works? No, but through a law of faith. For we reckon a person to be justified by faith without works of the law. Or is God of Jews only? Not also of nations? Yes, also of nations, since there is one God who will justify circumcision by faith and uncircumcision through the faith. And so, do we destroy law through faith? May it not be. But we support the law.

RESPONSORY   Ps 16:11

You will make known to me the path of life,…
   …fullness of joy in your presence.
Eternal pleasure at your right hand,…
   …fullness of joy in your presence.
Glory to the Father and to the Son and to the Holy Spirit:
   …You will make known to me the path of life,
   fullness of joy in your presence.

CANTICLE of MARY (The Magnificat)
LUKE 1:46-55

Antiphon *My spirit is beyond joy*
in God, my Savior

+ **My soul** is stretched full with praise of the Lord,
and my spirit, beyond joy in God, my Savior,
who chose to lay eyes on this humble servant.

Behold, now and forward,
each and every age will call me blessed,
for the Mighty One did great things to me.

Holy is the name and the mercy
to generations and generations,
the ones fearing the One,

Who scattered the haughty of mind and heart,
pulled the powerful off their high place,
and lifted with dignity the humble in need.

The hungering are filled with good things,
the rich are sent away empty,
and servant Israel is given relief

with a memory of mercy to remember,
the promise spoken to our ancestors,
to Abraham and his descendants forever.

Glory…

Antiphon

INTERCESSIONS

- For a culture of vocations all over the world…
- For all who have died…

- In gratitude for blessings…; Abba thank you.
- For the sins of this day…; Lord Jesus have mercy.
- With concerns over tomorrow…; Holy Spirit help.

PRAYER of the CONFIRMED   from the Rite of Confirmation

Almighty God,
Abba of our Lord Jesus Christ,
who brought your servants to new birth
by water and the Holy Spirit,
freeing us from sin:
send upon us, O Lord,
the Holy Spirit, the Paraclete;
give us the spirit of wisdom and understanding,
the spirit of counsel and fortitude,
the spirit of knowledge and piety;
fill us with the spirit of the fear of the Lord,
through Christ our Lord.
Amen.

OUR FATHER…

WEEK II
WEDNESDAY MORNING

+ *God, come to my assistance;* Psalm 70:2
  Lord, make haste to help me!

  Glory...

Praise, my soul, the King of heav-en;
To these feet your trib-ute bring.
Ran-somed, healed, re-stored, for-giv-en,
Ev-er-more God's prais-es sing:
Al-le-lu-ia! Al-le-lu-ia!
Praise the ev-er-last-ing King.

Praise for grace and fav-or giv-en
In our an-ces-tral dis-tress.
Praise God, still the same as ev-er,
Slow to chide and swift to bless.
Al-le-lu-ia! Al-le-lu-ia!
Glo-rious love and faith-ful-ness.

As a par-ent, tend-ing, spar-ing,
Well our fee-ble frame God knows.
Gent-ly bear-ing and res-cu-ing
Us from all who'd be our foes.
Al-le-lu-ia! Al-le-lu-ia!
Wide-ly yet the mer-cy flows.

121, Text: from Psalm 103, Henry F. Lyte, 1834, altered
Music: 87 87 87 LAUDA ANIMA, John Goss, 1869

PSALM 103

Antiphon   *Forgive each of your siblings*
           from your heart.   Mt 18:35

My soul, praise Adonai!
All my inmost being, praise the holy Name!
My soul, praise Adonai,
whose benefits are not to be forgotten:

forgiveness of all of your sins,
healing of all your diseases,
redemption of your life from the pit,
crowning you with love and compassion,
satisfying your desire with good,
renewing your youths like the eagle,
working vindication
and justice for all who are oppressed.

Adonai's ways are made known to Moses
and the deeds to peoples of Israel.

Compassionate and gracious is Adonai,
slow to anger and abundant in love,
neither accusing to always
nor harboring anger to forever,
neither treating us in accord with our sins
nor repaying us in accord with our iniquities.

As high as the heavens are above the earth
so great is the love for ones who fear Adonai.
As far as the east is from the west
so far from us are our transgressions removed.

As a father has compassion on his children,
so has Adonai compassion on ones fearing,
knowing our form and remembering we are dust.

The days of a human are like the grass
flourishing like flowers of the field,
for wind blows over and it is no more
and the place remembers it no more.

But the love of Adonai for the awestruck
is from everlasting to everlasting,
with favor for children of their children,
of those keeping the covenant
and remembering to obey the precepts.

Adonai established a throne in the heavens,
a reign to rule over all.
Praise Adonai, you angels,
you strong and mighty ones doing the bidding,
obeying the voice of the word.

Praise Adonai, you hosts,
you serving and doing the will.
Praise Adonai, all you works,
in all places of the dominion.
My soul, praise Adonai!

Glory... Antiphon

PSALM 39

Antiphon *You are the salt of the earth;*
you are the light of the cosmos.   Mt 5:13a,14a

I said, "I will watch my ways
of sinning with my tongue;
I will put on my mouth a muzzle
as long as temptation is in my presence."
So in silent stillness I said nothing,
and still my anguish increased.

My heart grew hot inside me;
in my meditation a fire burned.
I spoke with my tongue,
"Show me, Adonai, my end,
what is the number of my days;
let me know how fleeting I am.

See the handbreadths you made!
My days and my span are as nothing before you.
Indeed, each of all humanity stands as a breath.
Indeed, as a phantom the human goes out.
Indeed, vainly bustling about, heaping up wealth
without knowing who will get it."

But what am I looking for now, Lord?
My hope she is in you.
Save me from all my transgressions!
Make me not the scorn of fools.
I was silent and opened not my mouth,
for you, you have done it.

Remove your scourge from me;
from the touch of your hand I am overcome.
With a rebuke for sin you discipline the human
and you consume our wealth like a moth;
indeed we are each but a breath.

Hear my prayer, Adonai, and my cry for help;
listen, El, and be not deaf to my weeping.
For I am with you as a passing guest,
an alien stranger like all my ancestors.
Look away from me that I may rejoice
before I depart and am no more.

Glory…

                                                 Antiphon

In years to come when I
look back on my life in these
days, what will I wish had gotten
just a little bit more of my attention?

PSALM 77

Antiphon *Blessed are those who are persecuted*
for what is right, for theirs is
the reign of heaven. Mt 5:10

I cry aloud for God, indeed I cried for help.
My cry is for God to hear me.

In the day of my distress I sought the Lord,
my hand was stretched in the night without tiring;
my soul refused to be comforted.
I remembered God and I groaned;
I meditated and my spirit grew faint.

You kept open the lids of my eyes;
I was troubled and could not speak.
I thought of former days and of years long ago.
I remembered my song in the night;
my heart mused and searched my spirit,

"Will the Lord reject to forever,
never to show favor again?
Is the unfailing love vanished to forever?
Has the promise failed for all generations?
Has God forgotten mercy
or withheld compassion in anger?"

WEDNESDAY MORNING

Then I thought, "My appeal is this,
the years at the right hand of the Most High."
I will remember the deeds of Adonai;
yes, I will remember your long-ago miracles.
I will meditate on all of your works
and ponder your mighty deeds.

God in your holiness way,
what "god" is as great as God?
You are the God who does miracles;
you display among the peoples your power.
With your arm you redeemed your people,
the descendants of Jacob and Joseph.

The waters saw you, God,
the waters saw you and writhed;
indeed the depths were convulsed.
Clouds poured down waters,
thunder resounded in the skies,
and your arrows flashed around.

Your thunder sounded in the whirlwind,
lightnings lit up the world;
the earth trembled and quaked.
Through the sea is your path,
and your way through mighty waters,
though your footprints were not seen.

You led your people like the flock
by the hand of Moses and Aaron.

Glory...   Antiphon

PSALM 108

Antiphon *The one doing the truth*
comes to the light. Jn 3:21

My heart is steadfast, God; I will sing
and even my soul will make music.
Awake the harp and lyre;
I will wake up the dawn!

I will praise you among the nations, Adonai,
and I will sing of you among the peoples,
for greater than above the heavens is your love
and to the skies your fidelity.

Be exalted above the heavens, God,
your glory over all the earth
that your loved ones may be delivered.
Save your right hand, and help me!

God spoke from the sanctuary:
"I will triumph and parcel out Shechem,
and measure the valley of Succoth;
mine are Gilead and Manasseh,

Ephraim my head helmet,
Judah my scepter,
and Moab my washbasin;
On Edom I toss my sandals
and over Philistia I shout in triumph."

Who will bring me to the Fortress City?
Who will lead me into Edom?
Have you, God, not rejected us,
and not gone out, God, with our armies?

Against enmity give to us aid,
for worthless is human help.
In God will we gain victory…

Glory…

Antiphon

1 SAMUEL 2:1-10

Antiphon   *My spirit rejoices in God my Savior.*   Lk 1:47

My heart rejoices in Adonai,
my horn is lifted high in Adonai.

My mouth boasts over enmity,
for I delight in being delivered.
There is no Holy One like Adonai,
indeed there is no one who compares;
there is no Rock like our God.

Arrogant pride is coming from their mouth.
Do not keep talking so proudly
or proudly let arrogance come from your mouth,
for Adonai is God who knows,
by whom all deeds are weighed.

Bows of warriors are broken
but those stumbling are armed with strength.
The full hire themselves out for more food,
but the hungry ones hunger no more.
She who was barren bore seven sons;
blessed with many, another is pining away.

Adonai allows death and is making alive,
brings down to Sheol and is raising up.
Adonai allows poverty and is sending wealth,
humbling and exalting,
raising the poor from the dust
and the needy from ash-heaps
to sit with royals and inherit thrones of honor.

For Adonai's are the foundations of the earth,
setting the world upon them.
The feet of the saints will be guarded
but doers of the bad will be silenced in darkness.

For not by strength does the human prevail;
Adonai shatters opposition,
thundering from the heavens.
Adonai will judge the ends of the earth,
give strength, and raise the horn
of the one chosen and anointed.

Glory…

Antiphon

All shall be well
and all shall be well and
all manner of things shall be well.

Julian of Norwich, d. 1416

ISAIAH 61:10-62:5

Antiphon   *My God has clothed me*
            in garments of salvation.

To delight, I delight in Adonai,
my soul rejoices in my God,
who clothed me in garments of salvation
and arrayed me in a robe of justice,
as spouses dress their heads like priests
and adorn themselves with jewels,

for as the soil makes the sprout come up
and as a garden makes seeds to grow
so will Sovereign Adonai
make justice spring up
and praise before all the nations.

For the sake of Zion, I will not keep silent;
for the sake of Jerusalem I will not remain quiet,
till vindication comes out like the dawn
and salvation blazes like a torch.

The nations will see your vindication
and all the rulers your glory
and you will be called by a new name
that the mouth of Adonai will bestow.
You will be a crown of splendor
in the hand of Adonai
and a royal diadem in the hand of your God.

No longer will you be called One Being Deserted,
nor will your name be called Desolation,
but you will be called "my delight is in her"
and your land "espoused."
Adonai will delight in you
and your land will be married.

As young folks marry each other,
your Builder will marry you;
and as a newlywed rejoices over a spouse,
so will your God rejoice over you.

Glory...

                                                            Antiphon

---

Intimacy is a basic human need and
I tend to it or it will find unhealthy ways
to tend to me. It is the grace of being known,
the blessing of being with a friend or a spouse who
knows me so well that I am free to simply be who I am.
See *Being Spouses* by Stephen Joseph Wolf

PSALM 97

Antiphon　　*Fill the water pots with water;*
now draw and carry some
to the master of the feast.　　　Jn 2:7,8

Adonai reigns; let the earth be glad.
Let all the distant shores rejoice.
Clouds and thick darkness surround the throne
founded on justice and right.

Fire goes before,
consuming enmity on every side.
Lightnings light up the world;
the earth sees and trembles.

Mountains melt like wax before Adonai,
before the Lord of all the earth.
The heavens proclaim God's justice
and all peoples see the glory.

Let those who worship idols be shamed,
those boasting in their images.
Worship God, all you "gods."

Zion hears and rejoices
and the villages of Judah are glad
because of your judgments, Adonai.

WEDNESDAY MORNING

For you, Adonai,
are Most High over all the earth,
far exalted above all the "gods."

The bad is despised by lovers of Adonai,
who guards the lives of faithful ones
and delivers them from the hands
of doers of the bad.

Light dawns for the just
and joy for the honest of heart.
Rejoice in Adonai, you just,
and praise the holy name.

Glory…

Antiphon

Contemplation is the realization of
God in our life, not just realization
of an idea or something partial, but
a realization of the whole thing – the
realization that we belong totally to God
and God has given Godself totally to us.
It has all happened and it is going on now…
You don't really see this. It happens and you
see it and you don't. You get glimpses of it, you
believe it, your life is based on it, and sometimes it
seems to be in complete contradiction or impossible, and
yet it is there. It is the place we are always coming back to.
See *Why We Live In Community* by Thomas Merton

PSALM 146

Antiphon   *Blessed are the meek,*
            for they will inherit the earth.   Mt 5:5

Hallelujah!

Praise Adonai, my soul!
I will praise Adonai during my life;
I will sing praise to my God while I still am.

Trust neither royalty nor human beings
in whom there is no salvation.
Their spirit-breath departs,
and they return to the ground.
On that day their plans come to nothing.

Blessed are they whose help is the God of Jacob,
whose hope and God are Adonai,
the maker of heaven and earth
and the sea and all that is in them.

The one staying faithful to forever
defends justice for the oppressed
and gives food to the hungry.

Adonai sets prisoners free;
Adonai gives sight to the blind;
Adonai lifts those who are bowed down;
Adonai loves the just.

Adonai watches over alien strangers,
and sustains the orphan and the widow,
but frustrates the ways that are bad.
Adonai reigns to forever,
your God, Zion,
from generation to generation.

Hallelujah!

Glory…

                                                        Antiphon

---

God has
distributed gifts
and blessings in such
a way that every person
has a particular place and
purpose within society — and
thus everyone is equally necessary
for a society to function well…
How wonderful it would be if villages
and towns could become like large families.
Then heaven would come down to earth.

See *On Living Simply: the Golden Voice of John Chrysostom*
edited by Robert Van de Weyer

OFFICE OF READINGS and FIRST READING AT MASS

	Odd Years	**Even Years**
2 readings	*Romans 6:1-11*	*Genesis 14*
mass	Hebrews 7:1-3,15-17	1 Samuel 17:32-33,37
4 rdgs	*Romans 14*	*Genesis 31*
mass	Hebrews 12:4-7,11-15	2 Samuel 24:2,9-17
6 rdgs	*1 Corinthians 8*	*1 Thessalonians 5*
mass	Genesis 8:6-13,20-22	James 1:19-27
8 rdgs	*1 Corinthians 15:35-58*	*2 Corinthians 10:1-11:6*
mass	Ben Sira 36:1,5-6,10-17	1 Peter 1:18-25
10 rdgs	*Joshua 3 & 4*	*Philippians 2:12-30*
mass	2 Corinthians 3:4-11	1 Kings 18:20-39
12 rdgs	*1 Samuel 1:20-2:21*	*Ezra 7*
mass	Genesis 15:1-12,17-18	2 Kings 22:8-13;23:1-3
14 rdgs	*1 Samuel 21 & 22*	*Proverbs 9*
mass	Gen 41:51-57;42:5-7a,17-24a	Hosea 10:1-3,7-8,12
16 rdgs	*1 Chronicles 22*	*Job 18*
mass	Exodus 16:1-5,9-15	**Jeremiah** 1:1,4-10
18 rdgs	*2 Kings 1*	*Joel 3*
mass	Num 13:1-2a,25-14:1,26-29,34-35	Jeremiah 31:1-7
20 rdgs	*Ephesians 2:11-22*	*Ecclesiastes 5 & 6*
mass	Judges 9:6-15	Ezekiel 34:1-11

WEDNESDAY MORNING

	Odd Years	**Even Years**
22 rdgs	*Amos 3*	*2 Timothy 1*
mass	**Colossians** 1:1-8	1 Corinthians 3:1-9
24 rdgs	*Hosea 11*	*Esther C*
mass	1 Timothy 3:14-16	1 Corinthians 12:31-13:13
26 rdgs	*2 Kings 17:24-41*	*Judith 8 & 9*
mass	**Nehemiah** 2:1-8	Job 9:1-12,14-16
28 rdgs	*Jeremiah 3*	*Sirach 15*
mass	Romans 2:1-11	Galatians 5:18-25
30 rdgs	*Jeremiah 24*	*Wisdom 4*
mass	Romans 8:26-30	Ephesians 6:1-9
32 rdgs	*Ezekiel 10 & 11*	*2 Macabees 7:1-19*
mass	Wisdom 6:1-11	Titus 3:1-7
34 rdgs	*Ezekiel 38*	*Daniel 8*
mass	Daniel 5:1-6,13-14,16-17,23-28	Revelation 15:1-4

READING — **ROMANS 8:35,37-39**

Who will separate us from the love of Christ? Affliction? Distress? Persecution? Famine? Nakedness? Peril? The Sword? But in all these things we overconquer through the one who has loved us.

For I am persuaded that not death, nor life, nor angels, nor rulers, nor present things, nor things coming, nor powers, nor height, nor depth, nor any other creature will be able to separate us from the love of God in Christ Jesus, our Lord.

RESPONSORY — Ps 34:2

My soul will boast in the Lord...
   ...and at all times.
Praise always on my lips...
   ...and at all times.
Glory to the Father and to the Son and to the Holy Spirit:
   ...My soul will boast in the Lord, and at all times.

Gospel Canticle For Morning

Antiphon   *Show us, Lord, how mercy works,
and remember your holy covenant.*

Gospel Reading for Wednesday of
Week					
2	Mark 3:1-6	**14**	Matt 10:1-7	**26**	Luke 9:57-62
4	Mark 6:1-6	**16**	Matt 13:1-9	**28**	Lk 11:42-46
6	Mark 8:22-26	**18**	Matt 15:21-28	**30**	Lk 13:22-30
8	Mark 10:32-45	**20**	Matt 20:1-16	**32**	Lk 17:11-19
10	Matt 5:17-19	**22**	Luke 4:38-44	**34**	Lk 21:12-19
12	Matt 7:15-20	**24**	Luke 7:31-35		

CANTICLE of ZECHARIAH (The Benedictus)
LUKE 1:68-79

+ **Blessed be** the Lord the God of Israel
who chose a people to visit with redemption,
and raised salvation in the house of David,
saving strength from God's own servant,

speaking from the age of the prophets
through the mouth of the holy prophet:
Salvation out of enmity,
even out of those who hate us,

to show our ancestors how mercy works, -
and to remember the holy promise of the Lord,
the covenant made for our ancestor Abraham,
calming our fear and making us free
to serve with holy justice before God all our days.

And you also child -
will be called a prophet of the Most High
for you will go before the Lord to prepare his way
and give to people a knowledge of salvation
known in accepting forgiveness of their sins.

From the tender mercy of our God,
the sun rising from the height will visit with light
for those who sit in the dark or shadow of death
and to guide our feet into the way of peace.

Glory…

                                                              Antiphon

PETITIONS FOR THE CONSECRATION TO GOD
OF THE DAY AND ITS WORK

- For the Church and her ministry and apostolates…

- For secular authorities and all serving as stewards…

- For people who are poor or sick or in sorrow…

- For peace and the basic needs of each human being…

LENTEN PRAYER FOR VOCATIONS

> God of compassion,
> through honest awareness of sin
> and the grace of repentance
> you protect us from what could harm us
> and lead us to what will save us.
> Your Son, Jesus Christ, accepted the cross
> and redeemed your sons and daughters.
> Through prayer, fasting, and almsgiving
> you call us each to a unique vocation
> of health, healing and mercy.
> May we embrace the paschal mystery
> and faithful to the gospel of Christ
> become a people who worship you
> in spirit and in truth.

OUR FATHER…

Lord, do for me today what I cannot do for myself.
See *The Anonymous Disciple* by Gerard Goggins

WEEK II
WEDNESDAY EVENING

+ *God, come to my assistance;* Psalm 70:2
  Lord, make haste to help me!

  Glory...

A **Shep-herd of souls**, re-fresh and bless
Your cho-sen pil-grim flock
With man-na in the wil-der-ness,
And wa-ter from the rock.

Hung-ry and thirs-ty, mor-tal, weak,
As you would come and go:
Our souls the joys of heav-en seek
Which from your pass-ion flow.

We would not live by bread a-lone,
But by your Word of grace,
In strength of which we trav-el on
To our a-bi-ding place.

Be known to us in break-ing bread,
But do not then de-part;
Sa-vior, a-bide with us and spread
Your ta-ble in our heart.

124, Text: James Mongtomery, 1825, altered
Music: ST. AGNES, CM, John B. Dykes, 1866

B **All crea-tures of our God and King**
Lift up your voice and with us sing,
Al-le-lu-ia! Al-le-lu-ia!
You burn-ing sun with gold-en beam,
You sil-ver moon with soft-er gleam!
Al-le-lu-ia! Al-le-lu-ia!
Al-le-lu-ia! Al-le-lu-ia! Al-le-lu_-ia!

You flow-ing wa-ter, pure and clear,
Make mu-sic for your Lord to hear,
Al-le-lu-ia! Al-le-lu-ia!
You fire so mas-ter-ful and bright,
Giv-ing the hu-man warmth and light.
Al-le-lu-ia! Al-le-lu-ia!
Al-le-lu-ia! Al-le-lu-ia! Al-le-lu_-ia!

Dear moth-er earth, who day by day
Un-fold your bless-ings on our way,
Al-le-lu-ia! Al-le-lu-ia!
Flow-ers and fruits, all in you grown,
And God's own glo-ry let be shone.
Al-le-lu-ia! Al-le-lu-ia!
Al-le-lu-ia! Al-le-lu-ia! Al-le-lu_-ia!

You rush-ing winds that are so strong,
You clouds that sail in heav'n a-long,
Al-le-lu-ia! Al-le-lu-ia!
You ri-sing moon, in praise re-joice,
You lights of eve-ning, find a voice!
Al-le-lu-ia!   Al-le-lu-ia!
Al-le-lu-ia!   Al-le-lu-ia!   Al-le-lu_-ia!

And you most kind and gen-tle death,
Wait-ing to hush our la-test breath,
Al-le-lu-ia! Al-le-lu-ia!
You lead to home the child of God,
As Christ our Lord the way has trod.
Al-le-lu-ia!   Al-le-lu-ia!
Al-le-lu-ia!   Al-le-lu-ia!   Al-le-lu_-ia!

Let all things their Cre-a-tor bless,
And wor-ship God in hum-ble-ness,
Al-le-lu-ia! Al-le-lu-ia!
Praise, praise the Fa-ther, praise the Son,
And praise the Spir-it, Three in One!
Al-le-lu-ia!   Al-le-lu-ia!
Al-le-lu-ia!   Al-le-lu-ia!   Al-le-lu_-ia!

78, Text: Francis of Assisi, 1225; translated by William H. Draper,
Public School Hymn Book, 1919, altered.
Music: LASST UNS ERFREUEN, LM with alleluias;
Geistliche Kirchengesange, 1623

PSALM 52

Antiphon *Laying his hands
on each one brought to him,
Jesus healed those ailing with disease.* Lk 4:40b

Why, **mighty liar**, do you boast of the bad
to the disgrace of El all the day?
Your tongue plots destruction
like a sharpened razor, practicing deceit.

You love the bad rather than the good,
lies rather than honest speech.
Your tongue of deceit loves every harmful word.

Surely El will bring you down,
snatch you from your tent,
and uproot you from the land of the living.

Then the just will see and fear,
and they will laugh at you.
See the one who did not see God as the refuge,
but grew strong by destruction
and trusted in great wealth.

But I am like an olive tree
flourishing in the house of God;
I trust in God's unfailing love forever and ever.

I will praise you to forever
for what you have done,
and in the presence of your saints
I will hope in you
for your name is good.

Glory...

                                                            Antiphon

PSALM 75

Antiphon* *Let the one of you without sin
be the first to throw a stone.*   Jn 8:7

*One
adulterer
is there, the
other is not. A mob
of self-appointed judges
demands judgment. After
the words of the just judge, all
the stones drop to the earth, one by one,
beginning with the eldest, presumed to be the
most wise & just, but now with new understanding.

We give thanks to you, God;
we give thanks for your name is Near,
and they tell of your wonderful deeds.

You choose and appoint the time
to be the just judge.
The earth quakes, and all its people,
and you hold her pillars firm.

I say to the arrogant, "boast not,"
and to doers of the bad, "lift not your horn;
lift not your horns against the heavens
nor speak with arrogance."

For there is no one from east or from west
and no one from the desert to exalt.
But God is the one judge,
bringing low this one and raising another.

A cup is full in the hand of Adonai,
and wine foams and mixed spice pours out.
Indeed from this they drink to her dregs,
all doers of the bad on the earth.

And I will rejoice to forever,
and sing praise to the God of Jacob.
All the horns of doers of the bad will be cut off,
and the horns of the just will be lifted up.

Glory...

Antiphon

PSALM 94

Antiphon *Jesus touched her hand, the fever left her,*
and rising she began serving them.   Mt 8:15

God of vindication,
Adonai, God of vindication, shine forth!
Rise up, One Judge of the earth!
Pay back desserts to the proud!

Until when, Adonai, will doers of the bad?
Until when will doers of the bad be jubilant?
They pour out and speak arrogance;
all the doers of the bad make boast.

They crush your people, Adonai,
and they oppress your very own.
They slay the widow and alien;
they murder the orphan.

They say Adonai does not see
and the God of Jacob pays no heed.
Take heed, senseless ones among the people;
fools, when will you become wise?

Does the one who shapes the ear not hear?
Does the one who forms the eye not see?
Will the one who disciplines nations not punish?
Will the one who teaches have no knowledge?

Adonai knows the thoughts of humans,
that they are puffs of air.

Blessed is the one you instruct, Adonai,
the one you teach from your law
to grant relief from days of trouble
till a pit is dug for doers of the bad,

for the people of Adonai will not be rejected,
your very own never forsaken.
Judgment will again be just;
all the upright of heart will follow it.

Who will rise up for me against doers of the bad?
Who will take a stand against people doing bad?
Unless Adonai helps me,
I would as soon dwell in the silence of my self.

When I said, "My foot slips,"
your love, Adonai, supported me.
When my anxieties were great inside me
your consolations brought joy to my soul.

Can a throne of corruptions be allied with you,
one that brings misery by decree?
They band together against the life of the just
and condemn the innocent to death.

But Adonai became to me as a fortress,
and my God as a rock of refuge.
A rock of refuge is my God,
who will repay their sin to them
and destroy their bad ways.
Our God, Adonai, will destroy them.

Glory...   Antiphon

PSALM 62

Antiphon *Do not worry about tomorrow*
for tomorrow will worry about itself;
sufficient to the day is its own trouble. Mt 6:34

My soul finds rest in God alone,
from whom is my salvation,
alone my salvation and my rock,
my fortress never to be shaken.

Until when will you assault a human being,
will you throw down, all of you,
like a leaning wall or a tottering fence?

They fully intend to topple from the lofty place;
they delight in lies
and bless with their mouth
and curse in their heart.

My soul finds rest in God alone,
from whom is my hope,
alone my salvation and my rock,
my fortress not to be shaken.

From God is my salvation and my honor;
my mighty rock and refuge.
Trust in God at all times, people;
pour out your heart to God our refuge.

WEDNESDAY EVENING

Sons and daughters of humanity are but a breath;
the so-called great ones are an illusion.
On balanced scales they both rise;
together they are only a breath.

Trust not in extortion
and take no pride in stolen things;
even when riches increase
do not set your heart on them.

One thing God has spoken,
two things I have heard:
that to God is power
and to you, Lord, is love;
and surely you will reward to each
according to our deeds.

Glory...

Antiphon

---

*To be grateful is to recognize the love of
God in everything God has given us – and
God has given us everything. Every breath
we draw is a gift of God's love, every moment
of existence is a grace, for it brings with it immense
graces from God. Gratitude therefore takes nothing for
granted, is never unresponsive, is constantly awakening
to new wonder and to praise of the goodness of God. For
the grateful human know that God is good, not by hearsay
but by experience. And that is what makes all the difference.*

See *Thoughts in Solitude* by Thomas Merton

PSALM 139:1-18,23-24

Antiphon   *To you hearing I say,*
love your enemies
and do good to the ones hating you.   Lk 6:27

Adonai, you search me and you know me.
You know my sitting and my rising;
you perceive my thoughts from afar.
You mark my going and my lying down,
and you are familiar with all of my ways.

When a word is not yet on my tongue
you see it, Adonai; you know them all.
Behind and before you hem me in
and rest your hand upon me.
Too wonderful for me is this knowledge,
more lofty than what I can attain.

Where can I hide from your Spirit?
Where could I flee from your presences?
If I go up to the heavens, you are there;
if I make a bed in Sheol, you I see!

If I rise on the wings of dawn,
if I settle on the far side of the sea,
even there your hand will guide me
and your right hand will hold me…

WEDNESDAY EVENING

If I say, "Surely darkness will hide me
and the night will light around me,"
even darkness will not be dark to you
and night will shine as the day;
as the darkness, so the light.

For you created my inmost beings;
you knit me together in my mother's womb.
I praise you because I am full of fear and wonder;
my self knows well
how wonderful are your works.

My bones were not hidden from you
when I was made in the secret place,
woven together in the depths of earth.

Your eyes saw my body
and in your book were written and ordained
all the days before the first day was.

How precious to me, El, are your designs,
how vast are they, the sums of them;
if countable they number more than the sand.
Awake and still, I am with you.

Search me, El, and know my heart!
Test me, and know my anxious thoughts!
See if there is in me an offensive way,
then lead me in the way everlasting!

Glory...

Antiphon

PSALM 67

Antiphon *Peace I leave with you;*
my peace I give to you.   Jn 14:27a

May God be gracious to us and bless us,
may God's faces shine upon us.
How else can your ways be known on the earth
and your salvation among all the nations?

May the peoples praise you, God,
may the peoples praise you, all of them.

May the nations be glad and sing for joy
for you rule the peoples
and guide nations of the earth into justice.

May the peoples praise you, God,
may the peoples praise you, all of them.

The land will yield her harvest, God will bless us,
and all the ends of the earth will revere our God.

Glory…

Antiphon

Can we speak of the Christian as a
musical instrument played by the Holy Spirit?
Saint Gregory Nazianzen

COLOSSIANS 1:12-20

Antiphon *Who follows me will have the light of life.* Jn 8:12c

Give joyful thanks to the Father who made you fit
for your part of the lot of the saints in light,

who delivered us out of the authority of darkness,
transitioning us into the realm of the beloved Son
in whom we have redemption,
the forgiveness of our sins.

The Son is the image of the invisible God,
the firstborn of all creation.
In him all things were created,
in the heavens and on the earth,
the visible and the invisible,
whether thrones, lordships, rulers or authorities.

All creation has come to be through and for him.
He is before all things,
and in him all things hold together.

He is the head of the body, the church,
and the beginning, the firstborn from the dead,
so that in all things he may hold the first place.

In him all the fullness was well pleased to dwell,
and through him reconciliation to himself
of all things on earth and things in the heavens,
making peace through the blood of his cross.

Glory... Antiphon

READING — **1 PETER 5:1-7**

And so to presbyters among you, I exhort as a presbyter myself, a witness of the sufferings of Christ, and a share in the glory to be revealed. Shepherd the flock of God in your midst, not by compulsion but willingly according to God, not from eagerness for profit but eagerly, nor in exercising lordship over others but in being an example for the flock. And when the chief Shepherd appears, you will receive the unfading crown of glory.

Likewise, younger members submit yourselves to the presbyters, and all to one another gird yourselves in humility, because *God resists the arrogant, but gives grace to the humble.*

And so be humble under the mighty hand of God, who may then exalt you in time. Cast all of your anxiety on God, to whom everything about you matters.

RESPONSORY — Ps 17:8

Keep us, O Lord…
…as the apple of your eye.
Hide us in the shade of your wings…
…as the apple of your eye.
Glory to the Father and to the Son and to the Holy Spirit:
…Keep us, O Lord as the apple of your eye.

CANTICLE of MARY (The Magnificat)
LUKE 1:46-55

Antiphon

*The Mighty One has done
great things for me.*

+ **My soul** is stretched full with praise of the Lord,
and my spirit, beyond joy in God, my Savior,
who chose to lay eyes on this humble servant.

Behold, now and forward,
each and every age will call me blessed,
for the Mighty One did great things to me.

Holy is the name and the mercy
to generations and generations,
the ones fearing the One,

Who scattered the haughty of mind and heart,
pulled the powerful off their high place,
and lifted with dignity the humble in need.

The hungering are filled with good things,
the rich are sent away empty,
and servant Israel is given relief

with a memory of mercy to remember,
the promise spoken to our ancestors,
to Abraham and his descendants forever.

Glory...

Antiphon

INTERCESSIONS

- For all who have had a hard day at work…
- For all who have died…

- In gratitude for blessings…; Abba thank you.
- For the sins of this day…; Lord Jesus have mercy.
- With concerns over tomorrow…; Holy Spirit help.

FOR VOCATIONS

Father, you call us to the table of your Son,
renew us by word and sacrament,
and send us to labor in your harvest.
We are a people in need of the witness
of faithful marriages and priests,
generous single people and deacons,
religious sisters, brothers, monks and nuns.
Help each disciple to trust in your call,
make us able and willing to do what you ask,
keep us united in our gifted diversity,
and bring to maturity every seed you sow.
All this we ask through the Good Shepherd:
Jesus Christ, your Son and our Lord.

OUR FATHER…

Seeker, everybody is looking for God.
Disciple, Jesus has more to teach you.
Minister, whose feet are you washing?
Apostle, you are sent out as good news.

WEEK II
THURSDAY MORNING

+ *God, come to my assistance;* Psalm 70:2
  Lord, make haste to help me!

  Glory...

A O/ **breathe on me**, O/ **breath of God**,
Fill/ me with life a//-new,
That I may love what you have loved,
And do what you would do.

O/ breathe on me, O/ breath of God,
Un/-til my heart is// pure,
Un-til with you I will one will,
To do and to en-dure.

O/ breathe on me, O/ breath of God,
In/-spire my bu-sy// mind,
Un-til this earth-ly part of me
Glows with your fire div-ine.

O/ breathe on me, O/ breath of God,
My/ soul shall nev-er// die,
But live in your e-ter-nal life,
Your love the rea-son why.

116, Text: Edwin Hatch, 1878, altered
Music: ST. COLUMBA, CM; Gaelic Folk Melody
Popular melody for: *The King Of Love My Shepherd Is*

B Je-sus, my Lord\, my God/, my all\;
How late, my Je-sus, have I sought.
You pour down rich\-es of/ your grace\;
How can I love you as I ought?
Je-sus, our Lord, we you a-dore!
Call us to love you more/ and more\.
Call us to love you more and more.

Je-sus, what could you have found/ in me\
That you have dealt so pa-tient-ly?
How great the joy\ that you/ have brought\,
So far ex-ceed-ing hope or thought!
Je-sus, our Lord, we you a-dore!
Call us to love you more/ and more\.
Call us to love you more and more.

Had I but Ma\-ry's sin/-less heart\
With which to love you, dear-est King;
O! with what bursts\ of fer/-vent praise\
Your good-ness, Je-sus, would I sing.
Sweet Sac-ra-ment, we you a-dore!
Call us to love you more/ and more\.
Call us to love you more and more.

104, Text: Henry A. Collins, 1854, altered;
vs. 3 Frederick W. Faber, d. 1863, altered
Music: SWEET SACRAMENT, LM with refrain,
Romischkatholisches Gesanguchlein , 1826

PSALM 3

Antiphon *Whoever does and teaches
these commandments
will be called great in
the reign of heaven.* Mt 5:19

How many, Adonai,
are rising against me,
saying of me in enmity,
"No deliverance by God for this self!"

But you, Adonai, shield around me,
my glorious One, you lift my head.
My voice cries to Adonai
who answers me from the holy mountain.

I lie down and I sleep;
and I wake because Adonai sustains me.
I will have no fear of tens of thousands of people
who are drawn up on every side against me.

Arise, Adonai! Deliver me, my God!
You struck the jaw of enmity
and broke the teeth of bad doings.
From Adonai is the deliverance.
May your blessing be on your people.

Glory…

Antiphon

PSALM 6

Antiphon   *Young human, I say to you: Arise!*   Lk 7:14

Adonai, do not rebuke me in your anger
nor discipline me in your wrath.
Be merciful to me, Adonai, for I am weak.
Heal me, Adonai, for my bones are in agony
and my soul is in great anguish.

But you, Adonai, how long?
Turn, Adonai, and deliver my soul!
Save me because of your unfailing love!
Not from death are you remembered.
Who can praise you from Sheol?

I am worn out from my groaning;
through all the night I flood my bed with tears,
I drench my couch.
My eye grows weak with sorrow;
she weakens because of enmity.

Away from me, all doers of the bad,
for Adonai has heard the sound of my weeping.
Adonai has heard my cry for mercy.
Adonai accepts my prayer.
May enmity be ashamed and greatly dismayed,
and turn back in humble confusion.

Glory...

                                                                Antiphon

PSALM 44

Antiphon *The reign of heaven is like leaven*
a woman mixes into three measures
of flour until the whole is leavened.   Mt 13:33

With our ears, God, we have heard,
our ancestors told us the deed you did
in their days, in days long ago.

You drove out nations by your hand
and you planted them;
you crushed peoples so they could flourish.

For they won victory not by their sword and arm,
but by your right hand and arm
and the light of your faces,
for you loved them.

You are my Ruler and my God;
decree the victories of Jacob.
Through you we push back enmity;
through your name we trample opposition.

Indeed I trust not in my bow
and my sword does not bring me victory,
but you give to us victory over enmity
and shame the adversity.
In God we boast all the day
and we will praise your name to forever.

Psalm 44, continued

But you let us be rejected and humbled
and you do not go out with our armies.
You turned us back before enmity
and adversity plundered from us.

You gave us up like sheep devoured;
among the nations you scattered us.
You sold your people for no great price,
gaining nothing from their sale.

You made us a reproach to our neighbors,
scorn and derision to those around us.
You made us a byword among the nations,
a shaking of heads among the peoples.

All the day my disgrace is before me
and shame covers my face
at taunts of reproachers and revilers
because of avenging enmity.

All of this though we did not forget you
and were not false to your covenant.
Our hearts did not turn back
and our feet did not stray from your path,
but you pushed us into haunts of jackals
and you covered us over with deep darkness.

If we forgot the name of our God,
if we spread out our hands to a foreign "god,"
would God not have discovered this,
the One knowing the secrets of the heart?
Yet for you we face death all the day;
we are considered as sheep for slaughter.

Wake up, Lord! Why do you sleep?
Rouse yourself! Do not reject us to forever.
Why do you hide your faces
and forget our misery and oppression?

Indeed our self is brought down to the dust;
our body clings to the ground.
Rise up as our help and redeem us!
because of your unfailing love.

Glory...

Antiphon *The reign of heaven is like leaven
a woman mixes into three measures
of flour until the whole is leavened.* Mt 13:33

---

*A human has the right to act in conscience
and in freedom so as personally to make moral
decisions and 'must not be forced to act contrary to
their conscience. Nor must they be prevented from acting
according to their conscience, especially in religious matters.'*
See *Catechism* #1782, Vatican II *Declaration on Religious Freedom*

PSALM 80

Antiphon   *The reign of God will be given*
to a people who produce its fruit.   Mt 21:43

Hear us, One Shepherd of Israel,
you who lead Joseph like a flock.
From your throne on the cherubim, shine forth
before Ephraim, Benjamin and Manasseh!
Awaken your might! Come to our salvation!

O God, restore us!
Make your faces shine that we may be saved!

Until when, Adonai, God of Hosts,
will you smolder against
the prayer of your people?
You fed them with bread of tears
and you made them drink tears by the bowlful.
You made us a contention to our neighbors,
and enmity mocks us.

God of Hosts, restore us!
Make your faces shine that we may be saved!

Out from Egypt, you brought a vine;
you drove out the nations and you planted it.
You cleared the ground before her;
her roots took root and she filled the land.

Mountains were covered by her shade
and the mighty cedars by her branches.
She sent out her branches to the Sea,
and her shoots as far as the River.

Why have you broken down her walls?
All who pass by the way pluck her fruit.
The boar from the forest ravages her,
and creatures of the field feed on her.

God of Hosts, return now!
Look down from heaven!
See and watch over this vine,
this root that your right hand planted.
Some would burn it or cut it down;
at the rebuke of your faces may those plans perish.

Let your hand be on the one at your right hand,
the descendant of Adam you raised up for yourself.
Then we will not turn away from you;
you revive us and we will call on your name.

Adonai, God of Hosts, restore us!
Make your faces shine that we may be saved!

Glory... Antiphon

Do I qualify as an apostle, one who is sent? (see Acts 1:21-22)
How would I tell the great story of Jesus' baptism, ministry, death and resurrection to a neighbor who wants to understand who I am?

See *Forty Penances* by Stephen Joseph Wolf

PSALM 81

Antiphon *The sabbath was made for human beings,*
not human beings for the sabbath.   Mk 2:27

Sing for joy to God our strength!
Shout to the God of Jacob!

Begin the music! Strike the tambourine,
the melodious harp and the lyre!
Sound the ram horn at the new moon,
the full moon, the day of our feast!

For this is a decree for Israel,
an ordinance of the God of Jacob,
a statute established for Joseph
when time to go out from the land of Egypt.

I hear a tongue I do not know:
"I removed the burden from their shoulders,
their hands were freed from the basket.
In distress you called and I rescued you;

I answered from the thundercloud
and tested you at the waters of Meribah.
Hear, my people, and I will warn you, Israel,
if you will listen to me:

'No foreign "god" shall be among you;
you shall bow to no alien "god."
I am Adonai, your God,
who brought you out of the land of Egypt.
Open wide your mouth and I will fill it!'

But my people did not listen to my voice,
and Israel did not submit to me.
So I gave them to their stubborn heart
and they followed their devices.

If my people were listening to me,
if Israel would walk in my ways,
as quickly would I subdue enmity
and turn a firm hand to adversity.

Anyone hating Adonai would cringe
under punishment lasting to forever.
But I will feed my people with finest of wheat
and satisfy you with honey out of rock."

Glory…

                                                                     Antiphon

---

Now says Adonai, who
created and formed you, _____;   *(pray your name)*
fear not for I have redeemed you.
I have called you by name; you are mine…
You are precious in my eyes, honored and glorious,
and I love you. I will send help and ransom for your life.
Be not afraid for I am with you.   See Isaiah 43:1-5a

ISAIAH 12:1b-6

Antiphon   *The crowds asked John the Baptist,*
what then shall we do?   Lk 3:10

I will praise you, Adonai.
Though you were angry with me,
your anger turned away and you comforted me.

Surely God is my salvation!
I will trust and will not be afraid
for Yah is my strength and my song.

Adonai became for me salvation
and you will draw with joy
waters from wells of salvation…

Give thanks to Adonai! Call on the name!
Make the deeds known among the nations!
Proclaim that the name is exalted!

Sing to Adonai, who has done glory!
Let this be known to all the world.

Shout! And sing for joy, dwellers of Zion!
For great in your midst is the Holy One of Israel.

Glory…

Antiphon

Crowds, share your food and second coat with those in need.
Tax collectors, collect no more than what you know you ought.
Soldiers, do not extort anyone, and be satisfied with you wages.

ISAIAH 66:7-14a

Antiphon *Know this:*
the reign of God is at hand. Lk 10:11b

"**Before she goes into labor** she gives birth;
before pain comes upon her, she delivers a son.
Who has heard of such as this?
Who has seen such as these?

Can a country be born in one day
or a nation be brought forth in one moment?
Yet she is in labor,
then Zion gives birth to her children.

Do I bring to the moment of birth
and not give delivery?"
asks your God Adonai;
"Do I bring one to delivery and then close up?

Rejoice with Jerusalem and be glad for her!
All who love her, rejoice with her!
Rejoice, all who mourn over her,

for you will nurse and you will be satisfied
at the breast of her comforts,
for you will drink deeply and you will delight
in the overflow of her abundance."

Isaiah 66, continued

For this says Adonai:
"See, I extend peace to her like a river,
and wealth of nations like a flooding stream,
and you will nurse, being carried at her side,
and you will be playdanced on her knees.

As a child is comforted by a mother,
so will I comfort you
and over Jerusalem you will be comforted.

When you see, your heart will rejoice
and your bones will flourish like the grass."

Glory…

Antiphon	*Know this:* *the reign of God is at hand.*	Lk 10:11b

PSALM 143:1-11

Antiphon	*Go into all the cosmos and* *proclaim the gospel to all creation.*	Mk 16:15

Adonai, hear my prayer.
Listen in your fidelity to my cries for mercy.
Relieve me in your justice.
Bring not your servant into judgment
for not anyone alive is just before you.

Indeed enmity pursues my self
and crushes my life to the ground
and makes me dwell in dark places
like dead ones of long ago.
My spirit grows faint within me;
within me my heart is dismayed.

I remember days of long ago
and meditate on all of your work
and consider the deeds of your hands.
I stretch out my hands to you;
like land parched my soul thirsts for you.

Be quick! Answer me, Adonai! My spirit faints!
Hide not your faces from me
or I will be like and with ones going down the pit.

Bring in the morning your word of unfailing love,
for in you I trust.
Show me the way I should go
for to you I lift up my soul!

Rescue me, Adonai, from enmity; in you I hide.
Teach me to do your will, for you are my El.
May your good Spirit lead me on level ground.

For the sake of your Name, Adonai,
you keep me alive in your justice;
you bring my self out from trouble.

Glory...

Antiphon

OFFICE OF READINGS and FIRST READING AT MASS

	Odd Years	**Even Years**
2 readings	*Romans 6:12-23*	*Genesis 15*
mass	Hebrews 7:25-8:6	1 Samuel 18:6-9;19:1-7
4 rdgs	*Romans 15:1-13*	*Genesis 32*
mass	Hebrews 12:18-19,21-24	**1 Kings** 2:1-4,10-12
6 rdgs	*1 Corinthians 9:1-18*	*2 Thessalonians 1*
mass	Genesis 9:1-13	James 2:1-9
8 rdgs	*1 Corinthians 16*	*2 Corinthians 11:7-29*
mass	Ben Sira 42:15-25	1 Peter 2:2-5,9-12
10 rdgs	*Joshua 5 & 6*	*Philippians 3:1-16*
mass	2 Corinth 3:15-4:1,3-6	1 Kings 18:41-46
12 rdgs	*1 Samuel 2:22-36*	*Ezra 9 & 10*
mass	Genesis 16:1-12,15-16	2 Kings 24:8-17
14 rdgs	*1 Samuel 25*	*Proverbs 10*
mass	Gen 44:18-21,23b-29;45:1-5	Hosea 11:1,3-4,8c-9
16 rdgs	*1 Kings 1 & 2*	*Job 19*
mass	Ex 19:1-2,9-11,16-20b	Jeremiah 2:1-3,7-8,12-13
18 rdgs	*2 Kings 2*	*Joel 4*
mass	Numbers 20:1-13	Jeremiah 31:31-34
20 rdgs	*Ephesians 3:1-13*	*Ecclesiastes 7 & 8*
mass	Judges 11:29-39a	Ezekiel 36:23-28
22 rdgs	*Amos 4*	*2 Timothy 2:1-21*
mass	Colossians 1:9-14	1 Corinthians 3:18-23

	Odd Years	**Even Years**
24 rdgs	*Hosea 13*	*Esther 5 & 7*
mass	1 Timothy 4:12-16	1 Corinthians 15:1-11
26 rdgs	*2 Chronicles 29*	*Judith 10 & 11*
mass	Nehe 8:1-4a,5-6,7b-12	Job 19:12-27
28 rdgs	*Jeremiah 4*	*Sirach 16*
mass	Romans 3:21-29	**Ephesians** 1:3-10
30 rdgs	*Jeremiah 27*	*Wisdom 5*
mass	Romans 3:31b-39	Ephesians 6:10-20
32 rdgs	*Ezekiel 12*	*2 Macabees 7:20-42*
mass	Wisdom 7:22-8:1	**Philemon** 1:7-20
34 rdgs	*Ezekiel 39*	*Daniel 9*
mass	Daniel 6:11-28	Revelation 18:1-2,21-23

READING **ROMANS 14:13-19**

And so let us no longer judge one another, but rather judge ourselves thus: to put no stumbling block in the way of a brother or sister or any offense. I know and am persuaded by the Lord Jesus that nothing is unclean in itself, except to the one reckoning something unclean to whom it is unclean. For if your brother or sister is grieved because of food, you no longer walk in love. Do not destroy by food one on whose behalf Christ died. Do not let what is good to you be blasphemed.

Romans 14, continued

For the reign of God is not eating and drinking, but justice and peace and joy in the Holy Spirit. Those serving Christ in these are approved and well-pleasing to God and human beings. And so let us pursue the things of peace and the things of building up for one another.

RESPONSORY   Ps 63:7,8

On my bed through the watch of night…
　…*O Lord, I think of you.*
You who are my help,…
　…*O Lord, I think of you.*
Glory to the Father and to the Son and to the Holy Spirit:
　…*On my bed through the watch of night,*
　　O Lord, I think of you.

Gospel Canticle For Morning

Antiphon　　*Lord, give us knowledge of salvation known in the forgiveness of our sins.*

Gospel Reading for Thursday of
Week			
2	Mark 3:7-12	14 Matt 10:7-15	26 Luke 10:1-12
4	Mark 6:7-13	16 Matt 13:10-17	28 Lk 11:47-54
6	Mark 8:27-33	18 Matt 16:13-23	30 Lk 13:31-35
8	Mark 10:46-52	20 Matt 22:1-14	32 Lk 17:20-25
10	Matt 5:20-26	22 Luke 5:1-11	34 Lk 21:20-28
12	Matt 7:21-29	24 Luke 7:36-50	

THURSDAY MORNING

CANTICLE of ZECHARIAH (The Benedictus)
LUKE 1:68-79

+ Blessed be the Lord the God of Israel
who chose a people to visit with redemption,
and raised salvation in the house of David,
saving strength from God's own servant,

speaking from the age of the prophets
through the mouth of the holy prophet:
Salvation out of enmity,
even out of those who hate us,

to show our ancestors how mercy works, -
and to remember the holy promise of the Lord,
the covenant made for our ancestor Abraham,
calming our fear and making us free
to serve with holy justice before God all our days.

And you also child -
will be called a prophet of the Most High
for you will go before the Lord to prepare his way
and give to people a knowledge of salvation
known in accepting forgiveness of their sins.

From the tender mercy of our God,
the sun rising from the height will visit with light
for those who sit in the dark or shadow of death
and to guide our feet into the way of peace.

Glory...

Antiphon

PETITIONS FOR THE CONSECRATION TO GOD
OF THE DAY AND ITS WORK

- For the Church and her ministry and apostolates…
- For secular authorities and all serving as stewards…
- For people who are poor or sick or in sorrow…
- For peace and the basic needs of each human being…
- For a culture of vocations all over the world…

PONDER QUESTIONS for a CULTURE of VOCATIONS

My Lord and my God, help me to know how you have wired me for community, friendship and **love**. What is the form of life into which you are calling me that I may best love and be loved? Single? Married? Religious?

Lord, how have you made me in your image? With what gifts, virtues, talents and charisms? How are you calling me to participate in your ongoing **work** of creation?

Lord, for whom might you call me to place my life on the line? For what value, **truth**, reality, idea or person are you preparing me to give my life? How should I begin to live fully alive for this?

Lord, you know and love me even better than I know and love myself; how are you calling me to **be alone** with you in prayer? How are you calling me to participate in the redemptive, forgiving, healing mission of your Son, my Lord, Jesus Christ?

OUR FATHER…

WEEK II
THURSDAY EVENING

+ *God, come to my assistance;*   Psalm 70:2
Lord, make haste to help me!

Glory...

A   **Sing, my tongue, the Sa-vior's glo-ry,**
Of his flesh the mys-t'ry sing,
Of the blood, all price ex-ceed-ing,
Shed by our im-mort-al King,
Des-tined, for the world's re-demp-tion,
From a no-ble womb to spring.

On the night of that Last Sup-per,
Seat-ed with his cho-sen band,
He, the pas-chal vic-tim eat-ing,
First ful-fills the law's com-mand;
Then as food to all his sib-lings
Gives him-self with his own hand.

To the ev-er-last-ing Fa-ther,
And the Son who made us free,
And the Spir-it, God pro-ceed-ing,
From them each e-ter-nal-ly,
Be sal-va-tion, hon-or, bless-ing,
Might and end-less maj-es-ty.

53, Text: Thomas Aquinas, *Pange lingua gloriosi*, d. 1274,
translated by Edward Caswell, 1849, altered
Music: 87 87 87 ST. THOMAS (TANTUM ERGO) JohnF.Wade,d.1786
Popular melody for: *Down In Adoration Falling*

B **Lord, when at your
Last Sup-per you did pray**
That all your Church
might be for-ev-er one.
Grant us at ev'-ry
Eu-cha-rist to say
With long-ing heart and soul,
"Your will be done."
O may we all
one bread, one bod-y be,
Through this blest
Sac-ra-ment of U-ni-ty.

For all your Church,
O Lord, we in-ter-cede;
Make all our sad
div-is-ions soon to cease;
Draw us the near-er each,
to each we plead,
By draw-ing all to you,
O Prince of Peace;
Thus may we all
one bread, one bod-y be,
Through this blest
Sac-ra-ment of U-ni-ty.

We pray for all
who wan-der from your fold;
O bring them home,
Good Shep-herd of the sheep,
Back to the faith which
saints be-lieved of old,
Back to the Church which
still the faith does keep;
Soon may we all
one bread, one bod-y be,
Through this blest
Sac-ra-ment of U-ni-ty.

So, Lord, at length
when sac-ra-ments shall cease,
May we be one with
all your Church a-bove,
One with your saints
in one un-bro-ken peace,
One with your saints
in one un-bound-ed love;
More bless-ed still
in peace and love to be
One with the Trin-i-ty
in U-ni-ty.

106, Text: William H. Turton, 1859-1938, altered
Music: 10 10 10 10 10 10 UNDE ET MEMORES,
William H. Monk, 1823-1899

PSALM 56:2-7,9-14

Antiphon *The word of God is the seed.* Lk 8:11b

Be merciful to me, my God!
Human beings pursue me all the day,
attacking with oppression
and with slander all the day.

Indeed in their pride do the many attack me.
On the day I am afraid, in you I trust.
My praise is of God's word, in God I trust.
I will not be afraid; what can a mortal do to me?

All the day they twist my words against me;
all their plots are for harm.
They conspire, they lurk, they watch my steps;
they are eager for my life…

Record my lament, put my tears in your wineskin;
are they not in your record?
Enmity will turn back on the day I call;

I will know that God is for me.
In God whose word I praise,
in Adonai whose word I praise, in God I trust.
I will not be afraid; what can a human do to me?

Upon me, God, are my vows to you;
I will present thank offerings to you
for you delivered my soul from death
and my feet from stumbling,
to walk in God's presence
in the light of the living.

Glory…

Antiphon

PSALM 60:3-14a

Antiphon *Do not judge,*
lest you be judged. Mt 7:1

God you rejected us,
breaking our defenses;
you were angry, now restore us.

You shook the land and tore her open;
mend her fractures, for she quakes!
You showed your people a desperate time;
you made us drink wine to staggering.

For those who fear you, you raised a banner
to be unfurled against the bow,
that your beloved ones may be delivered.
Help us with your right hand and save us!

Psalm 60, continued

God spoke from the sanctuary:
"I will triumph and parcel out Shechem,
and measure out the valley of Succoth;
mine are Gilead and Manasseh,

Ephraim my head helmet,
Judah my scepter,
and Moab my washbasin;
On Edom I toss my sandal
and over Philistia I shout in triumph"

Who will bring me to the Fortress City?
Who will lead me to Edom?
Have you, God, not rejected us,
and not gone out, God, with our armies?

Against enmity give to us aid,
for worthless is human help.
In God will we gain the victory…

Glory…

Antiphon *Do not judge,*
lest you be judged. Mt 7:1

I can never really know what goes on
in the heart of another. Indeed I hardly
know what is going on in my own heart,
but God knows. Only God has all the data,
and so the job of judging belongs to God alone.

PSALM 128

Antiphon *Everyone having will be given more
and to abundance; but the one not having,
even that will be taken.* Mt 25:29

Blessed are all who fear Adonai
and walk in the way.

Indeed you will eat from the labor of your hands.
To you will be blessings and prosperity,
and your spouse like a fruitful vine
inside and outside your house,
sons and daughters around your table
like shoots of the olives.

See: one who fears Adonai is blessed;
may Adonai bless you from Zion.
See and enjoy the prosperity of Jerusalem
all the days of your life,
and the joy of the children of your children.

Peace be upon Israel.

Glory…

                                               Antiphon

---

*You sanctify
whatever you are grateful for.*
Anthony de Mello, Jesuit

PSALM 129

Antiphon *I am the bread of life; who comes to me does not hunger and who believes in me will never thirst.*   Jn 6:35

"**From my youths** they oppressed me greatly,"
let Israel now say.
"From my youths they oppressed me greatly,
but gained no victory over me.

On my back the plowers plowed;
long are the furrows they made.
Adonai the Just
cut free the cords of bad doings."

May all haters of Zion
be shamed and turned back;
May they be like grass on housetops
which withers before it grows,

which cannot fill one hand of the reaper
nor an arm of the gatherer,
and passers-by will not say,
"Blessing of Adonai upon you!
We bless you in the name of Adonai!"

Glory...

Antiphon

PSALM 72

Antiphon *Out of you, Bethlehem, will come forth a ruler
who will shepherd my people Israel.* Mt 2:6;
Micah 5:2

God, endow your justice to King Solomon
and your judgment to the royal heir,
to judge your people with integrity
and your afflicted with justice.

Mountains will bring prosperity to the people,
the hills too in abundance.
He is to defend people afflicted,
save the children of the needy,
and crush the oppressor.

They will fear you as long as the sun,
as long as the moon,
from generation to generations.
He is to be like rain falling on a mown field,
like showers watering the earth.

In his days the just are to flourish
in prosperous abundance til the moon is no more.
He will rule from sea to sea
and from the River to the ends of the earth.

Desert tribes will bow;
the royals of Tarshish and the distant shores
will bring tribute and present gifts
with royals of Sheba and Seba.   --

Psalm 72, continued

They will bow down to him;
the royals of all the nations will thus serve.

For he is to deliver the needy one crying out
and the afflicted one when no one is helping,
to take pity on the weak and the needy
and save the lives of the poor;

to rescue their lives
from oppression and violence,
for their lifeblood will be precious in his eyes.

May he live and be given gold of Sheba;
may all ever pray that he be blessed all the day.

May grain be abundant throughout the land,
on tops of hills, swaying like the fruit of Lebanon,
and people flourish and thrive like grass in a field.

May his name endure to forever
and continue as long as the sun;
being thus blessed, may the nations bless him.

Blessed be God, Adonai, God of Israel,
alone doing marvelous deeds.
Blessed be the glory of the name to forever;
may the earth be filled with the glory of God.
Amen and amen.

Glory…

Antiphon *Out of you, Bethlehem, will come forth a ruler who will shepherd my people Israel.* Mt 2:6; Micah 5:2

PSALM 144

Antiphon *Zaccheus, come down quickly,*
for this day it is fitting
for me to stay at your house. Lk 19:5

Praised be Adonai, my Rock,
who trains my hands for war, my fingers for battle,

my love and fortress, my stronghold and deliverer,
my shield in whom I take refuge,
who subdues peoples under me.

What, Adonai, is a human, that you care for us?
Children of humanity, that you think of them?
Like a breath is the human,
whose days are like a shadow passing.

Adonai, part your heavens and come down!
Touch the mountains so they smoke!
You send lightning lit to scatter enmity!
Shoot your arrows and you rout them!

Reach your hands from on high!
Deliver me! Rescue me from the mighty waters,
from the hand of foreign peoples speaking lies
whose right hands are the right hand of deceit.

Psalm 144, continued

I will sing a new song to you, God,
and on the lyre of ten make music to you,
the One giving victory to the rulers,
the One delivering your servant David
from the deadly sword.

Deliver me! Rescue me from foreign hands,
whose mouths speak the lie,
whose right hands are the right hand of deceit.

Our children in their youth
are like well nurtured plants,
like carved pillars adorning a palace,

our barns filled with provisions of every kind,
our sheep becoming thousands
and tens of thousands in our fields,
and our oxen drawing loads,

no break in the walls and no exile
nor a cry of distress in the streets:
Blessed are the people of whom all this is true;
blessed are the people whose God is Adonai.

Glory…

Antiphon *Zaccheus, come down quickly,
for this day it is fitting
for me to stay at your house.* Lk 19:5

REVELATION 11:17-18, 12:10-12a

Antiphon *Now have come*
the salvation, the power,
and the reign of our God.

We thank you, Lord God Almighty,
the One who is and who was;
you have taken your great power and reign.

The nations raged and your anger came,
and the time to judge the dead
and to reward your servants and prophets,
the saints, and those fearing your name,
the small and the great…

Now have come the salvation and power
and reign of our God
and the authority of Christ.
The accuser of our brothers and sisters was cast,
accusing them before our God day and night.

Their victory was because of the blood of the Lamb
and by the word of their witness.
They loved their life into their death,
and so be glad, you heavens,
and all you dwelling in them.

Glory…

Antiphon

READING — **1 PETER 1:22-25**

Your souls now purified by obedience to the truth of unfeigned love for brothers and sisters, love one another earnestly from the heart, having been regenerated not by corruptible seeds but incorruptible through the living and abiding word of God.

All flesh is as grass, and all its glory as a flower of grass; the grass dried up and the flower fell out, but the word of the Lord remains unto the age. This is the gospel word preached to you.

RESPONSORY — Ps 23:1

The Lord is my shepherd...
 ...nothing shall I lack.
My Lord lays me down in green pastures...
 ...nothing shall I lack.
Glory to the Father and to the Son and to the Holy Spirit:
 ...The Lord is my shepherd; nothing shall I lack.

CANTICLE of MARY (The Magnificat)
LUKE 1:46-55

Antiphon *God has exalted with dignity*
the humble in need.

+ My soul is stretched full with praise of the Lord,
and my spirit, beyond joy in God, my Savior,
who chose to lay eyes on this humble servant.

Behold, now and forward,
each and every age will call me blessed,
for the Mighty One did great things to me.

Holy is the name and the mercy
to generations and generations,
the ones fearing the One,

Who scattered the haughty of mind and heart,
pulled the powerful off their high place,
and lifted with dignity the humble in need.

The hungering are filled with good things,
the rich are sent away empty,
and servant Israel is given relief

with a memory of mercy to remember,
the promise spoken to our ancestors,
to Abraham and his descendants forever.

Glory...

Antiphon

INTERCESSIONS

- For ever deeper understanding of what Jesus taught when he washed the feet of his disciples…
- For the courage to wash feet…
- For all who have died…

- In gratitude for blessings…; Abba thank you.
- For the sins of this day…; Lord Jesus have mercy.
- With concerns over tomorrow…; Holy Spirit help.

AN ACT OF CONTRITION

My God,
I am heartily sorry for having offended you
and I detest all my sins
because of your just judgment
but especially that they offend you
who are all-mighty, all-good,
and deserving of all my love.
I firmly intend with the help of your grace
to do the good,
avoid situations that lead to sin,
and in penance amend my life.

OUR FATHER…

91, Text: *Liturgy of St. James*, 5th Century;
translated from Greek by Gerard Moultrie, 1864
Music: 87 87 87 PICARDY, *Chansons Populaires
des Provinces de France*, 1860

WEEK II
FRIDAY MORNING

+ *God, come to my assistance;*   Psalm 70:2
  Lord, make haste to help me!

Glory...

Let all mor-tal flesh keep\ si-lence,
And with fear and trem-bling\ stand;
Pon-der noth-ing earth-ly\ mind-ed,
For with bless-ing in his\ hand,
Christ our God to earth de-scend//\-eth,
Our full hom-age to de/-mand.

King of kings, yet born of\ Ma-ry,
As of old on earth he\ stood,
Lord of lords, in hu-man\ ves-ture,
In the bo-dy and the\ blood;
He will give to all the faith//\-ful
His own self for heav-en-ly food.

Rank on rank the host of\ heav-en
Spreads its van-guard on the\ Way,
As the Light of light de\-scend-eth
From the realms of end-less\ day,
That the pow'rs of hell may van//\-ish
As the dark-ness clears a/-way.

PSALM 38

Antiphon *If a house be divided against itself,
that house will be unabe to stand.*   Mk 3:25

Adonai, rebuke me not in your anger
nor discipline me in your wrath,
for your arrows have pierced into me
and your hand has come down upon me.

There is no health in my body
because of your anger;
my bones ache because of my sin.
Indeed my guilts overwhelm my head
like a heavy burden, too heavy for me.

I loathe them and they fester my wounds
because of my foolishness.
I am bowed down and brought very low;
all the day I go about mourning.

Indeed my backside is filled with searing
and there is no health in my body.
Numb and utterly crushed,
my heart groans in anguish.

Lord, before you is all of my longing;
my sighing is not hidden from you.
My heart pounds, my strength fails me,
and my eyes are without their light.

My friends and companions from the past
avoid being present to my woundedness,
and my neighbors stay far away.
People seeking my life set traps;
wanting to harm me, they talk of ruins
and plot deceptions all the day.

I am like the deaf and cannot hear,
like a mute unable to open my mouth.
I became like one who does not hear,
like one whose mouth gives no reply.

Indeed, I wait for you, Adonai;
you will answer, Lord my God.
For I said, "let them not gloat over me
nor puff themselves up when my foot does slip."

For my fall is near; my pain is ever with me.
Indeed I confess my iniquity
and am troubled by my sin.

Vigorous ones seek enmity;
many and numerous hate me for no reason.
When I seek the good they slander me,
repaying the good with the bad.

Forsake me not, Adonai;
my God, be not far from me.
Come quickly to help, my Lord, my salvation.

Glory...

Antiphon

PSALM 55:2-15,17-24

Antiphon *Whoever receives me*
receives the One who sent me.   Mk 9:37b

Listen, Elohim, to my prayer!
Ignore not my plea, but hear me and answer me,
as I am troubled by my thoughts
and groan at the voice of enmity,
at the stares of the faces of doers of the bad,
for they bring suffering down upon me
and revile me in anger.

My heart is in anguish within me
and the terrors of death assail me.
Fear and trembling harass me
and horror has overwhelmed me.

And I said, "If I had wings like the dove;
I would fly away and find rest.
See! I would flee far and stay in the desert.
I would hurry to my place of shelter
from the storm of the raging wind."

Confuse them, Lord; confound their scheming,
for I see violence and strife in the city.
By day and by night they prowl on her walls;
within her are malice and abuse.

Destructive forces are within her
and threats and lies never leave her streets. -

It is not insults of enmity rising against me;
from that I could hide and endure.

But it is you, my other self, my companion,
my friend with whom together
we shared close companionship
walking with the throng at the house of Elohim…

To Elohim I call and am saved by Adonai
who hears my voice when I cry out in distress
at dusk, dawn and noon,
who ransoms my whole self from battle
though many oppose me.

El enthroned forever will hear and let be afflicted
those who never allow themselves to change,
who have no fear of God,
who stretch hands against friends,
and violate covenants.

This one's mouth is smooth as butter,
yet war is in the heart,
speaking words more soothing than oil
that are yet drawn swords.

Cast your cares on Adonai, who will sustain you
and to forever let not the just fall.

But you, God, will bring bloody deceit
into the pit of corruption,
not living half their days;
And I will trust in you.

Glory…   Antiphon

PSALM 51

Antiphon   *One who loves one's life loses it.*   Jn 12:25

Have mercy on me, God,
in accord with your unfailing love;
in accord with your great compassion
blot out my transgressions.

Wash me of my many iniquities
and cleanse me from my sin,
for I know my transgressions
and my sin is before me always.

Against you yourself I sinned,
doing what is bad in your eyes.
You are proven right when you speak
and justified when you judge.
Surely we are sinners from birth,
from conception in a mother's womb.

Surely you desire truth in our inner parts;
in my inmost place you teach me wisdom.
You cleanse me with hyssop and I will be clean;
you wash me and I will be whiter than snow…

You let me hear joy and gladness;
let the bones you let be crushed now rejoice.
Hide your faces from my sins
and blot out all my iniquities.

A clean heart create in me, God!
Renew inside me a spirit to be steadfast.
Do not cast me from your presences,
nor take from me your Holy Spirit.

Restore to me the joy of your salvation
and sustain in me a willing spirit.
I will teach transgressors your ways
and sinners will turn back to you.

Save me from bloodguilt, God,
God of my salvation;
my tongue will sing of your justice.
Lord, open my lips
and my mouth will proclaim your praise.

Sacrifices give you no delight;
I could bring a burnt offering,
but it would give you no pleasure.
The sacrifices, God, you will not despise
are a broken spirit and a contrite heart.

Make Zion prosper in your pleasure,
and build up the walls of Jerusalem.
Then you will delight in the sacrifice of the just,
burnt offerings and whole offerings,
bulls offered on your altar.

Glory...

Antiphon

HABAKKUK 3:2-4,13a,15-19

Antiphon *Looking round on them with anger,*
Jesus grieved at their hardness of heart.   Mk 3:5

Adonai, I heard your fame;
I stand in awe of your deeds, Adonai.
Now, in the midst of years, renew them!
In the midst of years, make them known!
Even in wrath you remember mercy.

Eloah came from Teman,
the Holy One from the Mount of Paran.
The heavens are covered with glory
and the earth is filled with praise

like the splendor of the rays of the sunrise
or the hand from a hiding place of power…
You came out to deliver your people,
to deliver your anointed one…

You trample on the sea,
your horses churning up the great waters.
My heart heard and she trembled,
at the sound my lips quivered;

decay crept into my bones
and my legs trembled.
Yet, I will wait patiently for the day,
calamity to come on the nation invading.

Though the fig tree does not bud
and there is no grape on the vine,
the crops of the olive fail
and fields produce no food,

the sheep cut themselves off from the pen
and there are no cattle in the stalls,
yet will I rejoice in Adonai
and be joyful in the God of my salvation.

Sovereign Adonai, my strength,
makes my feet like that of the deer,
makes me go to the heights.

Glory…

Antiphon

Lord my God, it
has happened again
and anger is visiting me.
I still hear your gospel call to
love enemies, to pray for persecutors,
and to forgive. Trusting in your way I pray:
I am still angry with N. Judging is your job alone
for you alone have all the data. Like me, N. is created in
your image and loved by you without limit. But there seems to be
something unhealed in N.; I know not what it is, and N. may not know
either, but you, Lord, you know: and I believe that you want to heal it.
This I ask you to do. Lay onto N. your healing touch.

See *Anger the Jesus Way* (reflections on Mark 3:1-6, the only time
the gospels specify the word *anger* for Jesus) by Stephen Joseph Wolf

TOBIT 13:8-11,13-15

Antiphon *One of the seven angels showed me*
the holy city of Jerusalem
shining with the glory of God. Rev 21:10,11

Acknowledge the Lord in Jerusalem.

You Jerusalem, Holy City, will be scourged
for what your children have done.
The Lord will again have mercy
on the children of the just.

Acknowledge the Lord as is deserving
and bless the Ruler of the ages,
that your sanctuary will be built in you again
with joy and cheer by all who were exiles,
and love for all generations
those who were distressed.

A bright light will shine
to all the ends of the earth;
many nations will come from far away.

Those living in the most remote parts of earth
will come to your holy Name,
bearing in their hands
gifts for the Ruler of Heaven.

Generation to generation will give joyful praise
and the name of the Lord will be great forever…

Then, children of the just, rejoice and exult;
be gathered together
and bless the Lord of the ages.

Happy are those who love you,
and happy will be those
who rejoice in prosperity.

Happy also are all
who grieve over your afflictions
for they will rejoice with you
and give witness to your joy forever.

My soul, praise the Lord,
the mega Ruler.

Glory…

Antiphon

PSALM 147:1-11

Antiphon

*Let me preach also
in nearby villages.*   Mk 1:38

Name of God

Adonai *is
Hebrew for "My
Lord."* **YHVH**, *is
usually translated
LORD in all caps, for
most faithful Jews would
not speak the name* Yahweh,
but instead would say Adonai.
Yhvh *is the name revealed to Moses at
the burning bush, and means 'I am who
I am,' or 'I will be who I will be,' or simply
'I am.'* **El** *can mean any god, remembering that
nations and cities would have their own gods. The
plural for El is* **Elohim**, *which can mean many gods,
but in the psalms refers to the one* Yhvh *without any
sense of being multiple gods.* **El Shaddai** *(God Almighty)
is how the Patriarchs spoke of the one God.* **Yhvh Sabaoth**
(Lord of Hosts) refers to God enthroned with an army of angels.

Hallelujah!
How good it is to sing praise to our God!
How pleasant and fitting to give praise!

Adonai rebuilds Jerusalem, gathers Israel's exiles,
heals broken hearts and binds up wounds,
determines the number of the stars,
and calls to each of them by name.

Great and mighty in power is our Lord,
with unlimited understanding.
Adonai sustains the humble
and throws doers of the bad to the dust.
Sing to Adonai with thanksgiving!

Make music on the harp to our God,
who covers the skies with clouds
and supplies rain to the earth,
making grass to grow on the mountains,
providing food for cattle
and young ravens when they call.

Adonai finds pleasure
not in the strength of the horse
nor delight in the legs of the human,
but is delighting in those who fear Adonai
who hope in this unfailing love.

Glory…

Antiphon

PSALM 147:12-20

Antiphon *I am the living bread from heaven;*
anyone who eats of this bread
will live to the eon. Jn 6:51a

Glorify Adonai, Jerusalem!
Zion, now give praise!

Your God strengthens the bars of your gates,
blesses your peoples within you,
brings peace to your border,
and satisfies you with finest of wheat.

Your God sends a command to the earth,
and swiftly runs a word,
spreading snow like the wool
and scattering frost like the ash.

Hail is hurled like pebbles;
who can stand before the icy blast?
The word of the Lord is sent, and they melt;
wind stirs up and the waters flow.

The word of the Lord is revealed to Jacob,
decrees and laws of the Lord to Israel.
Not for another nation did the Lord do this;
they do not know these laws.
Hallelujah!

Glory…

Antiphon

FRIDAY MORNING

OFFICE OF READINGS and FIRST READING AT MASS

	Odd Years	**Even Years**
2 readings	*Romans 11:1-12*	*Genesis 24:33-67*
mass	Hebrews 8:6-13	1 Samuel 24:3-21
4 rdgs	*Romans 15:14-33*	*Genesis 35*
mass	Hebrews 13:1-8	Ben Sira 47:2-11
6 rdgs	*1 Corinthians 9:19-27*	*2 Thessalonians 2*
mass	Genesis 11:1-9	James 2:14-24,26
8 rdgs	*James 1:1-18*	*2 Corinthians 11:30-12:13*
mass	Ben Sira 44:1,9-13	1 Peter 4:7-13
10 rdgs	*Joshua 7*	*Philippians 3:17-4:9*
mass	2 Corinthians 4:7-15	1 Kings 19:9a,11-16
12 rdgs	*1 Samuel 3*	*Nehemiah 1*
mass	Genesis 17:1,9-10,15-22	2 Kings 25:1-12
14 rdgs	*1 Samuel 26*	*Proverbs 15 & 16*
mass	Genesis 46:1-7,28-30	Hosea 14:2-10
16 rdgs	*1 Kings 3*	*Job 22*
mass	Exodus 20:1-17	Jeremiah 3:14-17
18 rdgs	*2 Kings 3*	*Malachi 1 & 2*
mass	**Deuteronomy** 4:32-40	**Nahum** 2:1,3;3:1-3,6-7
20 rdgs	*Ephesians 3:14-21*	*Ecclesiastes 9 & 10*
mass	**Ruth** 1:1,3-6,14b-16,22	Ezekiel 37:1-14

	Odd Years	**Even Years**
22 rdgs	*Amos 5*	*2 Timothy 2:22-3:17*
mass	Colossians 1:15-20	1 Corinthians 4:1-5
24 rdgs	*Hosea 14*	*Baruch 1 & 2*
mass	1 Timothy 6:2c-12	1 Corinthians 15:12-20
26 rdgs	*Isaiah 20*	*Judith 12*
mass	**Baruch** 1:15-22	Job 38:1,12-21;40:3-5
28 rdgs	*Jeremiah 7*	*Sirach 17*
mass	Romans 4:1-8	Ephesians 1:11-14
30 rdgs	*Jeremiah 28*	*Wisdom 6*
mass	Romans 9:1-5	Philippians 1:1-11
32 rdgs	*Ezekiel 13*	*1 Macabees 2*
mass	Wisdom 13:1-9	**2 John** 1:4-9
34 rdgs	*Ezekiel 40*	*Daniel 10*
mass	Daniel 7:2-14	Rev 20:1-4;20:11-21:2

READING **EPHESIANS 2:11-22**

And so remember that when you were the nations in the flesh, called "uncircumcision" by those who were called "circumcision" in the flesh by the hand, that you were at that time without Christ, alienated from the commonwealth of Israel and strangers to the covenants of the promise, without hope and godless in the world. But now in Christ Jesus you who were then afar became near by the blood of Christ.

For he is our peace, the one who made both one, breaking the partition wall of enmity, abolishing in his flesh the law of commandments in decrees, that he might create in himself the two into one new human making peace, and might reconcile both in one body to God through the cross, ending in himself the enmity. And coming he preached peace to those afar and peace to those near, because through him we have access both by one Spirit and to the Father.

And so you are no longer strangers and aliens, but you are equal citizens with the saints and members of the family of God, having been built on the foundation of the apostles and prophets, with the very self of Christ Jesus as the cornerstone, in whom the whole building fits together and grows into a holy temple in the Lord, in whom you also are being built together into a dwelling place of God in the spirit.

RESPONSORY   Tobit 1:13

The Most High has kept me in favor…
   …*with all my heart I will keep God in mind.*
May the Most High rescue me from captivity…
   …*with all my heart I will keep God in mind.*
Glory to the Father and to the Son and to the Holy Spirit:
   …*The Most High has kept me in favor;*
      with all my heart I will keep God in mind.

Gospel Canticle For Morning

Antiphon   *God chose to visit God's people*
                  and brought redemption.

Gospel Reading for Friday of
Week			
2	Mark 3:13-19	14 Matt 10:16-23	26 Lk 10:13-16
4	Mark 6:14-29	16 Matt 13:18-23	28 Luke 12:1-7
6	Mark 8:34 - 9:1	18 Matt 16:24-28	30 Luke 14:1-6
8	Mark 11:11-26	20 Matt 22:34-40	32 Lk 17:26-37
10	Matt 5:27-32	22 Luke 5:33-39	34 Lk 21:29-33
12	Matt 8:1-4	24 Luke 8:1-3	

CANTICLE of ZECHARIAH (The Benedictus)
LUKE 1:68-79

+ **Blessed be** the Lord the God of Israel
who chose a people to visit with redemption,
and raised salvation in the house of David,
saving strength from God's own servant,

speaking from the age of the prophets
through the mouth of the holy prophet:
Salvation out of enmity,
even out of those who hate us,

to show our ancestors how mercy works, -
and to remember the holy promise of the Lord,
the covenant made for our ancestor Abraham,
calming our fear and making us free
to serve with holy justice before God all our days.

And you also child -
will be called a prophet of the Most High
for you will go before the Lord to prepare his way
and give to people a knowledge of salvation
known in accepting forgiveness of their sins.

From the tender mercy of our God,
the sun rising from the height will visit with light
for those who sit in the dark or shadow of death
and to guide our feet into the way of peace.

Glory…

                                                               Antiphon

PETITIONS FOR THE CONSECRATION TO GOD
OF THE DAY AND ITS WORK

- For the Church and her ministry and apostolates…

- For secular authorities and all serving as stewards…

- For people who are poor or sick or in sorrow…

- For peace and the basic needs of each human being…

- For guardian angel intercession for those considering use of violence…

- For any elders or children who feel abandoned…

- In gratitude for blessings and grace…

ANGELUS

The Angel of the Lord declared unto Mary.
And she conceived of the Holy Spirit.

Hail Mary full of grace, the Lord is with thee; Blessed art thou among women, and blessed is the fruit of thy womb, Jesus. Holy Mary, Mother of God, pray for us sinners, now and at the hour of our death. Amen.

Behold the handmaid of the Lord.
Be it done unto me according to your word.

Hail Mary . . .

And the Word became flesh.
And dwelt among us.

Hail Mary . . .

Pray for us, O Holy Mother of God;
That we may be made worthy of the promises of Christ.

OUR FATHER…

WEEK II
FRIDAY EVENING

+ *God, come to my assistance;*   Psalm 70:2
  Lord, make haste to help me!

Glory...

Crown him with ma-ny crowns
The Lamb up-on his throne;
Hark how the heav'n-ly an-them\ drowns
All mu-sic but its own.
A-wake, my soul, and sing
Of him who died for thee
And hail him as your King of kings
Through all e-ter-ni-ty.

Crown him the Lord of Love.
Be-hold his hands and side,
Rich wounds, yet vis-ib-le a\-bove,
In beau-ty glo-ri-fied.
No an-gel in the sky
Can ful-ly bear that sight,
But down-ward bends his wond'-ring eye
At mys-te-ry so bright!

46 (verses 1&2), Text: from Revevelation 19:12;
Verses by Matthew Bridges, 1851, altered
Music: DIADEMATA, George J. Elvey, 1868

PSALM 59:2-5,10-11a,17-18

Antiphon *The reign of heaven is like
a merchant who seeking fine pearls
finds one precious pearl and going away
sells everything and buys it.* Mt 13:45,46

Deliver me from enmity; protect me, God,
from those who rise up against me.
Deliver me from doers of the bad
and save me from bloody ways.

See, they lie in wait for my self;
fierce people conspire against me
for no offense of me nor sin, Adonai.
For no wrong they make ready to attack;
arise to help me and look!...

For you, my Strength, I watch,
for you God, my fortress,
you God are my love.

I will sing of your strength
and I will sing at dawn of your love,
for you are my fortress
and my refuge in times of trouble.

To you, my Strength, I sing praise
for you God, my fortress,
you God are my love.

Glory...

Antiphon

PSALM 133

Antiphon *The multitude of believers
was heart and soul one.* Acts 4:32a

See how good and how pleasant it is
to live as siblings
dwelling in unity.

Like the precious oil
running down on the head
and on the beard of Aaron,
running down on his collar and robes,

as if the dew of Hermon
was falling on Mount Zion,
there Adonai bestows
the blessing of life to forever.

Glory...

Antiphon

---

*God saw all that God made
and found it very good.* Genesis 1:31a

PSALM 140:1-9,13-14

Antiphon *Blessed are you when they disrespect
and persecute and tell all the lies
against you for my sake;
rejoice and be glad,
for great is your reward
in the heavens.*

Mt 5:11

Rescue me, Adonai,
from humans doing bad things;
protect me from humans of violence
who devise the bad in their hearts
and stir up conflict every day.
They make their tongues sharp as a serpent;
viper poison is on their lips.

Keep me, Adonai, from their hands;
protect me from humans of violence
who plan to trip up my feet.
Arrogance has hidden a snare for me,
spread a net of cords,
and set a trap for me beside the path.

I say to Adonai, "You are my God!"
Hear, Adonai, the cry of my cries for mercy!
Lord Adonai, my strength, my deliverance,
you shield my head on the day of battle.
Grant not, Adonai, their desires;
let not their plans to do the bad succeed…

I know that Adonai secures justice for the poor
and the cause of the needy.
Surely the just will praise your Name;
the upright will live before your faces.

Glory…

Antiphon

PSALM 116:1-9

Antiphon   *It is fitting for the Son of Humanity*
to suffer much and be rejected
and be killed, and rise after three days.   Mk 8:31

I love Adonai who heard my voice
and my cries for mercy, and turned an ear to me,
so all during my days I will call.

Cords of death entangled me
and worries over Sheol came upon me;
trouble and sorrow came over me.
Then I called on the name of Adonai:
"Oh, Adonai, save my self!"

Adonai is gracious and just,
our God the compassionate one.
Adonai protects the simple hearted;
I was in need and then I was saved.

Return, my soul, to your rest,
for good to you has been Adonai,
who freed my soul from death,
my eyes from tears, and my feet from stumbling,

that I may walk before Adonai
in the land of the living.

Glory...

Antiphon

PSALM 121

Antiphon   *When coming, will the Son of Humanity*
          find faith on earth?   Lk 18:8

I lift up my eyes to the mountains.
From where does my help come?
My help comes from Adonai,
Maker of heavens and earth,

who will not let your foot slip
nor slumber when guarding you.
Indeed the guardian of Israel
will not slumber and will not sleep.

Adonai is your guardian,
the Most High at your right hand.
By day the sun will not harm you,
nor the moon by the night.

Adonai will keep you from all harm
and guard your life.
Adonai will guard your going and coming
from now and to forevermore.

Glory…

                                        Antiphon

I think I'll just
let the mystery be.
Iris DeMent, songwriter

PSALM 145

Antiphon *The Son of Humanity came*
to seek and to save the lost. Lk 19:10

I will exalt you, my God the Ruler,
and I will praise your Name to forever.

In every day I will praise you
and I will bless your Name to forever.
Great is Adonai, and greatly being praised,
an unfathomable greatness.

Generation to generation commend your works
and tell of your mighty acts
and the glorious splendor of your majesty,
and I will meditate on your wonderful deeds.

They will tell of your awesome works
and I will proclaim your great deeds.
They will celebrate and remember
the abundance of your goodness
and they will sing of your justice.

Gracious and compassionate is Adonai,
slow to anger, rich in love, and good to all.
Adonai's compassion is on every creature.

All your works will praise you, Adonai,
and your saints will bless you.
They will tell of the glory of your reign
and speak your might to make known

to sons and daughters of humanity your acts
and the glorious splendor of your reign,
the realm of all the ages,
and your dominion through all
generation and generation.

Adonai is faithful to all the promises
and loving to all who are made.
Adonai upholds all who are falling
and lifts up all who are bowed down.

The eyes of all look to you
and you give them their food in due season,
opening your hand and satisfying the desire
of every living thing.

Just is Adonai in all ways,
and loving to all who are made.
Near is Adonai to all who call,
to all who call in truth.

Fulfilled is the desire
of all who fear and love Adonai,
who hears their cry and saves them
and watches over them.
But bad ways will be destroyed.

My mouth will speak praise of Adonai.
Let every creature praise the holy Name
to forever and ever.

Glory... Antiphon

REVELATION 15:3b-4

Antiphon
*They sang the song
of Moses the servant of God
and the song of the Lamb.*   Rev 15:3a

Great and wonderful are your works,
Lord God Almighty.
Just and true are your ways,
Ruler of the nations.

Who will not fear, O Lord,
or glorify your name?

Only you are holy.
All the nations will come
and worship before you;
your ordinances are shown to all.

Glory…

Antiphon

---

*The world is making a discovery that there
is and always has been a regularly occurring
non-pathological minority variant in the human
condition known in our time as being lesbian, gay,
bi-sexual, transgender, queer, intersex, asexual, +.
So what will we do with this discovery?*
See writings of James Alison, Theologian

READING   **1 CORINTHIANS 2:1-16**

Coming to you, brothers and sisters, I came not with excellence of speech or of wisdom announcing to you the testimony of God. For I decided to know nothing among you except Jesus Christ, and this one having been crucified. And I was with you in weakness and fear and much trembling. My speech and proclamation (*kerygma*) was not persuasive words of wisdom, but a demonstration of spirit and power, that your faith may be not in human wisdom but in the power of God.

We speak wisdom among the mature, but wisdom not of this age, nor of the leaders of this age being brought to naught. But we speak of God, a wisdom in mystery, hidden, which God foreordained before the ages for our glory, which none of the leaders of this age has known. For if they knew, they would not have crucified the Lord of glory. But as it has been written, *things which eye has not seen and ear has not heard and have not come upon the human heart, how many are prepared for those loving God,* it is revealed to us by God through the Spirit.

For the Spirit searches all things, even the deep things of God. Who of human beings knows the things of a human except the spirit in that human? So also no one has known the things of God except the Spirit of God. We have not received the spirit of the world but the Spirit from God, that we may know the things freely given to us by God, which we also speak not in teaching of human words of wisdom, but in teaching of the Spirit, comparing spiritual things with spiritual things.

A natural human does not receive the things of the Spirit of God, for they are folly to one who cannot know what is discerned spiritually. But the spiritual human discerns on one hand all things; on the other the Spirit is discerned by no one: *For who has known the mind of the Lord and so who will instruct?* But we have the mind of Christ.

RESPONSORY   1 Cor 15:3; Rom 5:8; 1 Ptr 3:18

Christ died for our sins...
   ...*while we were still sinners.*
Put to death, he rose to life in the Spirit...
   ...*while we were still sinners.*
Glory to the Father and to the Son and to the Holy Spirit:
   ...*Christ died for our sins while we were still sinners.*

CANTICLE of MARY (The Magnificat)
LUKE 1:46-55

Antiphon   *God has given relief to servant Israel*
with a memory of mercy to remember.

+ **My soul** is stretched full with praise of the Lord,
and my spirit, beyond joy in God, my Savior,
who chose to lay eyes on this humble servant.

Behold, now and forward,
each and every age will call me blessed,
for the Mighty One did great things to me.

Holy is the name and the mercy
to generations and generations,
the ones fearing the One,

Who scattered the haughty of mind and heart,
pulled the powerful off their high place,
and lifted with dignity the humble in need.

The hungering are filled with good things,
the rich are sent away empty,
and servant Israel is given relief

with a memory of mercy to remember,
the promise spoken to our ancestors,
to Abraham and his descendants forever.

Glory...

                                                             Antiphon

INTERCESSIONS   adapted from Intercessions
                                          of Good Friday

- Give unity to your Church.

- Protect N. our Pope and all our Bishops.

- Sanctify your faithful people by your Spirit.

- Increase the faith and understanding of seekers.

- Gather all Christians in unity.

- Be faithful to the Jewish people of the covenant.

- Hear the praise of all who worship the One God.

- Show the marks of your love in creation to those who do not yet see them.

- Guide the minds and hearts of those who govern us.

- Console all who are troubled.

- Have mercy on all who have died.

- In gratitude for blessings…; Abba thank you.

- For the sins of this day…; Lord Jesus have mercy.

- With concerns over tomorrow…; Holy Spirit help.

A LATIN AMERICAN PRAYER

> Lord, to those who have hunger,
> give bread;
> and to those who have bread,
> give hunger for justice.

OUR FATHER…

WEEK II
SATURDAY MORNING

+ *God, come to my assistance;* Psalm 70:2
  Lord, make haste to help me!

  Glory...

A

Refrain

> **On\ this day**, **O beau-ti-ful Mo-ther**,
> On\ this day we give you our love.
> Near you, Ma-don-na, fond-ly we hov-er,
> Trust-ing your gen-tle care/ to prove.

Verse 1
> **O**n this day we ask to share,
> Dear-est Mo-ther, your sweet care;
> Help us 'lest our feet\ a-stray\,
> Wand-'ring from your guid-ing way.

Refrain

Verse 2
> **Q**ueen of an-gels, deign to hear
> Lisp-ing chil-dren's hum-ble pray'r;
> Young hearts gain, O Vir\-gin pure\
> Sweet-ly to your-self al-lure.

Refrain

139, Text: Louis Lambillotte, SJ, 1796-1855, altered
Music: 77 77, BEAUTIFUL MOTHER,
Rohr's *Favorite Catholic Melodies*, 1857

B **Ho-ly\ Ma-ry/, grace-ful Mo-ther**,
Hear your\ sons and/ daugh-ters say,
Mo-ther\, Bless-ed/ a-mong wo-men,
for your\ sons and/ daugh-ters, pray.
May the\ grace of Christ our\ Sa-vior
And the\ Fa-ther's bound-less\ love
With the\ Ho-ly/ Spir-it's fa-vor
Rest up\-on us/ from a-bove.

Thus may\ we a/-bide in u-nion
With each\ oth-er/ and the Lord,
And pos\-sess, in/ sweet com-mu-nion,
Joys which\ earth can/-not af-ford.
May the\ grace of Christ our\ Sa-vior
And the\ Fa-ther's bound-less\ love
With the\ Ho-ly/ Spir-it's fa-vor
Rest up\-on us/ from a-bove.

136, Text: Verse 1a by Stephen J. Wolf, 2018;
Verses 1b & 2 by John Newton, *Olney Hymns*, 1779
Music: 87 87 D, PLEADING SAVIOR,
Joshua Leavitt, Christian Lyre, 1830
Popular melody for: *Sing of Mary, Pure and Lowly*

122, Text: Stan. 1,2, Foundling Hospital Collection, 1801;
Stan. 3, Edward Osler, 1836, altered
Music: 87 87 D, PLEADING SAVIOR,
Joshua Leavitt, Christian Lyre, 1830
Popular melody for: *Sing of Mary, Pure and Lowly*

C **Praise the\ Lord, you/ heav'ns, a-dore\;**
Praise you\ an-gels/ in the height;
Sun and\ Moon, re/-joice be-fore\;
Shine your\ praise, you/ stars of light.
Give praise\, for the Lord has\ spo-ken;
Might-y\ voice the worlds o\-beyed;
Laws which\ nev-er/ shall be bro-ken,
Guid-ance\ that the/ Lord has made.

Praise the\ Lord, the/ Lord is glo-rious,
Prom-is\-es that/ do not fail;
God has\ made the/ saints vic-tor-ious,
Sin and\ death shall/ not pre-vail.
Praise the\ God of our sal\-va-tion;
Hosts on\ high the pow'r pro\-claim;
Heav-en and earth and/ all cre-a-tion,
Praise and\ mag-ni/-fy the name.

Wor-ship\, hon-or/, glo-ry, bles-sing,
Lord, we\ off-er/ un-to thee;
Young and\ old, your/ praise ex-pres-sing,
In glad\ hom-age/ bend the knee.
All the\ saints in heav-en a-dore you,
We would\ bow be-fore your\ throne;
As your\ an-gels/ serve be-fore you,
So on\ earth your/ will be done.

D **Lord God/, Sab-a-oth, El, A-do-nai,**
   Proph-et E-ze-kiel's song we lift high:
   Spir-it and heart\, re-newed you pro-vide,
   You are our God.

Refrain **You are our God\,**
   your peo-ple are we, Al-le-lu-ia!

Take us out-side of our pride that div-ides,
Gath-er us in from all na\-tions wide,
Bring us back in-to your land at your side,
You are our God. *Refrain*

Sprink-le on-to us your wa\-ters clean,
From our im-pur-i-ties help us to wean,
Clean from i-dol-a-try let us be seen,
You are our God. *Refrain*

Take from our flesh\ these hearts\ of stone,
Make in us new hearts of flesh, not of bone,
In-side our be-ing your Spir-it be shown,
You are our God. *Refrain*

Praise to you Fa-ther, and praise to you Son,
Praise to you Spir-it, three prais-es in One.
Jus-tice and Mer-cy un-til days are done,
You are our God. *Refrain*

> 142, Text: Ezekiel 36:24-28, Stephen J. Wolf, 2016
> Music: 888, O FILII ET FILIAE; Chant Mode II,
> *Airs sur les hymnes sacrez, odes et noels,* 1623
> Popular melody for: *Ye Sons And Daughters*

PSALM 106:1-16,19-48

Antiphon *Whose sins you forgive, they are forgiven;*
  whose sins you hold, they are held.   Jn 20:23

Hallelujah!
Give thanks to Adonai who is good,
whose love is to forever.

Who can proclaim the mighty acts of Adonai?
Who can tell the fullness of praise?
Blessed are they who maintain justice,
doing just deeds at all times.

Remember me, Adonai, as you favor your people!
In your salvation, come with your aid for me
to enjoy the prosperity of your chosen ones,
to have joy in the joy of your nation,
and to give praise with your inheritance.

We have sinned as did our ancestors;
we have done wrong with bad deeds.
Our ancestors when in Egypt
gave no thought to your miracle deeds,
did not remember your many kindnesses,
and rebelled by *Yam Suf,* the Sea of Reeds.

Still you saved them for the sake of your name,
to make known your power.
You rebuked the Sea of Reeds; it dried up.
You led them through the depths as the desert.

Psalm 106, continued

And you saved them from the hands of hostility
and redeemed them from the power of enmity.

The waters covered the adversity;
not one of them survived.
Then they believed in the promises made,
and sang out praise.

But soon did they forget those deeds
and would not wait for good counsel.
They craved cravings in the desert
and in the wasteland they tested their El,
who gave them their request
but sent a wasting disease on their life.

They envied Moses in the camp
and Aaron, the consecrated of Adonai…
They made a calf at Horeb
and gave their worship to a cast idol.
They exchanged their Glory
for an image of a grass-eating bull.

They forgot El who had saved them,
doing great things in Egypt,
miracle deeds in the land of Ham
and awesome deeds by the Sea of Reeds.

By a word spoken they were to be destroyed,
except that Moses the chosen stood in the breach.
Then they despised the beautiful land
and did not believe the promise made.

They grumbled in their tents
and did not obey the voice of Adonai,
who lifted a hand to let them fall in the desert
and their descendants fall among the nations;
they were scattered through the lands.

They yoked themselves to Baal of Peor
and they ate of sacrifices to lifeless ones.
They provoked anger by their deeds
and a plague broke out among them.

Phinehas stood up and intervened
and the plague was checked;
this was credited to him as a just and good deed
for generation and generations to forever.

They angered by the waters of Meribah,
the cause of trouble for Moses,
who spoke rashly with his lips
when they made his spirit bitter.

They did not defeat the peoples as commanded,
but mingled with the nations
and adopted their customs.
They worshiped their idols
which became to them as a snare.

Psalm 106, continued

They sacrificed their sons and daughters.
They shed the innocent blood
of their own sons and daughters
whom they sacrificed to idols of Canaan,
desecrating the land by this blood.

They defiled themselves by their deeds
and prostituted themselves in their doings.
Against the people grew the anger of Adonai,
abhorring the promised inheritance.

Into the hands of nations they were given,
ruled by adversity, oppressed by enmity,
and made subject to their power.
Many times were they delivered,
but they rebelled in their decisions
and wasted away in their guilt.

And yet on hearing their cry
the Lord took note of their distress
and remembered for them the covenant
and relented in abundant love
bringing to them compassion
from even their captors.

Save us, Adonai our God!
Gather us from the nations
to give thanks to your holy name
and glory in your praise.

SATURDAY MORNING

Blessed be Adonai, God of Israel
from everlasting to everlasting
and let all the people say, "Amen!"
Hallelujah!

Glory...

Antiphon *Whose sins you forgive, they are forgiven;
whose sins you hold, they are held.* Jn 20:23

PSALM 50

Antiphon *I desire mercy and not sacrifice,
knowledge of God
rather than burnt offerings.* Mt 9:13a; 12:7;
Hosea 6:6

El Elohim Adonai
speaks and summons earth
from the rising of the sun to its setting.
From Zion, perfect of beauty, God shines forth.

Our God comes and will not be silent,
before whom a fire devours,
around whom a storm is fierce.
The heavens at above are summoned,
and the earth to judge the people:

Psalm 50, continued

"Gather the ones faithful to me,
the ones making my covenant by sacrifice."
The heavens proclaim the justice of God,
the One who is judge.

"Hear, my people, and I will speak, Israel,
and I will testify against you;
God, your God, am I.

Not for your sacrifices do I rebuke you,
or your burnt offerings ever before me.
I do not need a bull from your stall
or goats from your pen,

for every animal of the forest is mine,
cattle on the mountains, the thousands.
I know every bird in the air,
and every creature of fields is mine.

Were I hungry, I would not tell it to you,
for the world is mine and all in her.
Do I eat the flesh of bulls?
Drink the blood of goats?

Offer thanksgiving as your sacrifice to God!
And fulfill your vows to the Most High!
Call upon me in the day of trouble;
I will deliver you and you will honor me."

But God says to those who do the bad,
"What to you to recite my laws
or to take my covenant on your lips?
You hate instruction,
and cast my words behind you.

When you see a thief, you join in,
and cast your lot with doers of adultery.
You use your mouth for the bad
and harness your tongue to deceit.

You sit and speak against your brother and sister
and slander your mother's children.
You did these, and I kept silent;
you thought me to be like you?

...Consider now this: ...there is no one to rescue
...those who insist on forgetting God.
One offering thanksgiving offered as a sacrifice,
I will show that one to the salvation of God."

Glory...

Antiphon — *I desire mercy and not sacrifice,
knowledge of God
rather than burnt offerings.* Mt 9:13a; 12:7;
Hosea 6:6

---

*Break up for
yourselves a new field;
it is time to seek the Lord.* Hosea 10:12

PSALM 92:1-9,11,13-16

Antiphon *The reign of God is as when*
a human might throw seed on the earth
and sleep and rise night and day
and the seed sprouts and grows
without the human knowing how.   Mk 4:26,27

It is good to praise Adonai,
to make music to your name, Most High,
to proclaim your love in the morning
and your fidelity at night
on the ten-string and on the lyre,
and the melody of the harp.

For you make me glad by your deeds, Adonai;
at the works of your hands I sing for joy.
How great are your works, Adonai;
very profound are your thoughts.
The senseless human does not know
and the fool does not understand.

Though the bad springs up like grass
and doers of the bad seem to flourish,
their ways will be destroyed to forever.
But you, Adonai, are on high to forever…

You gave me strength like a wild ox
and I was anointed with fresh oil…
The just will flourish like the palm tree,
and grow like a cedar of Lebanon.

Planted in the house of Adonai,
in the courts of our God they will flourish.
In old age they will still bear fruit,
ever full of sap and still green,
to proclaim, "Adonai is just,
in my Rock there is no wrong."

Glory…

Antiphon

---

*Though the
psalms originated
very many centuries ago
in the East, they express accurately
the pain and hope, the unhappiness and trust,
of people of every age and country, and celebrate
especially faith in God, revelation and redemption…
The person who prays the psalms in the name of the
church can always find a reason for joy or sadness.*

See *Introduction to the Liturgy of the Hours,* 107

DEUTERONOMY 32:1-12

Antiphon   *Praise the greatness of our God.*

Listen, heavens, and I will speak:
Hear, earth, the words of my mouth.
Let my teaching fall like the rain,
let my word descend like the dew,
like showers on grass,
like abundant rains on plants.

The name of Adonai I will proclaim,
and praise the greatness of our God.
The work of the Rock is perfect indeed;
all the ways of our faithful God are just
and without wrong, upright and just.

The children acted corruptly with no shame,
a generation warped and crooked.
Foolish and unwise people,
you repay Adonai in this way?
Did not your Father create you
and make you and form you?

Remember the days of old!
Consider the years of generation and generation!
Ask your parents and they will tell you!
Ask your elders and they will explain to you

SATURDAY MORNING

how the Most High gave inheritance to nations,
dividing sons and daughters of humanity
and setting up boundaries of peoples
by numbers of sons and daughters of Israel.

For the portion of Adonai is the people,
Jacob the allotment of inheritance,
found in desert land,
a barren and howling waste,
shielded with care,
guarded as the apple of the eye,

like an eagle stirring up the nest
and hovering over the young ones,
spreading wings to catch them
and carrying them on its flight feathers.

Led by Adonai alone,
no foreign "god" was with them.

Glory…

                                                                     Antiphon

---

*Is God the greatest? To speak of
God with a superlative such as Most
Powerful or Most Beautiful or the Greatest
would be to see God as merely the best within
created categories, but God is beyond categories of
creation, and so better language may be to refer to God
as Greatness-Itself or Power-Itself or Beauty-Itself, though
this remains imperfect. And yet we cannot not talk about God.*

EZEKIEL 36:24-28

Antiphon
*Let any who thirst
come to me and drink.* Jn 7:37

I will take you out of the nations
and I will gather you from all the countries,
and I will bring you back into your land.

I will sprinkle on you clean waters,
and you will be clean from all your impurities,
and from all your idols I will cleanse you.

I will give you a new heart
and I will put inside you a new spirit,
and I will remove the stone-heart from your flesh
and I will give you a flesh-heart,

and I will put inside you my Spirit
and I will move you to follow in my decrees
and my laws you will be careful to keep,

and you will live in the land I gave your ancestors,
and you will be my people
and I will be your God.

Glory... Antiphon

---

*All repressed emotions are stored in the body...
The deep rest of contemplative prayer reduces the
defenses that hold these oppressive feelings in the unconscious.*
See *Divine Therapy & Addiction* by Thomas Keating, Trappist monk

PSALM 8

Antiphon *I have much more to tell you,*
but you cannot bear it yet. Jn 16:12

Adonai, our Lord!
How majestic is your name in all the earth!

Your glory is set above the heavens!
From lips of children and infants
you ordained strength to bring to silence
enmity, adversity and vengeance.

When I consider your heavens,
the works of your fingers,
the moon and stars which you set in place,
what is a human that you would be mindful,
a child of Adam and Eve that you would care?

And you made us little lower than a "god"
crowning us with glory and honor,
making us to rule over works of your hands,
putting everything under our feet,

all the flocks and herds and beasts of the field,
birds of the air and fishes of the sea,
all that swims through the paths of the seas.

Adonai, our Lord!
How majestic is your name in all the earth!

Glory…

Antiphon

OFFICE OF READINGS and FIRST READING AT MASS

	Odd Years	**Even Years**
2 readings	*Romans 7:14-25*	*Genesis 17*
mass	Hebrews 9:2-3,11-14	2 Samuel 1:1-4,11-12,19
4 rdgs	*Romans 16*	*Genesis 37*
mass	Hebrews 13:15-17,20-21	1 Kings 3:4-13
6 rdgs	*1 Corinthians 10:1-13*	*2 Thessalonians 3*
mass	Hebrews 11:1-7	James 3:1-10
8 rdgs	*James 1:19-27*	*2 Corinthians 12:14-21*
mass	Ben Sira 51:12b-20	**Jude** 1:17,20b-25
10 rdgs	*Joshua 10*	*Philippians 4:10-23*
mass	2 Corinthians 5:14-21	1 Kings 19:19-21
12 rdgs	*1 Samuel 4*	*Nehemiah 2*
mass	Genesis 18:1-15	Lamentat. 2:2,10-14,18-19
14 rdgs	*1 Samuel 27 & 28*	*Proverbs 31*
mass	Genesis 49:29-33;50:15-24	Isaiah 6:1-8
16 rdgs	*1 Kings 8*	*Job 23 & 24*
mass	Exodus 24:3-8	Jeremiah 7:1-11
18 rdgs	*2 Kings 4:1-7*	*Malachi 3*
mass	Deuteronomy 6:4-13	**Habakkuk** 1:12-2:4
20 rdgs	*Ephesians 4:1-16*	*Ecclesiastes 11 & 12*
mass	Ruth 2:1-3,8-11;4:13-17	Ezekiel 43:1-7a
22 rdgs	*Amos 6*	*2 Timothy 4*
mass	Colossians 1:21-23	1 Corinthians 4:9-15

SATURDAY MORNING

	Odd Years	Even Years
24 rdgs	*2 Kings 15 & 16*	*Baruch 3 & 4*
mass	1 Timothy 6:13-16	1 Corinth 15:36-37,42-49
26 rdgs	*2 Kings 20*	*Judith 13*
mass	Baruch 4:5-12,27-29	Job 42:1-3,5-6,12-17
28 rdgs	*Jeremiah 9*	*Sirach 24*
mass	Romans 4:13,16-18	Ephesians 1:15-23
30 rdgs	*Jeremiah 29*	*Wisdom 7*
mass	Rom 11:1-2a,11-12,25-29	Philippians 1:18b-26
32 rdgs	*Ezekiel 14 & 15*	*1 Macabees 3*
mass	Wisdom 18:14-16;19:6-9	**3 John** 1:5-8
34 rdgs	*Ezekiel 47*	*Daniel 12*
mass	Daniel 7:15-27	Revelation 22:1-7

READING **ROMANS 12:9-21**

Let love be unassumed. Shrinking from the bad, cleave to the good. Love one another warmly in filial love, giving preference in honor of one another, unslothful in zeal, burning in spirit, serving the Lord, rejoicing in hope, enduring in affliction, steadfast in prayer, imparting to the needs of the saints, and pursuing hospitality.

Bless your persecutors; bless and do not curse them. Rejoice with those rejoicing; weep with those weeping. Be of the same mind toward one another, not attentive to the high things, but being present to the humble. Do not become wise in your own mind.

Romans 12, continued

Instead of returning evil for evil, don't. Provide for good things before all people. If possible, as far as it rests on you, seek peace with all human beings.

Do not avenge yourselves, beloved, but leave room for the wrath, for it has been written, *Vengeance is mine; I will repay, says the Lord.*

But if your enemy is hungry, feed him or her; or if they are thirsty, give them drink. In doing this you will heap on their heads coals of fire. Be not conquered by the evil, but conquer the evil (*kakon*) by the good.

RESPONSORY   Ps 92:4,2

Made glad, Lord, by your deeds...
   ...*I make music to your name.*
At the works of your hands I sing for joy;...
   ...*I make music to your name.*
Glory to the Father and to the Son and to the Holy Spirit:
   ...*Made glad, Lord, by your deeds,*
   I make music to your name.

Gospel Canticle For Morning

Antiphon   *Lord, shine on those hidden in the shadows.*

Gospel Reading for Saturday of
Week **2** Mark 3:20-21   **14** Matt 10:24-33   **26** Lk 10:17-24
       4 Mark 6:30-34   **16** Matt 13:24-30   **28** Luke 12:8-12
       6 Mark 9:2-13   **18** Matt 17:14-20   **30** Lk 14:1,7-11
       8 Mark 11:27-33   **20** Matt 23:1-12   **32** Luke 18:1-8
      10 Matt 5:33-37   **22** Luke 6:1-5   **34** Lk 21:34-36
      12 Matt 8:5-17   **24** Luke 8:4-15

CANTICLE of ZECHARIAH (The Benedictus)
LUKE 1:68-79

+ Blessed be the Lord the God of Israel
who chose a people to visit with redemption,
and raised salvation in the house of David,
saving strength from God's own servant,

speaking from the age of the prophets
through the mouth of the holy prophet:
Salvation out of enmity,
even out of those who hate us,

to show our ancestors how mercy works, -
and to remember the holy promise of the Lord,
the covenant made for our ancestor Abraham,
calming our fear and making us free
to serve with holy justice before God all our days.

And you also child -
will be called a prophet of the Most High
for you will go before the Lord to prepare his way
and give to people a knowledge of salvation
known in accepting forgiveness of their sins.

From the tender mercy of our God,
the sun rising from the height will visit with light
for those who sit in the dark or shadow of death
and to guide our feet into the way of peace.

Glory...

                                                          Antiphon

PETITIONS FOR THE CONSECRATION TO GOD
OF THE DAY AND ITS WORK

- For the Church and her ministry and apostolates...
- For secular authorities and all serving as stewards...
- For people who are poor or sick or in sorrow...
- For the basic needs of each human being...
- For awareness of being created in the image of God...
- For discovery and discernment of our charisms...
- For consensus on both rights and responsibilities...
- For loving respect for folks who think differently...
- For God's healing of the core wounds of enemies...
- For the world peace that only God can give...
- For elders who feel abandoned...
- For just treatment of migrant workers and refugees...
- For the starving child awakening our conscience...
- For those suffering physical and mental torture...
- For people living in subhuman conditions...
- For human beings enslaved or unjustly imprisoned...
- For workers in degrading or unsafe conditions...
- For laborers where treated as mere tools for profit...
- For rejection of judging the inner guilt of others...
- For a culture of vocations all over the world...
- For those who have asked for my prayer...
- For those for whom I have promised to pray...
- For those who weigh on my heart...

OUR FATHER...

SOLEMNITIES in ORDINARY TIME

Holy Trinity Sunday (Sunday after Pentecost)
- A   John 3:16-18
- B   Matthew 28:16-20
- C   John 16:12-15

Body and Blood (Sunday after Trinity Sunday)
- A   John 6:51-58
- B   Mark 14:12-16,22-26
- C   Luke 9:11b-17

Sacred Heart (Friday after Body and Blood)
- A   Matthew 11:25-30
- B   John 19:31-37
- C   Luke 15:3-7

Birth of John the Baptist (June 24)
- Vigil: Luke 1:5-17
- Day: Luke 1:57-66,80

Peter and Paul, Apostles (June 29)
- Vigil: John 21:15-19
- Day: Matthew 16:13-19

Assumption of Mary (August 15)
- Vigil: Luke 11:27-28
- Day: Luke 1:39-56

All Saints (November 1)
- Matthew 5:1-12a

ACKNOWLEDGEMENTS, SOURCES & CHOICES MADE in this MEDITATION RENDERING

The official translation approved by the Catholic Church for the *Liturgy of the Hours* is a beautiful translation for chanting in monasteries and seminaries. As a parish priest for twenty-two years and now in retirement, almost all of my time with the Psalter is with the church universal but alone with God, whether in my room, in a chapel, or in the woods. Praying in *Lectio Divina*, trying to listen to the Lord, I have found much prayerful fruit in several translations.

I used the regular four-week cycle of the Liturgy of the Hours for a long time before switching to a two-week cycle. After a brief experiment with "all in one week," I went back to these two weeks.

This meditation rendering follows consciously these choices:

1. For the name *YHVH*, or *Yahweh*, the Hebrew word ***Adonai*** (ah-duh-nigh') meaning *My Lord*, is used. In several places the words *El* or *Elyon* or *Elohim* are retrieved, as is *Sabaoth* instead of *Mighty* or *Hosts*.

2. Following the Christian understanding of one God in the three persons of the Trinity, masculine pronouns for God are avoided (I really don't know why women tolerate them), except when God is referred to as Father, or specific references to Jesus. I do this as an openly gay cis-gender male.

3. Except in the traditional Lord's Prayer and doxology, rather than the Greek ***Father*** (*pater*) the more intimate Aramaic ***Abba*** is used (think Dad, Daddy, Papa) as in Mark 14:36. Among my family and friends, no one addresses their Daddy as Father. See also Saint Paul's use of *Abba* in Romans 8:15 and Galatians 4:6 (see pgs 23, 104).

4. In an admittedly imperfect effort to pray the gospel as well as the psalms, the word *enemy* is most often rendered as *enmity* and *foes* as *adversity*.

5. Where people are referred to as *evil*, the emphasis is shifted to those who *do* the bad, or *ways* that are bad.

6. Since *race* is a human construct, and we are all members of the one human race, words such as *tribe* and *family* are used.

FOR ORDINARY TIME

There are problems with all of these choices. Still, in my judgment, the benefits overwhelm the problems.

Any errors in this rendering are entirely my own. Let us be grateful for all those who do the real work of translating sacred scripture.

Most of the Antiphons for Ordinary Time are **Sayings of Jesus** drawn from Sunday Gospel readings: In the Sunday Lectionary, the Old Testament readings have connections with the Gospel reading, and the Responsorial Psalm is a response to the Old Testament reading. This means that on any given Sunday there is a relationship between the Gospel reading and the Psalm. The antiphons were chosen based on this relationship.

Some of the **intercessions and petitions** are drawn from *Guadium et Spes*, "Pastoral Constitution on the Church in the Modern World," Vatican II, 1965, paragraph 27.

SOURCES

The primary source for this work is the grace of three decades with the psalms, canticles and readings from many translations, including:

The Liturgy of the Hours (Four Volumes), Copyright © 1974 ICEL International Committee on English in the Liturgy, Inc.

New American Bible with Revised New Testament, (1986) **and Revised Psalms** (1991) Copyright © 1991, 1986, 1970 Confraternity of Christian Doctrine, Inc. Washington, D.C. All rights reserved. (*This is my favorite translation of the Psalms.*)

New American Bible Revised Edition (NABRE), Copyright © 2010, 1986 Confraternity of Christian Doctrine, Washington, D.C. All rights reserved. (*This is the current Catholic translation.*)

New Revised Standard Version Bible: Catholic Edition, Copyright © 1993 and 1989 by the Division of Christian Education of the National Council of the Churches of Christ in the U.S.A.

The New Jerusalem Bible, Copyright © 1985 by Darton, Longman & Todd, Ltd. & Doubleday, a division of Bantam Doubleday Dell Publishing Group, Inc.

The Jewish Study Bible, Copyright © 1985, 1999 by the Jewish Publication Society

Acknowledgments & Sources, continued

The Interlinear NIV Hebrew-English Old Testament, by John R. Kohlenberger III, Copyright © 1979, 1980, 1982, 1985, 1987 by the Zondervan Corporation

The NRSV-NIV Parallel New Testament in Greek and English, by Alfred Marshall, Copyright © 1990 by the Zondervan Corporation

The New Greek-English Interlinear New Testament, translators Robert K. Brown & Philip W. Comfort, Copyright © 1990 by Tyndale House Publishers

I am especially grateful for these three, and to all those who worked on the *New American Bible* Psalms of 1991.

These works were also very helpful:

The New Jerome Biblical Commentary, edited by Raymond E. Brown, S.S., Joseph A. Fitzmyer, S.J., and Roland E. Murphy, O.Carm., Copyright © 1990, 1968 by Prentice-Hall, Inc.

The following volumes from the **Anchor Bible**:

Psalms I (1-50); Psalms II (51-100); Psalms III (101-150), The Anchor Bible, Volumes 16, 17, and 17A, by Mitchell Dahood, S.J., Copyright © 1965,1966, © 1968, © 1970, Doubleday

The Wisdom of Ben Sira; The Anchor Bible, Vol. 39, by Patrick W. Skehan, Copyright © 1987, Doubleday & Company, Inc.

Tobit; The Anchor Bible, Vol. 40A, by Carey A. Moore, Copyright © 1996, Doubleday

The Wisdom of Solomon; The Anchor Bible, Vol. 43, by David Winston, Copyright © 1979, Doubleday & Company, Inc.

Daniel, Esher and Jeremiah, the Additions; The Anchor Bible, Vol.44, by Carey A. Moore, Copyright © 1977, Doubleday & Company, Inc.

The summary of *Lectio Divina* on page 69 comes from many guides, all of whom have my deep gratitude, expecially Rev. Paul Wachdorf of Mundelein Seminary, north of Chicago.

And a stack of dictionaries.

Stephen Joseph Wolf   Nashville, Tennessee   **www.idjc.org**

FOR ORDINARY TIME 515

PSALMS

1 I-Sun Morn, page 20
2 I-Sun Morning, 21
3 II-Thu Morning, 421
4 I-Sun Vigil, 6
5 I-Mon Morning, 54
6 I-Thu Morning, 422
7 I-Mon Evening, 72
8 II-Sat Morning, 505
9 I-Mon Morning, 52
10 I-Tue Morning, 86
11 I-Mon Evening, 77
12 II-Mon Evening, 327
13 II-Tue Evening, 367
14 I-Tue Evening, 108
15 I-Mon Evening, 78
16 II-Sunday Vigil, 258
17 I-Wed Evening, 144
18 I-Wed/ThuMrn,123,156
19 II-Mon Morning, 316
20 I-Tue Evening, 112
21 I-Tue Evening, 114
22 I-Fri Evening, 217
23 II-Sun Evening, 290
24 I-Tue Morning, 92
25 I-Thu Evening, 176
26 I-Fri Evening, 220
27 I-Wed Evening, 146
28 I-Wed Evening, 148
29 I-Mon Morning, 60
30 I-Thu Evening, 182
31 II-Mon Morning, 304
32 I-Thu Evening, 184
33 I-Tue Morning, 99
34 II-Sunday Vigil, 254
35 I-Fri Morning, 198
36 I-Wed Morning, 130
37 II-Tue Morning, 344
38 II-Fri Morning, 456
39 II-Wed Morning, 382
40 II-Mon Evening, 328
41 I-Fri Evening, 224
__42__ II-Mon Morning, 310
43 II-Tue Morning, 351
44 II-Thu Morning, 423
45 II-Mon Morning, 332
46 I-Fri Evening, 226
47 I-Wed Evening, 134
48 I-Thu Evening, 166
49 II-Tue Evening, 370
50 II-Sat Morning, 497
51 Fri Mornings, 200, 460
52 II-Wed Evening, 404
53 II-Tue Evening, 368
54 II-Tue Evening, 369
55 II-Fri Morning, 458
56 II-Thu Evening, 442
57 I-Thu Evening, 160
59 II-Fri Evening, 476
60 II-Thu Evening, 443
61 I-Sun Vigil, 7
62 II-Wed Evening, 410
63 I-Sun Morning, 23
64 I-Sun Evening, 42
65 II-Tue Evening, 358
66 II-Sun Morning, 272
67 I-TueMrn/II-WedEvg,101,414
68 I-Tue Morning, 88
69 I-Fri Morning, 195
70 I-Wed Evening, 143
71 I-Mon Evening, 74
72 II-Thu Evening, 447
__73__ II-Mon Morning, 307
74 I-Tue Evening, 109
75 II-Wed Evening, 406
76 II-Sun Evening, 291
77 II-Wed Morning, 384
78 *Lent & Easter only*
79 I-Thu Evening, 178
80 II-Thu Evening, 426
81 II-Thu Morning, 428
82 II-Mon Morning, 330
84 I-Mon Evening, 56
85 I-Tue Morning, 94
86 I-Thu Morning, 180
87 I-Thu Morning, 162
88 I-Fri Evening, 222
89 I-Wed/ThuMorn, 126, 158
__90__ II-Mon Morning, 318
91 I-Sun Evening, 40
92 II-Sat Morning, 500
93 I-Sun Morning, 24
94 II-Wed Morning, 408
95 I-Fri Morning, 206
96 I-Mon Morning, 62
97 II-Wed Morning, 392
98 I-Wed Morning, 135
99 I-Thu Morning, 168
100 I-Fri Morning, 207
101 II-Tue Morning, 352
102 II-Tue Morning, 348
103 II-Wed Morning, 380
104 II-Sun Morning, 268
105 I-Sat Morning, 234
106 II-Sat Morning, 493
__107__ I-Sat Morning, 238
108 II-Wed Morning, 386
110 Sun Evenings, 43, 293
111 I-Sun Morning, 44
112 I-Sun Evening, 294
113 I-Sun Vigil, 8
114 I-Sun Evening, 45
115 II-Sun Evening, 296
116 I-SunVig,II-FriEvg, 9, 480
117 I-Sat Evening, 247
118 II-Sun Morning, 274
119 I-SaMrn,246 II-SuVig,257
120 II-Mon Evening, 331
121 II-Fri Evening, 481
122 II-Sunday Vigil, 260
123 I-Mon Evening, 79
124 I-Mon Evening, 80
125 I-Tue Evening, 115
126 I-Wed Evening, 149
127 I-Wed Evening, 150
128 II-Thu Evening, 445
129 II-Thu Evening, 446
130 II-Sunday Vigil, 261
131 I-Tue Evening, 116
132 I-Thu Evening, 186
133 II-Fri Evening, 477
134 II-Sunday Vigil, 256
135 I-Fri Evening, 227
136 II-Mon Evening, 334
137 II-Tue Evening, 372
138 II-Tue Evening, 373
139 II-Wed Evening, 412
140 II-Fri Evening, 478
141 I-Sun Vigil, 10
142 I-Sun Vigil, 12
143 II-Thu Morning, 432
144 II-Thu Evening, 449
145 II-Fri Morning, 482
146 II-Wed Morning, 394
147 II-Fri Morning, 466, 468
148 I-Sun Morning, 27
149 I-Sun Morning, 29
150 II-Sun Morning, 278

"Sunday Vigil" is Saturday Evening   Psalms 58, 83, & 109 omitted as in *Liturgy of the Hours*

PSALTER COMPARISON

PSALMS of the FOUR-WEEK PSALTER

	Office of Readings				*Morning Prayer*			
	I	II	III	IV	I	II	III	IV
SUN	1 2 3	104	145	24 66	63 149	118 150	93 148	118 150
MON	6 9A	31	50	73	5 29	42 19A	84 96	90 135
TUE	10 12	37	68	102	24 33	43 65	85 67	101 144
WED	18A	39 52	89A	103	36 47	77 97	86 98	108 146
THU	18B	44	89B 90	44	57 48	80 81	87 99	143 147A
FRI	35	38	69	55	51 100	51 147B	51 100	51 147B
SAT	132	136	107	50	119-19 117	92 8	119-14 117	92 8

DAWN & DUSK WEEK ONE

	Morning Prayer	*Evening Prayer*
VIGIL		4 *61* 113 116 141 142
SUN	*1 2* 63 93 148 149	*64 91* 110 111 114
MON	*5 9* 29 84 96	*7 71* 11 15 123 124
TUE	*10 68* 24 33 67 85	*14 74* 20 21 125 131
WED	*18A 89A* 36 47 98	*17 28* 70 27 126 127
THU	*18B 89B* 48 57 87 99	*25 79* 30 32 86 132
FRI	*35 69* 51 95 100	*22 26* 88 41 46 135
SAT	*105 107* 117 119	

PSALTER COMPARISON

PSALMS of the FOUR-WEEK PSALTER

| | \multicolumn{4}{c}{Daytime Prayer} | \multicolumn{4}{c}{Evening Prayer} | Night |

	Daytime Prayer I	II	III	IV	Evening Prayer I	II	III	IV	Night
SUN	118	23 76	118	23 76	110 114	110 115	110 111	110 112	91
MON	19B 7	119-6 40	119-12 71	119-17 82 120	11 15	45	123 124	136	86
TUE	119-1 13 14	119-7 53 54	119-13 74	119-18 88	20 21	49	125 131	137 138	143
WED	119-2 17	119-8 55	119-14 70 75	119-19 94	27	62 67	126 127	139	31 130
THU	119-3 25	119-9 56 57	119-15 79 80	119-20 128 129	30 32	72	132	144	16
FRI	119-4 26 28	119-10 59 60	22	119-21 133 140	41 46	116A 121	135	145	88
SAT	119-5 34	119-11 61 64	119-10 34	119-22 45	119-14 16	113 116B	122 130	141 142	4 134

DAWN & DUSK WEEK TWO

	Morning Prayer	*Evening Prayer*
VIGIL		*34 134* 16 119 122 130
SUN	*66 104* 118 150	*23 76* 110 112 115
MON	*31 73* 19 42 90	*12 40 82 120* 45 136
TUE	*37 102* 43 65 101	*13 53 54* 49 137 138
WED	*39 103* 77 97 108 146	*52 75 94* 62 67 139
THU	*3 6 44* 80 81 143	*56 60 128 129* 72 144
FRI	*38 55* 51 147	*59 133 140* 116 121 145
SAT	*50 106* 8 92	

CANTICLES, READINGS & ANTIPHONS

OLD TESTAMENT CANTICLES

Exodus 15:1b-4,8-13,17-18 I-Sat Morning, page 242
Deuteronomy 32:1-12 II-Sat Morning, 502
1 Samuel 2:1-10 II- Wed Morning, 388
1 Chronicles 29:10b-13 I-Mon Morning, 59
Tobit 13:1b-8 I-Tue Morning, 96
Tobit 13:8-11,13-15 II-Fri Morning, 464
Judith 16:1,13-15 I-Wed Morning, 132
Wisdom 9:1-6,9-11 I-Sat Morning, 244
Sirach 36:1-6,13-22 II-Mon Morning, 312
Isaiah 2:2-5 I-Mon Morning, 58
Isaiah 12:1b-6 II-Thu Morning, 430
Isaiah 26:1b-4,7-9,12 I-Tue Morning, 98
Isaiah 33:13-16 I-Wed Morning, 133
Isaiah 38:10-14,17b-20 II-Tue Morning, 354
Isaiah 40:10-17 I-Thu Morning, 164
Isaiah 42:10-16 II-Mon Morning, 314
Isaiah 45:15-25 I-Fri Morning, 202
Isaiah 61:10-62:5 II-Wed Morning, 390
Isaiah 66:7-14a II-Thu Morning, 431
Jeremiah 14:17b-22 I- Fri Morning, 204
Jeremiah 31:10-14 I-Thu Morning, 163
Ezekiel 36:24-28 II-Sat Morning, 504 (& 492)
Daniel 3:26-27,29,34-41 II-Tue Morning, 356
Daniel 3:52-57 II- Sun Morning, 277
Daniel 3:57-90 I-Sun Morning, 25
Habakkuk 3:2-4,13a,15-19 II-Fri Morning, 462

OLD TESTAMENT READINGS

Tobit 4:15-19 I-Wed Morning, 138
Isaiah 66:1-2 I-Thu Morning, 172
Jeremiah 15:16 II-Mon Morning, 322
Ezekiel 36:22-26 II-Sun Morning, 282

NEW TESTAMENT CANTICLES

Luke 1:46-55 – Evenings, first on pg 17
Luke 1:68-79 – Mornings, first on pg 35
Luke 2:29-32 I-Wed Evening, 144
Ephesians 1 – Mon Evenings, 81, 336
Philippians 2 – Sun Vigils, 13, 262
Colossians 1 – Wed Evenings, 151, 415
Revelation 4&5 – Tue Evenings, 117, 375
Revelation 11&12 -ThuEvenings,188,451
Revelation 15 – Fri Evenings, 229, 484
Revelation 19 – Sun Evenings, 46, 298

NEW TESTAMENT READINGS

Romans 3:21-31 II-Tue Evening, 375
Romans 8:35,37-39 II-Wed Morning, 398
Romans 11:30-36 I-Sunday Vigil, 15
Romans 12:9-21 II-Sat Morning, 507
Romans 13:11-14 I-Tue Morning, 104
Romans 14:13-19 II-Thu Morning, 435
Romans 15:1-6 I-Fri Evening, 230
1 Corinthians 2:1-16 II-Fri Evening, 485
2 Corinthians 1:3-7 I-Sun Evening, 47
Ephesians 2:11-12 II-Fri Morning, 471
Ephesians 4:25-32 I-Fri Morning, 209
Colossians 1:3-6 I-Sunday Vigil, 263
Colossians 1:9b-14 I-Mon Evening, 82
1 Thessalonians 2:13 II-Mon Evng, 338
1 Thess. 5:1-11 II-Wed Morning, 361
2 Thessalonians 2:13-17 II- Sun Evg, 299
2 Thessalonians 3:7-13 I-Mon Evg, 65
James 1:19-27 I-Wed Evening, 152
1 Peter 1:3-9 I-Thu Evening, 189
1 Peter 1:22-25 II-Thu Evening, 452
1 Peter 5:1-7 II-Wed Evening, 416
2 Peter 1:3-11 I-Sat Morning, 249
1 John 3:1-2 I-Tue Evening, 118
Revelation 7:9-12 I-Sun Morning, 32

SAYINGS & RESPONSORY VERSES

Be not afraid, 256

Matthew 1:21, 92   Matthew 1:23, 367   Matthew 2:6, 447   Matthew 3:17, 60
Matthew 4:19, 146   Matthew 5:3, 20   Matthew 5:4, 351   Matthew 5:5, 394   Matthew 5:6, 294
Matthew 5:7, 10   Matthew 5:8, 78   Matthew 5:9, 58   Matthew 5:10, 384   Matthew 5:11, 478
Matthew 5:13a,14a, 382   Matthew 5:16, 12   Matthew 5:19, 421   Matthew 5:38,39, 143
Matthew 5:40, 54   Matthew 6:6, 271   Matthew 6:24b,21, 370   Matthew 6:26, 150

FOR ORDINARY TIME 519

SAYINGS & RESPONSORY VERSES, continued

Matthew 6:34, 410   Matthew 7:1, 443   Matthew 7:24, 304   Matthew 8:15, 408
Matthew 8:17, 109   Matthew 9:13a, 12:7, 497   Matthew 10:6, 207   Matthew 10:28, 195
Matthew 10:37, 126   Matthew 10:38, 158   Matthew 10:39, 80   Matthew 11:28,30, 7
Matthew 13:16,17a, 130   Matthew 13:23, 358   Matthew 13:30, 180   Matthew 13:33, 423
Matthew 13:45,46, 476   Matthew 13:52, 257   Matthew 14:27,29, 94   Matthew 14:31, 44
Matthew 15:28, 101   Matthew 16:26, 227   Matthew 18:20, 206   Matthew 18:22, 45
Matthew 18:35, 380   Matthew 21:31, 220   Matthew 21:43, 426   Matthew 22:21, 62
Matthew 22:37,39, 123   Matthew 23:3b,4, 116   Matthew 25:13, 23   Matthew 25:29, 445
Matthew 25:35,36, 290   Matthew 28:20, 134

Mark 1:3, 164   Mark 1:15, 176   Mark 1:38, 466   Mark 2:9-11, 224   Mark 2:15, 114
Mark 2:22, 86   Mark 2:27, 428   Mark 2:28, 291   Mark 3:5, 462   Mark 3:25, 456
Mark 3:35, 261   Mark 4:25, 186   Mark 4:26,27, 500   Mark 4:41, 238   Mark 5:30, 182
Mark 5:41, 79   Mark 6:7a, 81   Mark 6:8, 166   Mark 6:31, 336   Mark 7:15, 344
Mark 7:21,22, 347   Mark 8:31, 480   Mark 9:7, 327   Mark 9:31, 369   Mark 9:37b, 458
Mark 10:15, 368   Mark 10:45, 331   Mark 10:51,52, 149   Mark 12:29, 156
Mark 13:31, 258   Mark 16:15, 432

Luke 1:47, 388   Luke 2:29-32, 144, 234   Luke 2:49, 56   Luke 2:52, 244   Luke 3:10, 430
Luke 4:4, 40   Luke 4:18, 112   Luke 4:24, 74   Luke 4:40b, 404   Luke 5:4, 373
Luke 6:20b, 77   Luke 6:23, 332   Luke 6:27, 412   Luke 6:36, 278   Luke 6:41, 72
Luke 7:6,7, 247   Luke 7:14, 422   Luke 7:16, 352   Luke 7:44,47, 184   Luke 8:11b, 442
Luke 9:13a, 43   Luke 9:14, 293   Luke 9:16, 25   Luke 9:50, 348   Luke 9:58, 52
Luke 9:60, 222   Luke 10:2, 272   Luke 10:11b, 431   Luke 10:29, 161   Luke 10:37, 316
Luke 11:9, 246   Luke 11:13, 115   Luke 12:15, 318   Luke 12:34, 99   Luke 12:49, 328
Luke 13:30, 91   Luke 14:10,11, 88   Luke 14:33, 307   Luke 16:13, 8   Luke 17:17, 168
Luke 18:8, 481   Luke 18:13, 198   Luke 18:13; 22:69, 32   Luke 19:5, 449
Luke 19:10, 482   Luke 19:42a, 178   Luke 20:38, 144   Luke 21:15, 135
Luke 23:34, 42   Luke 23:43, 260   Luke 24:46, 6

John 2:7,8, 392   John 3:8, 21   John 3:16, 372   John 3:17, 277   John 3:21, 386   John 3:30, 29
John 4:34, 334   John 5:6, 226   John 6:35, 446   John 6:51a, 468   John 6:51b, 254
John 7:37, 504   John 8:7, 406   John 8:12c, 151, 415   John 10:4, 310   John 10:14, 274
John 10:30, 162   John 12:24, 181   John 12:25, 460   John 12:26b, 200   John 13:14, 9
John 14:23, 296   John 14:27a, 414   John 15:1, 217   John 15:12, 160   John 15:17, 27
John 16:12, 505   John 18:34, 24   John 20:21, 268   John 20:23, 493, 311

Acts 1:21-22, 427   Acts 4:32a, 477   Romans 14:17, 202   1 Cor 15:3; Rom 5:8; 1 Ptr 3:18, 486
1 Timothy 2:2, 148   1 Timothy 2:3b,4, 149   Philippians 2:3, 13, 262   Hebrews 11:29a, 242
James 4:12, 330   1 John 1:8,9, 108   Revelation 1:5,6, 230   Revelation 1:8, 188
Revelation 4:8b, 117, 375   Revelation 15:3a, 229, 484   Revelation 21:5b, 96   Rev 21:10,11, 464

Genesis 1:31a, 477   Leviticus 19:18, 123   Deuteronomy 6:5, 123   1 Chronicles 29:14b, 59
Tobit 1:13, 472   Psalm 16:11, 376   Psalm 17:8, 416   Psalm 23:1, 452   Psalm 25:4, 138
Psalm 26:9,11, 152   Psalm 34, 312   Psalm 34:2, 398   Psalm 41:5, 82   Psalm 63:7,8, 436
Psalm 70:2, 4   Psalm 71:1,5, 104   Psalm 72:18,19, 66   Psalm 81:16b, 189   Psalm 92:4,2, 508
Psalm 100:5, 118   Psalm 111:2,4,10, 15   Psalm 113:3,4, 263   Ps 119:147, 362   Psalm 130:1, 172
Psalm 138:4,5, 47   Psalm 141:2, 338   Psalm 142:6,7a, 250   Psalm 143:8, 210   Psalm 147:2, 322
Psalm 147:5, 299   Psalm 148, 314   Isaiah 12:4,5, 282   Isaiah 42:6a, 314   Isaiah 43:1-5a, 429   Isaiah 53:4, 109
Isaiah 58:6;61:1-2, 112   Jeremiah 1:5, 204   Jeremiah 24:7b, 163   Job 38-42, 165
Hosea 6:6, 497   Hosea 10:12, 499   Micah 5:2, 447

DAWN & DUSK RAINBOW

CORNER NOTES

All Shall Be Well, 389
A Living Gospel, 125
Anger the Jesus Way, 463
Apostle, One Who is Sent, 427
Apostleship of Prayer, 400
As a Child Rests, 116
A Subordinate Caste, 87
Awareness, 350
Babylonian Exile, 243, 372
Beatitudes, 10
Be Not Afraid, 194, 256
Big Stories of the Old Testament, 243
Chapter-a-Day Reading Plan, 14
Comfort, 47
Conscience, 425
Contemplative Life, 22, 393, 504
Culture of Vocations, 273, 317, 438
Debasement, 131
Do Not Judge, 444
Easter makes all the difference, 311, 355
Every Age & Country, 501
Fear, 194, 333
Friendship, 46
Garden of Eden, 101
God Questions, 165
God's Universal Salvific Will, 149
Grain of Wheat, 181
Grace, 28
Gratitude, 411
Hallel Psalms, 276
Hallelujah!, 271
Harmony of Tensions, 174
Humility, 131
Idolatry, 313, 112
Insert Your Name, 429
Intimacy, 391
In Years to Come, 383
Is God the Greatest?, 503
Job Answers, 165
Justice, 112
Lamentations, 111
Lectio Divina, 69

LGBTQIA+ Discovery, 484
List, My, 129
Mary, Mother of God, 233
Monks, 167, 179, 183, 501
Mountain, 162
My Cross, 159
Mystery, 481
Name of God, 466
Note about Readings, 15
One adulterer is there, 406
Parable of the Latrine, 347
Paranoia, 73
Parents, 116
Perfection, 157
Personal Vocation, 133
Place of Business, 319
Pope's Prayer Network, 400
Possessions, 309
Praying Deeper, 295
Priest-Prophet-Royal-Lover, 79
Principal & Foundation, 185
Psalm Attributions, 6
Psalm Doesn't Apply to Me, 221
Psalm of the Elders, 76
Religious Freedom, 425
Respect, Compassion & Sensitivity, 150
Sandwiches, 115
Seeker-Disciple-Minister-Apostle, 418
Servant Songs, 292
Simplicity, 395
Singing, 132, 278, 414
Son of Humanity, 292
Sophia Lady Wisdom, 245
Suffering Servant, 292
Take off your sandals, 80
The Tricky Part, 55
Way of a Pilgrim, 32
What the Prophet Does, 97
Who Am I to Judge?, 203
Who Is My Neighbor?, 317
Widows, Orphans & Aliens, 112
You Want to be a Saint, 117

IMAGES by Stephen Joseph Wolf

Alleluia, 258
Anger the Jesus Way, 404
Away from the Cross, 486
Baptism of the Lord, 60
Cosmology of the Ancients, 315
Crucifixion, 478
Footwasher, 336
Hildegard Mandala, 95

Holy Family, 118
Jesus on the Cross, 352
Light of Christ, 169
Mother of Tenderness, 190
Nativity, 92
Nativiy Cross, 387
Unity in the Trinity, 374
Unity Cross, 465

FOR ORDINARY TIME 521

QUOTES & NOTES

James Allison, 484
Herbert Alphonso, S.J., 133
Sister Wendy Beckett, 187
Fr Phillip Breen, 263
Frederick Buechner, 306
Breton Fishers, 24
Will D. Campbell, 297
Catechism of the Catholic Church, 150, 425
Jean-Pierre de Caussade, S.J., 125
Anthony de Mello, S.J, 229, 359, 445
Iris DeMent, 481
Serafina Di Giacomo, 82
Sister Ruth Fox, OSB, 364
Pope Francis, 174, 203, 400
Mahatma Gandhi, 143
Gerard Goggins, 400
Sister Thelma Hall, R.C., 80
Hasidic saying, 61
Mychal Judge, OFM, 324
Julian of Norwich, 389
Thomas Keating, OCSO, 504
Soren Kierkegaard, 12
Jonathan Larson, 369
Mark Link, S.J., 204
Gabriel Marcel, 161
Thomas Merton, 20, 22, 50, 117, 245, 393, 411
Martin Moran, 55
Reinhold Niebuhr, 232, 214

D.T. Niles on Evangelization, 298
Henri Nouwen, 157
Evagrius Ponticus, 53, 120, 277
John Jacob Raub, 71
Sister Helen Prejean, 28
Saint Anthony of Egypt, 277
Saint Augustine of Hippo, 46, 132, 298, 340
Saint Benedict of Nursia, 183
Saint Francis of Assisi, 84, 183, 30
Saint Gregory Nazianzen, 414
Saint John Chrysostum, 395
Saint John the Baptist, 430
Saint Ignatius of Loyola,
    120, 174, 185, 204, 214
Saint Irenaeus, 261
Saint John Gabriel Perboyre, 192
Saint Paul of Tarsus, 59
Saint Pope Paul VI, 63
Saint Teresa of Avila, 357
Saint Teresa of Kolkata, 225
Maria Sktodowska-Curie, 333
Mark E, Thibodeaux, S.J., 295
James Thurber, 350
Paul Wachdorf, 68
Benedicta Ward, 179
Isabel Wilkerson, 87
Greg Wolf, 129
Anthony Zoghby, 247

PRAYERS

Our Father, 18, 36, 266, 286
Act of Contrition, 454
A Franciscan Blessing, 364
A Latin American Prayer, 488
Angelus, 474
Come Holy Spirit, 140
Consciousness Examen, 204
Doxology, 3, 230
Easter Prayer for Vocations, 302
For Vocations, 418
Hail Mary, 474
Jesus Prayer, 32
Lenten Prayer for Vocations, 400
Lord Take Me, 324

Morning Offering, 212
Night Prayer, 41, 481
Ponder Questions for Vocations, 438
Prayer for Generosity, 120
Prayer in an Addictive Culture, 154
Prayer of Saint Francis, 84
Prayer of the Confirmed, 378
Restless Heart, 340
Serenity Prayer, 232, 214
Suscipe of Mother McAuley, 106
Take Lord Receive, 174
Te Deum, 37, 287
The Road Ahead, 50
Vincentian Mission Prayer, 192
Workers in Offices, Shops & Markets, 68

SONGS

All Creatures of Our God & King: LASST UNS ERFREUEN	II-Wed Morning, 402
All Glory, Laud, and Honor: ST. THEODULPH	I-Fri Evening, 216
Amazing Grace: NEW BRITAIN	I-Wed Morning, 121
As Abba Loves You: BUNESSAN	I-Wed Morning, 122

DAWN & DUSK RAINBOW

Songs, continued

Song	Reference
Beautiful Savior: ST. ELIZABETH	I-Thu Evening, 175
Be Still My Soul: FINLANDIA	II-Tue Evening, 366
Blessed Be The God and Father: HYMN TO JOY	I-Wed Evening, 141
Come, Holy Spirit Whoever One: LAMBILLOTTE	I-Sun Morning, 19
Crown Him With Many Crowns: DIADEMATA	II-Fri Morning, 475
For The Beauty Of The Earth: DIX	I-Mon Evening, 70
From All That Dwell Below: DUKE STREET	I-Mon Morning, 51
Holy God We Praise Your Name: GROSSER GOTT	I-Sun Evening, 39
Holy, Holy, Holy, Lord God Almighty: NICAEA	II-Sun Morning, 267
Holy Mary, Graceful Mother: STUTTGART	II-Sat Morning, 490
How Can I Keep From Singing: ENDLESS SONG	I-Fri Evening, 215
How Lovely Is Your Dwelling Place: O WALY WALY	II-Tue Evg, 365
I Know That My Redeemer Lives: DUKE STREET	II-Mon Morning, 303
I Sing The Mighty Pow'r of God: ELLACOMBE	II-Mon Evening, 326
In Christ There Is No East or West: MCKEE	II-Tue Morning, 341
In God's Eye All Are Black and White: MCKEE	II-Tue Morning, 342
Jesus My Lord My God My All: SWEET SACRAMENT	II-Thur Morn, 420
Joyful, Joyful, We Adore You: HYMN TO JOY	II-Sun Evening, 288
Let All Mortal Flesh Keep Silence: PICARDY	II-Fri Evening, 455
Lord God Sabaoth El Adonai: O FILII ET FILIAE	II-Sat Morning, 492
Lord of All Being Throned: JESU DULCIS MEMORIA	I-Tue Morn, 85
Lord When At Your Last…: UNDE ET MEMORES	II-Thu Evening, 440
Love Divine All Love Excelling: HYFRYDOL	II-Sun Evening, 289
My Life Flows On In: ENDLESS SONG	I-Fri Evening, 215
Now Thank We All Our God: NUN DANKET	I-Sun Vigil, 4
O Breathe On Me O Breath of God: ST. COLUMBA	II-Thu Morning, 419
O God Grant Me Serenity: TALLIS CANON	I-Fri Evening, 214
On This Day O: BEAUTIFUL MOTHER	II-Sat Morning, 489
O Sanctissima: O DU FROLICHE	I-Sat Morning, 233
Praise God, from Whom All…: OLD HUNDREDTH	I-Sun Evening, 38
Praise My Soul the King of Heaven: LAUDA ANIMA	II-Wed Morn, 379
Praise the Lord You Heavens: PLEADING SAVIOR	II-Sat Morning, 491
Praise To The Lord: LOBE DEN HERREN	II-Sun Vigil, 253
Prophets Out of Ancient Times: HYFRYDOL	II-Tue Morning, 343
Shepherd of Souls: ST. AGNES	II-Wed Evening, 401
Sing My Tongue: ST. THOMAS (Tantum Ergo)	II-Thu Evening, 439
Take Lord Receive: TALLIS CANON	I-Fri Evening, 214
Take Up Your Cross: ERHALT UNS HERR	I-Fri Morning, 194
The Church's One Foundation: AURELIA	II-Mon Evening, 325
The King of Love My Shepherd Is: ST. COLUMBA	I-Thur Morn, 155
There's A Wideness In God's Mercy: HYFRYDOL	I-Wed Evg, 142
We Gather Together: KREMSER	I-Sunday Vigil, 5
We Walk By Faith: ST. AGNES	I-Fri Evening, 193
What a Friend We Have In Jesus: FRIEND	I-Tues Evening, 107
When I Survey the Wondrous Cross: HAMBURG	I-Fri Evening, 213

The number given below each song's lyrics is the page number of *Fr Steve's Three-Finger-Chord Ukulele Hymns*. www.idjc.org/ukulele. Most of the songs have been altered, and some are marked for an alternate melody. Original texts for most of these and music tunes are available on www.nethymnal.org.

Books by Stephen Joseph Wolf

PRAYER BOOKS	FOR FAITH-SHARING
Rainbow Prayer	God's Ones: Living in the Lord
Dawn & Dusk Rainbow for Ordinary Time	The Passion in the Great Story of Jesus
	Being Spouses
Dawn & Dusk Rainbow Prayer (ordinary time & the seasons)	Forty Penances for Spiritual Exercise
	Tree of Life
A Jesus Breviary	Pondering Our Faith
31 Days of God's Love-Call	Twelve-Step Spirituality for Christians
POETRY & ESSAY	Anger the Jesus Way
Seeking Holy Honesty	God's Money
Gay Respect in the Good News	Planning My Own Funeral?
UKULELE SONGBOOKS	Fr Steve's Three-Finger Chord Ukulele Hymns
	Three-Finger Chord Ukulele Old-Timey Songs

Stephen Joseph Wolf is retired, a former parish priest (22 lents & holy weeks), spiritual director and retreat leader, and former certified public accountant (14 tax seasons), and before that worked as a landscaper, desk clerk, laundry worker, janitor, and paper boy, growing up the second of eight sons of a parish secretary and Nashville's best television repairman. He continues to write for faith-sharing groups and retreats, paint folk art icons, sing baritone for the LGBTQ+ chorus Nashville in Harmony, play the ukulele with Music for Seniors and others, volunteer as bookkeeper for two non-profits, serve on the board of PFLAG Nashville, and live in Nashville with his husband Billy. **www.idjc.org**

www.ingramcontent.com/pod-product-compliance
Lightning Source LLC
Chambersburg PA
CBHW071948110526
44592CB00012B/1033